Theories of Power
and Domination

Theories of Power and Domination

The Politics of Empowerment in Late Modernity

Angus Stewart

SAGE Publications
London • Thousand Oaks • New Delhi

SAGE Publications Ltd
6 Bonhill Street
London EC2A 4PU

SAGE Publications Inc
2455 Teller Road
Thousand Oaks, California 91320

SAGE Publications India Pvt Ltd
32, M-Block Market
Greater Kailash - I
New Delhi 110 048

British Library Cataloguing in Publication data

A catalogue record for this book is available from
the British Library

ISBN 0 7619 6658 7
ISBN 0 7619 6659 5 (pbk)

Library of Congress catalog card record available

Typeset by SIVA Math Setters, Chennai, India
Printed in Great Britain by Biddles Ltd, Guildford, Surrey

Contents

Acknowledgements

I have had the pleasure of discussing and debating changing perspectives on politics and society with successive generations of students at the London School of Economics, most recently in the Graduate Programme in Political Sociology and the Research Workshop in Political Sociology. Our mutual wish that the seminar be a forum for engaged argumentation, reflection and development was realised with pleasing frequency. I also wish to express my sincere thanks to Ruth Dar, whose enthusiasm and resourcefulness in the pursuit of bibliographic sources invariably went well beyond the best of friendships; and to Phillip Derbyshire whose efficient and informed efforts acquiring much needed sources has restored my faith in booksellers. To my children, Amy, Calum, Daniel and Jonathan, go my thanks for their love, support and inspiration. Finally, I express my love, gratitude and respect to my wife, Elizabeth, a true partner, for her unflagging enthusiasm and indispensable practical support.

Introduction

... in the hope ... of at least breaking the appearance of unanimity which is the greater part of the symbolic force of the dominant discourse. (Bourdieu 1998: viii)

Modernists know this is possible: the fact that the world has changed so much is proof that it can change still more. They can, in a striking phrase of Hegel's, 'look the negative in the face and live with it'. (Berman 1998: 33)

This book addresses the nature and possibilities of transformative politics in the present epoch of late modernity. In doing so, it pursues a thematic conceptual strategy, challenging what Bourdieu identifies in the above quotation as 'the symbolic force of the dominant discourse'. This discourse is identified as that which in contemporary political and social theory both conventionally and conceptually equates power and domination. Such an equation is argued to preclude critical analytic and political possibilities, possibilities concerning the distinctive nature of a politics of domination and a politics of empowerment.

There are of course many reasons to view such an undertaking with hesitation, if not downright scepticism. At the beginning of the twenty-first century, there is widespread disenchantment with both the forms and the possibilities of politics. The electoral rigidities of 'cultures of contentment', the limitations of bureaucratic government as a mechanism for the implementation of intended social change, the very apparent interpenetration of money and political, particularly electoral, competition expressed in significant part in the dominant role of television, the perception and reality of widespread corruption at every level of public life,[1] the proliferation of multiple cultures and minority groups pursuing distinctive political agendas (and frequently, apparently incompatible versions of the good life), the accelerating momentum of resurgent tribalisms of ethnicity and region, the chronic, ubiquitous and apparently irresistible pressures of destabilising international economic forces: together – and in various permutations – all these developments foster feelings of indifference, impotence and cynicism. Against such a background, realistic possibilities of human empowerment, understood as the enhancement of autonomy and solidarity, can seem very limited.

A M o d e r n i s t   S t a n c e

Against the background of such an apparently unconducive political terrain, this book addresses the possibilities of transformative politics in late modernity. The epochal specification is important for two reasons in particular. The first is methodological: a central presupposition here is that meaningful understanding of the major characteristics of domination and power as social phenomena must be historically contextualised. This being so, the purpose of the book is to consider the possibilities for transformative politics in a particular epoch. The second reason is substantive and concerns the dominant intellectual and political ethos. It is undoubtedly the case that the single largest challenge to the study of power and by extension of politics in the closing decades of the twentieth century came from 'the postmodern turn' (Seidman 1994). With certain notable exceptions, this post-modernist turn in political and social theory involved variations on the proposition that the definitive characteristics of the social forms and forces which had provided the central dynamic of the modern world had changed so fundamentally as to necessitate a new conceptual vocabulary of social analysis, that of postmodernism (Crook et al. 1992; Harvey 1989; Jameson 1995).[2]

The present argument dissents from such a position but does so in a specific way. As will become clear in following chapters, the present epoch is characterised by enormous changes in, for example, those forms of economic and political organisation central to both the for-mation and continuing development of modernity as an identifiable period in world history. Further, in relation to the dominant mode of political organisation definitive of the modern world, namely, that of the states system, the possibility is addressed on a number of occa-sions that this mode is in various ways losing its pre-eminence (see, for example, Chapters 4, 7 and 8). Nevertheless, a basic develop-mental continuity in both the structures of domination and processes of empowerment makes it both meaningful and desirable to retain modernity as a general context of explanation as against some putative postmodernity. Why late modernity? Here, I follow Giddens (1991b) in his general assessment that the present epoch is defined by an iden-tifiably distinctive configuration which represents a universalising of modernity; in Habermasian terms, the present epoch is considered as a globalisation of societal rationalisation, both spatially and tempo-rally, implicating struggles of redistribution and recognition centring on processes of communicative democracy. I endorse and analyse such emergent universalisation in relation to both domination and empowerment.

There is a third critical reason for emphasising that the following argument addresses domination, power and politics specifically in late modernity. This reason is most easily specified in relation to an understanding of modernity in terms of the ideas of justice and of the political as pertaining to matters of public concern and their determination through processes of self-government.[3] The contestation of just such an understanding has of course been central to the postmodernist project. Thus, 'the overall challenge of postmodern thinking might be rendered into the assertion that we are far too ready to attach the adjective "just" to cognitive, ethical and political arrangements that are far better understood as phenomena of power' (White 1991: 115). Apart from the work of Foucault, whose general argument is addressed in Chapter 1, the seminal text here is Lyotard's *The Postmodern Condition* (1984). There, the central proposition is that, in a distinctive postmodern era, legitimation has become 'plural, local and immanent' (Fraser and Nicholson 1989). Arguing that scientists no longer adhere to prescriptive philosophies of science, Lyotard suggested that something similar was – or ought to be – happening in relation to the crucial matter of political legitimation. Rather than a single, overarching theory of justice, which, he proposed, must inevitably be a discourse of power, obscuring difference and normalising diversity, we require a 'justice of multiplicities'. As Fraser and Nicholson note, however, the meaning of this proposition is far from clear. Are we to understand a normative vision, a delineation of the good society incorporating a decentralised plurality of democratic, self-managing groups and institutions whose members problematise their normativity and modify it in appropriate situational ways?[4] Or are we rather to understand a contextualised political relativism which *precludes* both the normative political theorising *required* to legitimise such a 'justice of multiplicities' and any possibility of the 'identification and critique of [those] macrostructures of inequality and injustice which cut across the boundaries separating relatively discrete practices and institutions'? (ibid.: 23).[5] As we shall see, issues of normativity and the critique of domination have been central to the modernist vision and remain so in late modernity.

Lyotard wishes to refute any critical theory positing general sites of domination on the grounds that 'the social' is heterogeneous and non-totalisable. In this account, therefore, what distinguishes modernity and postmodernity as perspectives upon power and politics is the latter's prohibition of the use of general frameworks of analysis such as those of capitalism and patriarchy. 'From the premise that criticism cannot be grounded by a foundationalist philosophical metanarrative, [Lyotard] infers the illegitimacy of large historical stories, normative theories of justice, and social-theoretical accounts of macro-structures which institutionalise inequality' (ibid.: 24). While recognising important analytic and political insights arising from postmodernism, the present argument nevertheless endorses the centrality of just such normative theories of justice and social-theoretical accounts of macro-structures to the analysis of domination and power and to the articulation of models of politics generated in relation to them.[6]

Of course, the postmodern turn can serve to reinforce, if that were necessary, the need for social and political theory to be historical in the sense of recognising the specificity of different societies and periods. Postmodernist accounts have served to greatly sensitise us to what Connolly, speaking in particular of Foucault, has vividly described as an 'ontology of discord' (1984: 371). In such a project, we are directed to the ways in which difference is not merely suppressed but also created in unproblematised schemes of justice. We are in effect encouraged to cultivate 'a responsibility to otherness' as an appropriate and constructive stance to the plurality of modernity. However, recognising such a responsibility and with it the consequence that within modernity all institutional arrangements must be viewed as contingent and problematic,[7] need not and should not be at the cost of denying the equally important 'responsibility to act', above all to act politically in pursuit of projects of empowerment (White 1991: x).[8]

To the extent that power and politics are thought of *exclusively* in terms of the elaboration of an ontology of discord, we privilege an ultimate aestheticisation of politics, a perspective of unbounded fluidity of practices and identities. Such a perspective may and can certainly offer us a salutary reminder of possibilities for the radical regeneration of political forms by way of the pursuit of new configurations of plurality and difference. The renewed deliberations of radical democracy in whatever setting may indeed be seen as 'oases in the desert', episodes both historical and historic, which highlight the 'conventionality, fallibility, precariousness and revisability of all political arrangements' (ibid.: 52).[9] Within the present argument, such episodes are proposed to be expressions of *power (to)* in the context of various modes of domination. But to the extent that they represent a postmodernist appropriation of politics, they are subject to a crippling limitation: the absence of a 'why'? Possible answers to such 'why' questions require that collective action in the context of inequality and difference be mobilised in relation to the goal of generating and sustaining procedures of transformative politics, a politics based in the chronic mutual interrogation of competing models of justice and plural versions of the good life. Recognising and accepting postmodernism's valorisation of difference, we can identify the politics of late modernity as thematising the standpoint of the 'concrete collective other', an intermediate focus between unique self-actualising individuality and 'universal humanity' (Fraser 1986). The result is 'an ethic of solidarity', an affirmation of difference, pointing towards struggles of recognition oriented towards the realisation of immanent ethical communities, contesting the discursive practices of dominant groups. Equally, an adequate and coherent politics of late modernity requires an equal consideration of the generation of minimalist norms of universalist justice via processes of communicative democracy. A continuing commitment to the contestation of injustice combined with a valorisation of difference thus emerges as definitive of transformative politics in late modernity.[10]

This emphasis upon difference is important not merely in relation to a recognition of the irreducible plurality of the modern world but also in relation to the central issue of domination in late modernity. The emergence of processes variously subsumed under such labels as 'the informational society', 'the consumer society' or 'fast capitalism' points to two salient facts as far as the issue of domination is concerned. First, it indicates that 'commodity fetishism' has become a pervasive aspect of the dominant rationale of modern societies representing a naturalisation of a particular social order, capitalist modernity, including its determined/collusive support in dominant political forms, which parallels the 'socialisation' of the 'natural world' (Beck 1992). Secondly, this 'culture of the economic' is expressed in increasingly dominant discourses and institutions which so structure 'public' meanings and relationships as to make projects of difference increasingly difficult to articulate, let alone sustain.

The chapters that follow identify and analyse a wide range of processes of social change: successive periods of capitalist development, changing modes of the organisation of production, cycles of capitalist expansion and stagnation, globalisation, the rise and possible faltering of a uniquely modern form of political order in the international system of states, the implication of citizenship in modernity, the contemporary proliferation of social movements. In most, if not all, cases, the analysis of their implications in processes of domination and empowerment requires a consideration of structures and groups. Such analyses and the explication of the consequences for a political theorisation of the potential of modernity have been central to the modernist project. The deficiencies of earlier modernist models regarding the nature and possibilities of a politics directed towards the goal of a democratic expansion of publicly focused procedures of interest determination and control (many of which have been cogently identified by postmodernist perspectives) do not provide a sufficient basis upon which to abandon the ceaseless but historically inescapable project of a politics of empowerment.

Structure of the Argument

The argument proceeds as follows. Chapter 1 sets out the main conceptual and analytic problem addressed in the book. This concerns the major division in discussions of power, which is identified as between those which focus upon the analysis of an understanding of power as domination, conceived as the strategic capacity to achieve goals ('power over'), and those which focus upon the analysis of power as the expression of collective autonomy, conceived as the intersubjective generation of specific forms of solidarity ('power to'). Whereas 'power over' discussions identify various parameters in terms of which strategic capacities – organisational, ideological, structural – may be specified, 'power to' analyses are concerned to conceptualise the political conditions, characteristics and implications of power as action in concert.

The dominant tradition of power analysis uses a strategic conception of power and, in so doing, *effectively equates power with domination*: that is, it proposes the logical and empirical *implication* of power to and power over. This dominant tradition is explicated here through a critical exploration of the work of Lukes, Parsons, Giddens, Foucault and Mann. In this perspective, a politics of power necessarily becomes a politics of strategic success through appropriate resource mobilisation. The chapter concludes with the argument that, from such a standpoint, the very *possibility* of a political theory and practice concerned with processes of empowerment is precluded.

The second chapter proposes that an alternative lexicon of power and politics required by a critical theory of empowerment can be constructed from sources outside the dominant tradition of power studies. A distinctive and positive conception of power is elaborated through a critical appropriation of Arendt's critique of the fundamental assumptions of Western political theory and Habermas' consequent articulation of the possibilities of social relations grounded in communication in relation to the social and political conditions prevalent in late modernity. Three relationships are identified as of central importance here: those between power and community, power and interests, and power and domination. These are explored in relation to central debates about power in contemporary social and political theory.

Having distinguished between power and domination, the argument then considers the relationship between them. Key to this relationship is the recognition that structures of domination are not mechanically monolithic and self-equilibrating but are above all *sites of struggle*. Such struggles must be seen as non-equivalent to routinised processes of conflict resolution and resource distribution, but as relatable to identifiable possibilities for social transformation through processes of empowerment. The dynamic of such processes is identified in the contradictory character of structures of domination and the complementary transformative struggles expressive of alternative conceptions of immanent community, whether such communities are those of interest or of recognition.

The next two chapters explore the dialectical relations of domination and empowerment with respect to two major sites of domination and struggle in late modernity: capitalism and the states system. In explicating the *structuring* of capitalist domination and the implication of *variable processes* of domination in the realisation and reproduction of capitalism, Chapter 3 emphasises the significance of capitalism as *a dynamic historical process*. Three major sites of struggle are identified and analysed: markets, the organisation of production and political organisation. The relationship between contemporary capitalist restructuring and the development of 'the informational age' is explored through a critical analysis of the work of Castells and others. The chapter concludes with a consideration of the tendencies towards domination inherent in contemporary characteristics of capital mobility.

Chapter 4 discusses states as sites of domination and struggle in late modernity. The state system is explicated as the *modern* system of rule, the distinctive feature of which has been territorially defined spaces of legitimate domination. A contrast is made between 'capitalism' and 'territorialism' as distinctive and opposite modes of rule within modernity. Following a critical analysis of the dominant Weberian definition of the modern state, the necessity is proposed of distinguishing between a state-centred politics of domination and a government-centred politics of empowerment. Possibilities regarding the contemporary transformation of the dominant state form in late modernity are then explored through a critical analysis of competing perspectives on welfare statism. The chapter concludes with a consideration of recent arguments that globalisation has resulted in a 'powerless state' and with a positive proposition concerning the relevance of the public/private distinction under late modernity.

Building on the conceptual and substantive issues explored in Part I, Part II discusses the possibilities for political empowerment identified within three main analytic frameworks: those of the public sphere (Chapters 5 and 6), citizenship (Chapter 7) and new social movements (Chapter 8), respectively. Two main issues are explored in relation to these frameworks. The first of these concerns the relationship between the relevant context of empowerment and the structures of domination explicated in Part I. Thus, for example, the discussion of the public sphere is located within the context of the relationship between capitalism and democracy, and citizenship within the context of the relationship between state power and a politics of difference. The second issue, particularly exemplified in the discussion of social movements, concerns the degree to which transformative possibilities for empowerment are proposed as alternative or complementary to dominant institutional forms.

Chapters 5 and 6 explore the potential for political empowerment offered by the idea of the democratic public sphere. Both the possibilities and the limitations of a politics of the public sphere have been centrally identified with Habermas' discussion of the concept. Chapter 5 locates this discussion within the overall trajectory of Habermas' political theory, a theory chronically concerned with the relationship between domination and empowerment in modernity. Chapter 6 completes this analysis, identifies and explains the limitations of the Habermasian project and advances a critical appropriation of the idea of the public sphere as a site of empowerment expressive of concerted action. This appropriation focuses upon the possibilities for empowerment implicated in 'democratic breakouts' (empirically identifiable phenomena embodying the experience of the political) and novel modes of political discourse rooted in concrete experience.

The articulation and institutional grounding of citizenship has been central to the politics of modernity. Chapter 7 explores competing conceptions of citizenship in terms of their relationship to power and domination. A dominant form is identified in a state-centred, territorially bound conception of citizenship focusing above all on passive membership status and on issues of inclusion/exclusion. The critique of such a conception from the standpoint of difference, elaborated with respect to critical dimensions of gender and multiculturalism, leads to a democratic conception of citizenship centred on the constitution of immanent political communities as new sites of power generation and struggle in late modernity. Chapter 8 then examines contemporary social movements in relation to domination and empowerment. Transformative social movements in struggle are considered as alternative sites for the mobilisation of alternative immanent value communities in late modernity. Particular attention is paid to the vital question as to whether social movements offer the possibility for realisation of a non-territorially based arena of empowerment and political struggle at this juncture in late modernity.

Notes

1. At the time of writing, Germany is engulfed in an ever-widening political scandal, the *Parteispendenaffäre*, focused on the architect of Germany's economic miracle and the process of European integration, former Chancellor Helmut Kohl. Simultaneously, another member of the European Community, Austria, is being trenchantly criticised for the introduction into a governmental coalition of the Far Right Freedom Party led by Jorg Haider. The 27 per cent level of electoral support for the People's Party, which makes such a development possible, is widely explained by several decades of institutionalised cronyism at every level of Austrian politics.

2. Of course, the more fundamental challenge has been not primarily analytic but epistemological and, as we shall see, political.

3. For a useful specification of the distinction between the political and politics, see S. Wolin, 'Fugitive Democracy' in Benhabib 1996a: 31–45. Whereas politics refers to the 'legitimised and public contestation, primarily by organised and unequal social powers, over access to the resources available to the public authorities of the collectivity' (that is, strategic action), the political is 'an expression of the idea that a free society composed of diversities can nonetheless enjoy moments of commonality when, through public deliberations, collective power is used to promote or protect the well-being of the collectivity'.

4. As will become clear in subsequent chapters, the present argument would have no difficulty in principle with such a vision, which can be read as a processual specification of the mutual interrogation of a praxis of justice and praxes of the good life. For a general discussion of such possibilities, see Stewart 2000.

5. See Chapter 1 for a discussion of the same limitation in the work of Foucault.

6. As Fraser and Nicholson also note, Lyotard's own argument about the nature of postmodern society does itself incorporate one such general structural tendency which he argues requires a coordinated political response. This is the tendency to universalise instrumental reason, that is, to subject the plurality of discursive practices indiscriminately to the single overriding

criterion of efficiency or 'performativity'. See Lyotard 1984: 47–67; Fraser and Nicholson 1989: 25.

7. Thus, for all the positive possibilities opened up in a general way by Habermas' argument about intersubjectivity and communicative rationalisation for the explication of an understanding of power as collective action, it remains limited by his proposal that the divisions and differences within modernity can be resolved in principle by procedural frameworks. On the intertwinings of discussions of justice and discussions of the good life, see Benhabib 1992 and Stewart 2000.

8. As White notes, 'political reflection pursued under the pull of the responsibility to act in the world will generate cognitive machinery attuned to problems of action coordination; and, conversely, ... political reflection pursued under the responsibility to otherness will use the world disclosing capacity of language to loosen the hold of that machinery, as well as of the dominant modes of identity and action coordination connected with it' (1991: 28).

9. The phrase 'oases in the desert' is used by Hannah Arendt to describe short periods of radical democracy in the history of various revolutions from the eighteenth to the twentieth centuries. See Arendt 1963.

10. The issue of difference and its relation to a politics of justice is central to the analysis of empowerment in late modernity. See Part II below.

Part I

1

Power and Domination: The Dominant Perspective

The general argument presented here may be simply stated. First, relations of power and domination have been and continue to be significantly constitutive of social relations in modern societies.[1] This may seem an unexceptional statement but it is one which is more complex and more analytically promising than might appear at first sight. The key to both the complexity and the analytic promise lies in a further proposition regarding the necessity of identifying and maintaining a clear distinction between concepts and relations of power and domination. This necessity is semantic, conceptual and political.[2] A similar necessity underlines a third proposition: that in late modernity, any emancipatory politics must be fundamentally and consistently determined by a politics of power as distinct from a politics of domination.

What is the importance of distinguishing between power and domination? The simplest, most straightforward answer might appear to be on grounds of parsimony. If one has a concept which identifies a specific set of analytic problems and, of equal importance, political possibilities, why confuse the issues by involving a second? There is considerable merit in this answer but, as with most questions, a fuller answer is more revealing and, of particular importance here, more politically relevant. Even a limited acquaintance with the literature on power in the human sciences indicates two characteristics: a thematic distinction between power to and power over, combined with an overwhelming preoccupation with the conceptual, theoretical, empirical and political explication of the latter.

Consider four arguments which have been central to discussions of power in the social sciences in recent decades: Lukes' *Power: A Radical*

View (1974), Parsons' 'On the Concept of Political Power' (1967a), Giddens' structuration theory (1976, 1977, 1979, 1984), Foucault's elaboration of disciplinary power (1977, 1979, 1980, 1982), and Mann's exploration of the sources of social power (1986, 1993). Appearances to the contrary notwithstanding, the predominant preoccupation of all this work has been with power over. That Lukes focuses upon questions of power over to the virtual exclusion of the issue of power seems beyond dispute. In his seminal text, which continues to provide a major focus for the discussion of power analysis in the social sciences, Lukes states: 'The three views we have been considering [Lukes' now standard agenda setting out one-, two- and three-dimensional views of power] can be seen as alternative interpretations and applications of one and the same underlying concept of power, according to which A exercises *power over* B when A affects B in a manner contrary to B's interests' (1974: 27, emphasis mine*).

Parsons: an Authoritative Conceptualisation of Power?

Lukes goes on to note that there are of course alternative ways of conceptualising power. Of the two that he chooses to consider, one is that advanced by Talcott Parsons. In his equally seminal paper, Parsons defines power as follows: 'Power is … the generalised capacity to secure the performance of binding obligations by units in a system of collective organisation when the obligations are legitimised with reference to their bearing on collective goals and when in the case of recalcitrance there is a presumption of enforcement by negative situational sanctions – whatever the actual agency of that enforcement' (Parsons 1967a: 308). Discussion of this Parsonian conceptualisation of power has focused upon Parsons' equation of power and authority and has generally sought to distinguish – and frequently attack – such a conception by (and for) its emphasis upon mobilisation deriving from consensus and upon the pursuit of collective goals as 'facilitative', as opposed to the 'distributive' character of conceptualisations concerned with conflicts of interest and the coercive and sectional pursuit and achievement of goals.[3] (Parsons' argument concerning power was elaborated by way of a critical response to an outstanding example of the distributive, coercive model, advanced by C. Wright Mills in *The Power Elite*, 1956.)[4]

---

* All emphasis is in the original unless otherwise stated.

In contrast to its general initial reception and its critical interrogation by Anthony Giddens, Parsons' argument has come to be regarded as providing an alternative, indeed a opposing, conception to the distributive argument. Yet, in a very important way, such a view is profoundly misleading. Appropriately abstracted from the clash of theoretical and empirical arguments which provided its original context, Parsons' argument can be accurately understood as occupying the same conceptual space as the view(s) against which it was elaborated, at least as far as its conceptualisation of power is concerned. Power for Parsons, as for the various exponents of the three dimensions of Lukes' discussion, is conceived of in terms of the same basically *teleological* model of action, wherein 'an individual subject (or a group that can be regarded as an individual) chooses the appropriate means to realise a goal that it has set for itself' (Habermas 1977: 3–23). As Habermas noted, Parsons effectively repeats at the level of systems theory 'the same teleological concept of power (as the potential to realise goals) that Weber pursued at the level of action theory' (ibid.: 5). Such a conception is clearly expressed in Parsons' stipulation: 'I have defined power as the capacity of a social system to mobilise resources to realise collective goals' (1967b: 193) and further directly linked to the distributive perspective in the following statement: the 'power of *A* over *B* is, in its legitimised form, the "right" of *A* as a decision-making unit involved in the collective process, to make decisions which take precedence over those of *B*, in the interests of the collective operation as a whole' (Parsons 1967a: 318).[5]

Viewed correctly, therefore, Parsons' conception of power must be seen, not as an alternative to the mainstream 'power-over' model, but as a variant within it. Recognition of this key possibility was lacking in the initial engagement with the issue of power by Anthony Giddens. Indeed, it was the central point of that engagement, a robustly critical discussion of Parsons' argument concerning power, that 'what slips away from sight almost completely in the Parsonian analysis is the very fact that power, even as Parsons defines it, is always exercised over someone! ... Parsons virtually ignores, quite consciously and deliberately, the necessarily hierarchical character of power, and the divisions of interest which are frequently consequent upon it' (Giddens 1977: 341). In reality, of course, Parsons' theoretical framework *as a whole* has adequate scope to identify and address *issues of power over* as stipulated in such concepts as force and influence. He rather seeks to restrict the specific *concept* of power to the analysis of legitimised power used for mobilisation in relation to collective (i.e. generalised) goals. Of course, this sanitisation of power relations has crucial political implications and Giddens was correct to signal these. Nevertheless, the key point remains: viewed in general terms, Parsons' system-appropriation of power remains a variant on the power over perspective.

Giddens: Power as Dependency and Domination

What is clear from the position that Giddens adopts throughout the essay on Parsons is that his own conception of *social* power is a hierarchical one of power over, as we can see from the preceding quotation. It is important to emphasise this as, in discussions of power analysis, Giddens has been most frequently criticised for privileging power as agency to the neglect of a meaningful conception of domination. This criticism has largely tended to obscure the fact that Giddens' concept of power *in the context of interaction* is couched in terms of domination. Thus, in a direct exposition of his own conception of power, he distinguishes between two senses in which we may usefully speak of power, one broad, the other narrow. Power in the broad sense can be seen as the 'transformative capacity of human agency', where such capacity refers to 'the capability of the actor to intervene in a series of events so as to alter their course … it is the "can" which mediates between intentions and wants and the actual realisation of the outcomes sought after'. By contrast, power in the narrower sense is relational, a property of interaction, and may be defined 'as the capability to secure outcomes where the realisation of these outcomes depends upon the agency of *others*' (Giddens 1976: 111).

Here then we have an understanding of specifically social power as inherently interactive and relational, a specification of 'the transformative capacity of human agency' which might be viewed as potentially emphasising the relational, even the concerted, character of social power to. However, Giddens immediately makes it clear that such an interpretation is not what he intends by qualifying and exemplifying his narrower sense of power as follows: 'It is in this sense that men have power "over" others; this is power as *domination*' (ibid.). Thus, where 'transformative capacity' is dependent upon the agency of others, manifestations of power are so implicated with domination as to make the two terms virtually synonymous. *In this perspective, dependency upon the agency of others promotes the pursuit of domination and compliance, not mutuality and concert.* Such a conclusion is reinforced by Giddens' argument that the use of power in interaction can be understood in terms of the resources or facilities which participants bring to and mobilise as elements of its production, thus directing its course. These include the skills whereby the interaction is constituted as 'meaningful', but also ... any other resources which a participant is capable of bringing to bear *so as to influence or control the conduct of others* who are parties to that interaction, including the possession of 'authority' and the threat or use of force. (ibid.: 112, emphasis mine)

The clear emphasis upon 'power over', upon power as intended domination, in this argument is inescapable. Such an argument effectively equates social power with domination to the extent that it proposes, not merely a necessary empirical link between relations of power and relations of domination but, more fundamentally, an integral conceptual link: an affirmative, productive conception of social power (to) is made conceptually subordinate to a concept of domination of power over.

In a way that follows logically (and, as Layder, Barbalet and Clegg argue, ontologically) from a fundamentally teleological conception of power, Giddens' concept of social power is overwhelmingly strategic: it is basically preoccupied with the acquisition and utilisation of power (Layder 1985: 131–49; Barbalet 1987: 1–24; Clegg 1989: 138–47).[6] But what of the generation of social power? This question Giddens treats in an unproblematic and reductionist manner, which, in spite of his emphatic and much-criticised commitment to the priority of human agency in social analysis, fails to take seriously the specific qualities of human empowering with respect to the generation of social power.[7]

Basically, Giddens conceives of power in terms of the acquisition and use of resources or capabilities, expressed in struggles and subordination. Thus, in a relatively early formulation, 'Power in either the broad or the restricted sense, refers to *capabilities*. Unlike the communication of meaning, power does not come into being only when being "exercised", even if ultimately there is no other criterion whereby one can demonstrate what power actors possess. This is important, because we can talk of power being "stored up" for future occasions of use' (1976: 111). A later formulation addresses the conceptual scope of power and indicates the exclusion of the question of the generation of power.

[P]ower can be related to interaction in a dual sense: *as involved institutionally in processes of interaction, and as used to accomplish outcomes in strategic conduct.* Even the most casual encounter instances elements *of the totality as a structure of domination* [emphasis mine]; but structural properties are at the same time drawn upon, and reproduced through, the activities of participants in systems of interaction .... *Power as transformative capacity can ... be taken to refer to agents' capabilities of reaching such outcomes.* (1979: 88)

Even more directly on the issue of generation, in the text setting out what must regarded as the definitive formulation of the 'structuration theory' which has provided the emergent theoretical framework within which Giddens' various discussions of power are located: 'Power ... is generated in and through the reproduction of structures of domination. The resources which constitute structures of domination are of two sorts – allocative and authoritative' (1984: 258).

Giddens' conceptualisation of social power in exclusively strategic terms has a number of important consequences: it excludes from consideration the issue of the generation of power, an issue which it will be argued below is crucial when addressing those questions of autonomy and dependence which Giddens quite rightly recognises as central to non-zero-sum analyses of power relations. In spite of Giddens' formal commitment to possibilities of 'making a difference', it effectively makes power a function of the distribution of resources, subject only to actors' capabilities to draw upon such resources effectively. On this latter point, a major vein of criticism of Giddens' attempt to *transcend* the dualism which he sees as characteristic of much traditional social theory has been that, given that any such attempt must end up by privileging one half of the dualism or another, Giddens' argument favours agency over structure, subjectivity over objectivity (see, for example, Layder 1985: 140–47). The present argument seeks to emphasise the converse; namely, whatever the limitations of the notion of the duality of structure, in particular the apparent evanescence of any conception of domination, Giddens' specification of social power makes socially transformative capacity substantially dependent upon 'existing' structures of domination. Such a stance denies the significance of the proposition that 'the analysis of "power to" is logically prior to that of "power over", since, although "power over" always entails "power to", *the reverse is not the case*' (Benton 1981: 174, emphasis mine).[8]

What of the objection that to argue that Giddens effectively reduces 'power to' to 'power over' is to ignore his recognition of the relational nature of social power? This emphasis is most directly expressed in Giddens' arguments concerning 'the dialectic of control'. In elaborating such arguments, Giddens rejects the idea that power relations can ever be meaningfully thought of in zero-sum terms, proposing that all actors always have some possibilities of *exercising* power. Thus,

> actors in subordinate positions are never wholly dependent, and are often very adept at converting whatever resources they possess into some degree of control over the conditions of reproduction of the system.

> In all social systems there is a *dialectic of control*, such that there are normally continually shifting balances of resources, altering the overall distribution of power. (Giddens 1982b: 32)

While this was and remains an important corrective to mechanical, determinist formulations of the nature of social power, even here Giddens' concern is with the relational character of *strategic* power relations, that is, with the historical and situated character of relations of power over.

It is true that in the course of the development of his work Giddens has increasingly come to stress the 'productive', enabling characteristics of power, as opposed to the purely repressive, subordinating aspect. Thus, he writes, 'power is not inherently oppressive'. Substantially modifying his earlier position, he continues: 'The barrage of critical attacks which Parsons' analysis of power provoked should not allow us to ignore the basic correctives which he helped to introduce into the literature. Power is the capacity to achieve outcomes ... [and] is not, as such, an obstacle to freedom or emancipation but is their very medium – although it would be foolish, of course, to ignore its constraining properties' (1984: 257).[9] But although the judgement upon Parsons is reversed, the linkage and subordination of 'power to' to 'power over' is not. Thus, 'The existence of power presumes structures of domination whereby power that "flows smoothly" in processes of social reproduction (and is, as it were, 'unseen') operates' (ibid.). The reality is that, while one can fully appreciate Giddens' wish to set out a humanist perspective which focuses upon the possibility of knowledgeable actors making a difference, the purposes and premises of structuration theory preclude a coherent conceptualisation and discussion of power and domination and their interrelations.[10] Giddens' analytic starting point in the development of his theory is the rejection of a dualism involving a radical opposition which must be transcended if an adequate and comprehensive account of social process is to be produced. This results in the effective collapsing of a necessary and meaningful distinction between power as concerted agency and domination as structured and durable constraint into an ersatz resolution in which strategic power as transformative capacity expresses an empirically determining but untheorised 'institutional mediation' or 'overall distribution of power'. Consequently, in spite of Giddens' identification of 'the dialectic of control' as expressing the necessarily relational character of power, the framework of structuration theory dissolves that very idea of dialectic between power and structural domination into the illusory soup of an evanescent duality.

Foucault: The Denial of Normativity

If the explication of structuration theory's *de facto* subordination of the conceptual and political autonomy of social power to structures of domination appears contentious, the proposition that the central characteristic of the Foucauldian perspective is the identification of power with domination – conceptually, methodologically and, therefore, politically – may seem commonplace, if not banal. Almost certainly, Foucault's principal substantive contribution to social analysis is seen to lie in his delineation of distinctly modern forms of domination, that is, those of disciplinary power and bio-power respectively. The distinctiveness of disciplinary power is indicated by means of a contrast with what Foucault proposes to be the pervasive form of pre-modern domination, namely, sovereign power. Whereas sovereign power was substantially periodic and, due to limitations upon the available technologies of power, of a relatively low level of social penetration, disciplinary power is in principle constant and all pervasive (see Foucault 1977: esp. Part Three, and 1980: Chs 5–8). The difference between the two materialisations of power is most graphically expressed in the contrasting position of actors within each model. Fundamental to the classical sovereignty model is the 'givenness' of the actors involved, whether individual or collective. It is precisely a contrasting constitution of actors (or 'subjectivisation' as Foucault terms it) which lies at the very heart of the disciplinary model, identifying as it does the emergence of a novel, distinctively modern power configuration with the emergence of disciplines, viewed both as bodies of specialist, procedural knowledge and as related sets of practices.

It may be objected that to see the argument expressed in *Discipline and Punish* in terms of a contrast between classical and modern forms of power is to obscure the most important conceptual difference between these forms. This difference concerns what Foucault proposes to be the *sine qua non* of disciplinary power: its inherently productive quality, as opposed to the repressive, coercive quality of sovereign power.[11] Whereas sovereign power may direct, mobilise, coerce or repress those who are subject to it, while leaving their basic integrity intact, disciplinary power constructs that subjectivity which is necessary to the successful operation of a particular regime of power/knowledge.

Clearly, a key difference is proposed here regarding the character of modern as opposed to classical power. Nonetheless, the differences are still located within the framework of power over, that is, of domination. The difference may be expressed as follows: domination in the sovereignty model is expressed through the prohibition and, if that fails, the punishment of the censured action, while domination in the disciplinary model inculcates the required action by making it the desired action within the inescapable framework of political rationalities and technologies of power. The difference is important but should not obscure the common foundation in domination.[12] As Peter Dews noted, 'Foucault seeks to establish a direct unequivocal relation between "subjectification" and "subjection"' (Dews 1984: 87).[13] Such a position is entirely supported by the following passage from Foucault's fullest exposition of his conception of power:

> This (modern) form of power applies itself to everyday life which categorises the individual, marks him by his own individuality, attaches him to his own identity, imposes a law of truth on him which he must recognise and which others have to recognise in him. It is a form of power which makes individuals subjects. There are two meanings of the word *subject*: subject to someone else by control and dependence, and tied to his own identity by a conscience or self-knowledge. Both meanings suggest a form of power which subjugates and makes subject to. (Foucault 1982: 212)

Later, in the same text, it is proposed that 'the analysis of power relations demands that a certain number of points be established'. Among these are:

1) *The system of differentiations* which permits one **to act upon** the actions of others ...
2) *The types of objectives* pursued by those **who act upon** the actions of others .... (ibid.: 223, emphasis mine).

There are thus two key propositions around which Foucault's argument about the distinctive character of modern disciplinary power relations is articulated: that the defining mechanism of such modern power is the constitution of appropriate forms of subjectivity corresponding to the disciplines of 'regimes of truth' and that the hermetic character of all modern regimes of power/knowledge means that power relations are necessarily and exclusively relations of domination. The thematic emphasis upon hierarchy, asymmetry and control conveyed by these statements is quite clear. It is this emphasis, combined with a formally complete eschewal of any basis for a global, public-oriented emancipatory politics (as opposed to localised struggles which, to the extent that they articulate constructive alternatives as opposed to negative 'refusals', must necessarily contain the elements of a further variant of disciplinary power) which has given rise to the now commonplace accusations of fatalism against Foucault.[14] A panorama of 'histories' reveals a range of monolithic and incomparable regimes of power/ knowledge whose only real similarity lies in their hermetically sealed inaccessibility to any freedom, individual or collective, beyond the constitutive constraints of yet further such regimes. On this view, power and domination are indeed merely synonyms.[15]

To recognise this is to recognise that, in order to establish a meaningful distinction between power and domination, one is required both to demonstrate the lack of coherence in Foucault's argument regarding power analysis and to explicate a defensible relationship between power and freedom upon which we can ground a critical analysis of structures of domination and explore the possibilities for a distinctively conceived and constituted power relations. Such exploration must of course accept the necessity that any and all power relations are only contextually meaningful while rejecting as illogical the presumption that this equates with contextual derivation and determination.

We can establish the 'regime-autonomy' of freedom, that is, the conceptual and empirical independence of freedom in relation to both systematised bodies of knowledge and structures of dominant practices, in the following way. First of all, from a purely empirical and historical point of view, we can recognise Foucault's failure to address what Charles Taylor calls 'the ambivalence of these new disciplines' (Taylor 1986: 81). Foucault writes illuminatingly about the structuring of new forms of domination around the interrelationship of new disciplines (in his dual sense of the term) but fails to acknowledge and assess the contribution of such disciplines to the development of the potential for and the actuality of individual and collective self-disciplines as attributes of self-governing, participatory societies. Foucault's treatment of disciplines as necessarily and wholly productive of compliant subjectivities and illusory free subjects eliminates any viable distinction between power as domination and power as agency but offers us no discussion of alternative, even contradictory possibilities. To that extent, as Taylor remarks, his analyses are 'absurdly one-sided' (1986: 83). As such, they signally fail to acknowledge that collective disciplines can function both as structures of domination and as essential elements of agentic power and thereby preclude the possibility of adequately analysing the dynamic relationship between power and domination.[16]

The one-sided logic of Foucault's argument leads to an inability to recognise, let alone engage with in a theoretically coherent way, the difference between political regimes which have at the very least a principled commitment to the 'intrinsic principles' of their constituent disciplines and to the maintenance of their limits and those which permit and facilitate the systemisation of discipline into a structure of domination (Walzer 1986: 66). As Walzer notes, 'it is the state that establishes the general framework within which all other disciplinary institutions operate. It is the state that holds open or radically shuts down the possibility of local resistance' (ibid.).

Of equal importance with these empirical and historical considerations in a critical assessment of Foucault's position is a consideration of the semantic and logical limitations of that position. These limitations have been clearly stated by Charles Taylor. The key question to be addressed is: 'can there really be an analysis which uses the notion of power, and which leaves no place for freedom, or truth?' (1986: 90). To the extent that Foucault's power as domination relates to the idea of imposition on 'our significant desires/purposes' and consequently to the idea of the removal of this restraint, the answer to this key question must be an emphatic negative. Although the central thrust of Foucault's position is 'to discredit … the very idea of liberation from power', the reality, Taylor argues, is that 'power, in his [Foucault's] sense, *does not make sense* without at least the idea of liberation' (1986: 92). The meaningfulness of Foucault's power-as-domination-as-imposition argument requires not only an idea of freedom but also a conception of truth as that which is masked through imposition. Thus, the 'Foucauldian notion of power not only requires for its sense the correlative notions of truth and liberation, but even the standard link between them, which makes truth the condition of liberation. *To speak of power, and to want to deny a place to "liberation" and "truth", as well as the link between them, is to speak incoherently*' (ibid.: 93, emphasis mine).

To state the argument more positively: a coherent account of domination and empowerment can only be grounded in an acceptance of the *normativity* of political engagement and resistance. Foucault seeks to bracket or even reject the need for such normativity by proposing the substitution of a strategic, specifically military, perspective on power: the dichotomy legitimate/illegitimate is to be replaced by the contrast between struggle and submission. As Fraser notes, however, Foucault is not consistent in his application of such a strategic perspective (1989a: 29). But, even if he were to be so, the resultant argument would fail to provide a basis for that resistance to domination for which Foucault calls and which he argues is inevitably generated by and within the very character of power relations when viewed strategically. Fraser states the point graphically: 'Why is struggle preferable to submission? Why ought domination be resisted? Only with the introduction of normative notions of some kind could Foucault begin to answer such questions' (ibid.: 29).[17]

If normative confusion is both a source and a consequence of Foucault's denial of a meaningful distinction between power and domination, between power to and power over, an equally important source is the promiscuity of his application of the concept of power. Just as Giddens insists that power is logically and intrinsically tied to agency, so Foucault's Nietzschean methodology within which a will-to-truth and a will-to-power are simply opposite sides of the same coin leads to his argument that power is ubiquitous and ineliminable. As Fraser notes, the resultant equation of power and social constraint obscures the vital difference between phenomena which are indeed ineliminable and normatively neutral and those which are arguably or, in some cases most certainly, not (Fraser 1989a: 31–2; McCarthy 1990: 446).

Foucault's commitment to a Nietzschean perspective thus precludes the possibility of an emancipatory conception of power as human agency and produces that incoherence of which Taylor writes so eloquently when the attempt is made to explore the possibility of liberation. This incoherence accounts for the most striking characteristic of 'The Subject and Power', namely, an elaboration of power relations in terms of the familiar equation with that domination which is identifiable in the mechanisms of disciplinary power – that is, with hierarchy, asymmetry and control – juxtaposed with a programmatic commitment to the analysis of power relations from the point of resistance. The incoherence of the Foucauldian perspective is most evident at those points where Foucault attempts to incorporate important insights regarding the necessarily contingent character of power relations – specifically, power relations are only such to the extent that they are precisely not relations of domination but rather open strategic games – into an argument whose premises exclude possibilities of liberation.[18] The solution to this incoherence proposed here involves the rejection of the Foucauldian premise by way of the semantic, methodological, ontological and, most importantly, political affirmation of the necessary and viable distinction between power and domination, where the former focuses upon human freedom and agency, recognised as necessarily relational and contextual, and the latter focuses upon structures of imposition and closure.[19]

Mann: Power as the Complexities of 'Caging'

A sharp focus upon the analysis and explication of power as 'power over' similarly characterises Michael Mann's magisterial study of *The*

Sources of Social Power (1986 and 1993). Indeed, it is the central aim of Mann's power project to argue that, in general terms, social analysis cannot be pursued in relation to diverse conceptions of 'society' as an unproblematic, unitary totality but rather in relation to a conception of societies as 'multiple overlapping and intersecting power networks' (1986: 2). This latter conception is famously – and with quite clear Parsonian resonance – elaborated in the IEMP framework which proposes that 'a general account of societies, their structure, and their history can best be given in terms of the interrelations of ... the four sources of social power: ideological, economic, military, and political relationships' (ibid.). These sources of power are initially specified not as dimensions, levels or factors but as 'overlapping *networks* of social interaction' (emphasis mine). This is immediately qualified with the statement that the sources of social power are also 'organisations, institutional means of attaining human goals'. Mann is emphatic that the central problems in power analysis concern 'organisation, control, logistics, communication – the capacity to organise and control people, materials, and territories, and the development of this capacity throughout history. *The four sources of social power offer alternative organisational means of social control*' (ibid.: 2–3, emphasis mine). Here, the equation of power relations with hierarchical relations of subordination could not be clearer.

In agreement with Giddens, Mann argues that power is not usefully regarded as a resource; resources are most usefully seen as the media through which power is exercised. The task of power analysis therefore is twofold: the identification of the major alternative media or, as Mann prefers, power sources, through which power is exercised and the development of a methodology to facilitate the study of such media. The opening pages of his first volume endorse a general teleological, strategic perspective on power as 'the ability to pursue and attain goals through mastery of one's environment' and then proceed to consider the question of social power (1986: 6). Two aspects of social power are proposed, one distributive, the other collective: whereas distributive power refers to 'mastery exercised over other people', collective power, following Parsons, is to be understood functionally as referring to those aspects of power 'whereby persons in cooperation can enhance their joint power over third parties or over nature' (ibid.). It may appear that such a distinction contradicts the proposition that we are dealing with a singular conception of power over. The difficulties in endorsing such a position are, however, twofold: the first concerns the use of the term 'cooperation' in the characterisation of the collective 'aspect' of social power. Diverse characterisations of 'collective power' throughout the two volumes lead one to seriously question the meaning to be attached to such a term. For example, the development of capitalism is spoken of as having qualitatively transformed the extent of collective power. The general meaning of such a proposition, in terms of the development of interdependent relationships of historically unique scope whether intensively or extensively, nationally, internationally and transnationally, is clear. But to characterise such a development as cooperation, rather than for example coordination, may be seen as both misleading – in the subjectless world of functional relationships, persons (unless purposely choosing) have no place; how then are the norms governing such functional 'cooperation' determined? – and as obscuring a central issue in power analysis: the question of the terms upon which social relationships are produced and reproduced.

Following the discussion of Parsons' conceptualisation of power above, the argument elaborated by Mann may be proposed to advance a distinction without a difference. Parsons' proposition should be correctly seen as locating power on the same conceptual plane as the distributive approach, proposing that the notion of collective power relates not to distinctive, critical and circumscribed political and social possibilities (power to) but rather to *a particular kind of power over*, that is legitimised with respect to institutionally specified 'collective goals'. Indeed, Mann goes some way towards recognising this when he states, 'In most social relations, both aspects of power, distributive and collective, exploitative and functional, operate simultaneously and are intertwined' (1986: 6). It emerges even more clearly from Mann's explication of his central concept, that of *organisational power*. Here, he emphasises the extent to which the implementation of collective goals necessitates organisation and a division of function and, as a consequence, is subject to 'an inherent tendency' to distributive power; in particular, the power of the top over the whole.

In adopting such a stance, Mann takes us into the familiar world of classical elite theory; indeed, he cites Mosca in support of his argument. To the extent that this is so, the argument potentially opens up the extensive literature on the sociological determinism of Mosca, Michels and their elitist successors (Michels 1959; Mosca 1939). But even on its own terms, Mann's discussion presents us with difficulties. Most immediately, there is a lack of clarity in his explanation of the source of that compliance which provides the stability of organisational power: on the one hand, he proposes that relations of domination within organisations are due to the fact that the 'few at the top can keep the masses at the bottom compliant, provided their control is *institutionalised* in the laws and norms of the social group in which both operate' (ibid.: 7). Here, law and not coercion is specified as the ultimate basis of social control. Subsequently, however, we are told that the 'masses comply because they lack collective organisation to do otherwise, because they are embedded within collective and distributive power organisations controlled by others. They are *organisationally outflanked*' (ibid.). Here, it appears that the key to successful domination as represented by mass compliance lies in organisational superiority, whatever its fluctuating basis in different media. As Mann notes, it is this latter argument which is developed and documented extensively throughout the volume as a whole.

Elaborating his organisational perspective on power, Mann distinguishes extensive and intensive power, and authoritative and diffused power: the former distinction contrasts the 'ability to organise large numbers of people over far-flung territories in order to engage in minimally stable cooperation' with 'the ability to organise tightly and command a high level of mobilisation or commitment from the participants, whether the area covered is large or small' (ibid.: 7–8). Lest such a distinction should encourage the perception that emergent social networks are the expression of the historically variable relationship between large, authoritative power organisations, Mann introduces the second distinction in which authoritative power is identified as that which is 'actually willed by groups and institutions' and 'comprises definite commands and conscious obedience'. This is contrasted with diffused power which 'spreads in a more, spontaneous, unconscious, decentered way throughout a population, resulting in similar social practices that embody power relations but are not explicitly commanded'.[20] The typical content of diffused power is then specified as 'an understanding that these practices are natural or moral or result from self-evident common interest'. That is, the central aspect of diffused power is normalisation. Elaborating this notion of diffused power, Mann proposes that on the whole it embodies 'a larger ratio of collective to distributive power' – that is, of functional cooperation to dominative coordination – while noting that this is not invariably so. Diffused power can result in the typical 'outflanking' of subordinate classes so that they consider resistance pointless. Thus, 'the diffuse power of the contemporary world capitalist market outflanks authoritative, organised working-class movements in individual nation-states today' (ibid.).

Mann's explication of the distinction between authoritative and diffused power should be seen as important for two reasons: first, it involves a significant equivocation about the significance of organisation as the central focus of power in so far as Mann's discussion raises the possibility that market exchanges, for example, embody symmetrical interactions whereby all the participants achieve their separate goals. (That is, there is no necessity to consider in sociospatial and organisational terms the way in which differential realities of market exchange embody different logics of collective action.) Secondly, in contrast, the possibility is also raised that relationships which may appear – presumably critically in analysing power relations – as 'natural' or the result of 'self-evident common interest' may in fact embody definitive asymmetries of power, as in the example of the domination of the world capitalist market, which is in Mann's view ultimately not the expression of authoritative power but is nonetheless proposed to be dominant in relation to working-class movements.

In general terms, however, Mann is quite unequivocal in his formulation of an argument about power which, while being flexible and fluid about the complex intertwinings and crystallisations which characterise the historical realisation of successive configurations of power, consistently views power relations in terms of variable forms of domination as embodied in distinctive while empirically composite infrastructural forms. Amidst the enormously impressive and original comparative macro-sociological explications of the second volume, a central theme emerges in Mann's chronicling of the diverse realisations of the modern world: whatever the range of comparative crystallisations of the proposed media of power, modernity may be primarily equated with a qualitative expansion of infrastructural power (over) identified as entrapment within nation-state cages (1993: e.g. at 20, 250–52). Nowhere is this more starkly stated than in Mann's explication of his conception of political power. Such power, he proposes, 'derives from the usefulness of territorial and centralised regulation. Political power means *state* power. It is essentially authoritative, commanded and willed from a center. State organisation', he continues, 'is twofold: Domestically, it is "territorially centralised"; externally, it involves geopolitics' (1993: 9).

Because modern states have massively enlarged their institutional infrastructures, they have played a critical role in structuring the diverse configurations of mediatic power that are the history of the modern world (ibid.: 88). States have shaped the structuring of both classes and nations, while being variably influenced by their differential impact according to their prior configuration. In the 'sea changes' that characterise the process of modernisation in and through those Western states embodied in that states system which shaped the contours of the modern – although by no means globalised – globe, states, through their civilian functions, politicised more and more aspects of social life. In particular, larger and more penetrative states 'impacted considerably on the relations between states and civil societies' (ibid.: 504). Reinforcing his proposition that *the* referent and the only referent of political power is state power, Mann relates both enhanced administrative coordination/regulation and processes of political representation to the development of modern state power. He proposes that modern states crystallised 'more overtly as capitalist states than as anything else'.[21] This proposition is, however, typically qualified by two further propositions: first, in Foucauldian mode, that the growth in state infrastructural powers reinforced the general politicisation of social life in which 'unconsciously ... power networks were redirected toward the terrain of the state's territories, *caging*, naturalising social life, even in its more intimate sphere, and ... territorialising social conceptions of identity and interest, eventuating in the crystallisation of the modern state as the nation-state';[22] secondly, such nation-state crystallisations 'entwined with long-lived political struggles over how centralised and national or decentralised and federal the state should become, producing interstitial forms of national centralisation' (ibid.: 505).

Clearly central to Mann's perspective is an analysis of social determination as the result of a multi-logic causality – entwinings, crystallisations and so forth – and an interpretation of the modern world as expressive of a multi-actor structuration which is both contingent and illustrative of the critical impact of unintended consequences. At the same time, within all the sensitivity to and emphasis upon comparative differences, certain dynamics are prioritised as central to the shaping of the modern world; above all, those of 'state caging' and the diffused power of an increasingly worldwide capitalism. One of the relatively unqualified statements essayed in the second volume is that the power networks of the established modern world are predominantly those of economic and political media (capitalism and the states system) and decreasingly those of ideological and militaristic media, at least as far as the period with which Volume II deals.[23]

Yet ideological power is proposed 'as an essential and autonomous part of the rise of bourgeois classes and nations' (ibid.: 35). Such ideological power is proposed to derive from issues of meaning, the promulgation of and mobilisation in terms of norms as shared understandings of how people should act in their relations with each other and aesthetic/ritual practices (1986: 22). In keeping with Mann's general argument, the significance of such ideological power is proposed to lie in its consequential organisational contours. These are stipulated in terms of two main types: the first more autonomous form is sociospatially transcendent. It 'develops a powerful autonomous role when emergent properties of social life create the possibility of greater cooperation or exploitation that transcend the organisational reach of secular authorities.... [As such] ideological organisations may be unusually dependent on ... diffused power techniques, and therefore boosted by the extension of such "universal infrastructures" as literacy, coinage, and markets' (ibid.: 23). The second type is ideology as imma-nent morale, 'intensifying the cohesion, the confidence, and therefore, the power of an already established social group' (ibid.: 24). This latter type is proposed to be 'less dramatically autonomous in its impact, *for it largely strengthens what is there*' (ibid.).

Mann argues that we can meaningfully relate intensity of social and political mobilisation to two possibilities: either to its funda-mental location in micro-contexts of face-to-face relations ('Protest was more passionate because the injustice of bread prices, of regres-sive sales and land taxes, and of conscription immediately concerned not merely self but also intimate loved ones' – 1993: 227);[24] or where mobilisation takes place in terms of an extensive solidarity, through the critical presence of media of communication. On this basis Mann proposes that the first protonational phase of modern development should be seen as dominated by churches as they diffused broader social identities through sponsorship of mass discursive literacy. In a second phase, churches were replaced by commercial capitalism – and military states – as the main communicator between intensive and extensive levels. Eighteenth-century infrastructures of ideologi-cal power are seen as containing three critical transitivities: what had been specialised knowledge, narrowly confined to one or other domain of instrumental activity, now became generalist moralising knowl-edge;[25] discursive literacy diffused through and down from the old regime and networks of discursive literacy used comparative reference points, thereby relativising social practices.[26] 'Transitivity became a potent weapon. Ideologists could find allies to outflank old regimes, expose their particularistic corruptions to moral principles, mobilise democratic sentiments and relativise sacred traditions' (1993: 233). A second emergent ideological power is identified by Mann as appearing in rare revolutionary crises. In such 'moments', ideological power elites arrived at principled messages that derived partly from their prior experience of discursive networks (ibid.: 235).

Two aspects of this discussion of ideological power are important in the present context: first, while Mann is at pains to emphasise the autonomous impact of ideological power in early modernity, whether revolutionary or not, quite meaningfully linking this impact to the question of available media and resistance to domination, the general thrust of his argument is such as to stress either the transience of the ideas and practices involved or to see their durability in the way in which they serve to shape subsequent processes of caging. Secondly, while Mann writes most illuminatingly about the emergence and significance of ideological power in early modernity, he is, as noted above, clear about its declining significance.[27] So in this account, for example, the ideological power of citizenship has not fuelled continuing debate and struggle over the nature and forms of democracy; rather, it is assimilated only to the comparative analysis of elite strategies for containment and subordination. Power over absorbs power to.

So there we have it: within Mann's imposing lexicon of power, political power can only be understood as state power and ideological power can only express new possibilities for the crystallisation of an organisational materialist caging of collective resistance to exploitation and aspirations for justice. Those processes of social change that have determined the modern world may well have been multiple and complexly interpenetrating but the most insightful guides can be identified as Mosca and Foucault: modern crystallisations of power, as they emerge from Mann's two volumes, represent the historical entwinement of authoritative structures of incomparable infrastructural reach and decentred, subjectless systems of functional rationality.

Taken together, these two propositions present us with two distinct explanations of relations of domination: (1) that such relations are to be explained by the comprehensively hierarchical nature of organisational relations as embodied in the laws and norms of the organisation as a whole;[28] (2) that such relations are to be explained because subordinates lack autonomous organisational resources, presumably either within those structures of domination whose goals and methods of implementation are largely heteronomously determined or outside such structures. In spite of the emphasis that Mann places on institutionalisation in the opening conceptual section of his first volume, an emphasis which is maintained throughout both the volumes, he offers us an unqualified rejection of the first possibility: the 'simple answer to the question of why the masses do not revolt … does not concern value consensus, or force, or exchange in the usual sense of those sociological explanations' (ibid.).

We are left with our second possibility: that compliance within relations of domination is to be accounted for by the absence of organisational alternatives. It would seem reasonable to translate such a possibility into the proposition that compliance within relations may be explained, not by a lack of resistance, but by the absence of means to implement such resistance. (Whether such a proposition is empirically correct is a separate issue.) Subordinate compliance is understood in such an argument as the inability to translate the 'power to' of concerted resistance into a socially effective instrumentality of organised 'power over'. But to view the possibilities in this way runs counter to both Mann's conceptual starting point and his consequent empirical proposition. That starting point distinguishes between the distributive and the collective aspects of power relations, the former centring on subordination, the latter on cooperation. The consequent empirical proposition specifies that both aspects 'operate simultaneously and intertwined'. But the subsequent elaboration regarding the explanation of compliance effectively identifies the notion of a meaningful collective aspect sociologically *with the possibility, probability, or indeed even virtual inescapability of distributive power.* The possibility, the significance, indeed the very meaning(fulness) of collective, cooperative power relations once again becomes a function of relations of domination.

Such an argument flies in the face of the conceptual and analytic possibilities illustrated in the proposition by Benton cited above: 'the analysis of "power to" is logically prior to that of "power over", since, although "power over" always entails "power to", the reverse is not the case'. This is certainly so to the extent that Mann appears to find it difficult to envisage instances of cooperative, collective relations which are not subject to transformation into relations of super- and subordination due to the effects of organisational power. Since Mann is explicit about the limits of relations of domination ('the masses comply because they lack collective organisation to do otherwise'), power relations (whatever the intertwined sources) are to be understood in strategic terms. The linkage of power to and power over excludes the possibility of a conception of concerted power, a conception which can generate a critical assessment of the ways in which processes of social differentiation are subverted into relations of social stratification.

For all the emphatic eschewal of holistic models and evolutionary processes in *The Sources of Social Power*, the cumulative impression is of an account of societal development as expressed in the steady, at times explosive, growth of infrastructural power. The narrative of such societal development is, however, dialectically structured. In particular, the dialectic between state and civil society provides a recursive theme. Civil society generates certain requirements which can only be met by states; in meeting these requirements states acquire new resources which may enhance their despotic powers but only by generating infrastructural powers, which may subsequently be re-appropriated by civil society.

Whatever the formal lip service paid to a conceptual distinction between power to and power over, the overwhelming preoccupation of contemporary social theory is with the latter, that is, with power and domination understood as integrally related concepts. As was stated at the outset, the consequence of this preoccupation is the substantial neglect of a direct engagement with both the analytic possibilities and political implications of a distinctive concept of power to. The following chapter will identify the distinctive referents of a concept of 'power to' and consider the relationship between power so conceived and a now distinguishable domination.

Notes

1. For the present I take modern societies to be those relatively stable patterns of social interaction bounded by differential institutionalisations of state/economy interrelationships. As part of this proposition, I further propose that modern states are *qualitatively distinct* political, social and cultural entities.

2. As Holton notes: 'When trying to interpret and decode any linguistic discourse, two interrelated problems arise. First, there is the issue of how far distinctions between concepts refer to distinctions between different kinds of observable social events, processes, and phenomena, distinctions that can be subjected to empirical analysis. Second, there is the problem of how far distinctions arise from variations in the purposes of observers' (Holton 1998: 17). Paraphrasing and adapting his next sentence, one might propose in the present context, that to ignore the second issue is to ignore the ways in which the terms such as 'power' and 'domination' are implicated not merely in intellectual analysis but also in the contestation between different political projects regarding the nature of modernity.

3. See, for example, Giddens 1979: 333–49.

4. 'Power is thus facilitative in Parsons' ... schema: it produces, or rather *facilitates* the production of, binding obligations within organisational settings' (Clegg 1989: 136). Of course, as Clegg notes in his typically lucid and insightful discussion of the Parsonian perspective, the key question is: facilitative for whose goals? Thus, 'Power is facilitative for those who are As rather than Bs, since it is the As who decide what are the collective goals to be facilitated, at least as far as Bs are concerned' (ibid.: 134). See the discussion of Mann's argument concerning collective goals below.

5. This last sentence is quoted by Lukes in *Power* (1974), but he fails to engage with its implications for his argument about 'alternative' conceptions of power. At first sight, it might seem that Lukes' own, third-dimensional approach is itself the exception to the teleological model which comprehends Parsons and the first- and second-dimensional approaches, focusing as it

does on the discrepancy between the subjective and real interests of those subordinated within a particular political and social order. But Lukes himself makes it clear that he regards such discrepancy as the result of the *imposition* – by whatever mechanisms – of 'perceptions, cognitions and preferences' compatible with a given status quo. Thus, 'is it not the supreme exercise of power to get another or others to have the desires you want them to have – that is, to secure their compliance by controlling their thoughts and desires?' (1974: 23). My argument here is completely supported – indeed, reinforced – by Lukes' emphatic linkage of power and agency, in his later foray into the discussion of power in 'Power and Structure' in *Essays in Social Theory*, 1977.

6. In this, Giddens follows his mentor, Max Weber.

7. On Giddens' neglect of the partly autonomous and therefore causally contributive character of situated action, see D. Layder, *Modern Social Theory* (1997: 164): 'As a result, Giddens' approach compresses and ultimately dissolves various dimensions and characteristics of situated power into the notion of transformative capacity and thus they are lost to analysis'.

8. In the traditional language of the 'three faces' discussion, Benton continues: 'Where A's objectives do not conflict with the achievement of any of B's actual or possible objectives, then A's "power to" achieve A's objectives entails no "power over" B'.

9. Giddens himself acknowledges the reversal.

10. I believe it unnecessary to rehearse the relevant arguments for the purposes of the present discussion. While, as will become clear, I do not find myself in total agreement with either, I am in general agreement with the critiques of structuration theory set out by Layder and Clegg. See Layder 1985 and 1997: 164–71 and Clegg 1989: 135–47.

11. While adopting a critical stance towards the particular formulations of a productive conception of power, Giddens nevertheless significantly emphasises the importance of both Parsons' and Foucault's emphasis upon such a conception. See *The Constitution of Society* (1984: 257). See also Ransom 1997, Chapters 1 and 2.

12. Foucault himself is quite explicit about the common basis of domination, while emphasising the distinctive forms of domination emerging in modern societies: 'In speaking of domination I do not have in mind that solid and global kind of domination that one person exercises over others, or one group over another, but the manifold forms of domination that can be exercised within society. Not the domination of the king in his central position, but that of his subjects in their mutual relations: not the uniform edifice of sovereignty, but the multiple forms of subjugation that have a place and function within the social organism' (*Power/Knowledge*, 1980: 96; and Dallmayr 1985).

13. Charles Taylor among others has noted the way in which Foucault's fundamentally Nietzschean premises preclude the possibility of comparing regimes, let alone meaningfully moving from one set of practices to another: 'the move from one context to another cannot be seen as a liberation because there is no common measure between the impositions of the one and those of the other' (1986: 92). On the intimate connection between 'the methodological, genealogical strategies that generate Foucault's accounts of

modern structures of disciplinary power and the normative ambiguities that surround, one might almost say, suffuse his work', see the discussion by Nancy Fraser. Like Taylor, Fraser also remarks upon the centrality of non-comparability to Foucault's intellectual project: 'he concerns himself with the holistic and historically relative study of the formation and functioning of *incommensurable* networks of social practices involving the mutual inter-relationship of constraint and discourse' (Fraser 1989b: 20, emphasis mine).

14. See for example, Fred Dallmayr, 'Pluralism Old and New: Foucault on Power' in *Praxis and Polis* (1985: 90).

15. This conclusion is in no way diminished by recognising Foucault's chronic insistence on the interdependence of the realities of power and resistance. This insistence is fatally weakened by Foucault's equally chronic and, given his premises, unavoidable, refusal to link resistance to the capacity of competent subjects to say, with good reason, 'yes' or 'no' to the claims made on them by others. See McCarthy 1990. For a contrary view, see Ransom 1997, Chapter 5.

16. See the critical comments by Habermas regarding Foucault's 'levelling of ambiguous phenomena' in Habermas, 'Some Questions regarding the Theory of Power: Foucault Again', Lecture X in 1990b, esp. pp. 288–92.

17. Habermas notes the force of this formulation in his critical discussion of Foucault's position in *The Philosophical Discourse of Modernity* (1990b).

18. It might be argued that in 'The Subject and Power' Foucault recognises the necessity for the inextricable link between freedom and power relations which is the source of incoherence in his earlier – and as it has been absorbed into social theory generally, definitive – work. This is the position adopted, for example, by Fred Dallmayr. Dallmayr regards the formulations of 'The Subject and Power' as a significant advance over Foucault's earlier discussions of power, tying as these formulations do power relations to the necessity of free individuals in their integrity acting within a field of possibilities. Nevertheless, the formulations can only be read as involving the conceptualisation of power relations exclusively in strategic terms, as opposed to possibilities of communicative interaction which are explicitly excluded by Foucault. The overall effect of 'The Subject and Power' smacks of the attempt to synthesise a functionalism, albeit a pluralistic one, with an ungrounded theory of political action involving strategic agency of a particular kind. The earlier and later explications are united by a focus on a teleological model of power, Foucault's – and Dallmayr's – disclaimers notwithstanding. See Dallmayr 1985: 90–6. On the centrality of strategic interaction in Foucault's final ontology of power and the way in which this conceptualisation privileges strategic modes of power relations to the exclusion of possibilities of communicative action, see McCarthy 1990: 454–5. Again, a more positive assessment of the political possibilities of Foucault's work is advanced in Ransom 1997, Chapter 6.

19. In identifying the actualisation of power understood in this way as resistance, we should be aware of the possibility of indirect connections between alternative symbolic forms and possibilities for liberation. As Taylor importantly argues in his critical analysis of the implications of Foucault's work, it is certainly possible to conceive of and identify examples of intelligible 'purposefulness without purpose' involving explicable social processes

which are not consciously willed. 'It is certainly not the case that all patterns *issue* from conscious action, but all patterns have to be made *intelligible* in relation to conscious action.' The importance of this consideration will become clear in Chapter 2. See Taylor 1986: 86–8.

20. The Foucauldian overtones are inescapable.

21. In an usually unequivocal statement Mann states: 'Overall, these states had crystallised more overtly as capitalist states than as anything else. Domestically, the state was in this respect less an actor, more a place in the arena of power. *Its singular purpose conferred a degree of cohesion upon state institutions*' (1993: 505, emphasis mine).

22. Why Mann should propose the nation-state as opposed to the national-state here is unclear. Of course, he is quite clear about his 'modernist' stance on the question of nationalism and therefore on the broadly causal relationship between, as he views it, state caging, projects of consequent 'democratisation' and, as a further consequence, nationalist projects. That nationalist mobilisation was an identifiable regime strategy may well be a reasonable and supportable proposition (Anderson 1980). That this is a supportable generalisation regarding modern state building processes is more questionable. In addition, Mann has consistently remained sceptical about propositions regarding both conceptions and political projects of both identity and interest outside the framework of states.

23. This generalisation is qualified with respect to the military source of power to the extent that this is seen as maintaining a continuing significance which is both circumscribed in its general impact upon state crystallisations but of great, even overwhelming, consequence due to the super-technologisation of militarism.

24. Moore advances a similar argument regarding the counter-revolutionary mobilisation in the Vendée, proposing that this can be meaningfully understood not in terms of ideological mobilisation but as a response to what was perceived to be the very network integrity of Vendée communal relations. See Moore 1966.

25. See the following chapter for a discussion of struggles around diverse conceptions of ethical community in modernity and Chapter 5 for a discussion of Habermas' specification of the historical development of the public sphere.

26. As I shall argue below, such effectively reflexive problematising of existing social practices is an essential part of modernity and an integral element of the possibilities of transformative politics.

27. With the caveat noted previously that Mann indicates that he will deal at greater length with the ideological dimension of social and nationalism in Vol. III.

28. On the critical and largely neglected significance of hierarchy in the structuring of domination, see Mouzelis 1991: chs 4 and 5.

2

Analysing Power and Domination

The previous chapter identified and explored the ways in which dominant forms of contemporary political and social theory treat power and domination as substantial synonyms. This situation arises in particular from the effective privileging of a strategic conception of power. The consequence is the practical reduction of power analysis to a focus upon the production or reproduction of relations of subordination, the analysis of 'power over'. As we saw in the work of Michael Mann, for example, discussion of what is identified as a distinctive conception, aspect or dimension of power, a conception which focuses upon the cooperative nature of the social relations involved or 'power to', is incorporated into the analysis of power over. Even where there is a formal emphasis upon the 'positive', creative nature of power relations, as in the work of Foucault, the accompanying argument is elaborated within a theoretical framework which either privileges a proposed inevitability of relations of domination or singularly fails to ground dissonant arguments regarding resistance in relation to possibilities of transformation.

Several critical losses occur as a result of this elision of power and domination, losses which can be seen as not only analytic but most importantly political. First of all, there is a failure to recognise or a denial of the possibility of the distinctive character of any emancipatory conception of social power. Secondly, the possibility of analysing the historically, variable contextualised relations between social power (conceived of as a distinctive and irreducible aspect of human relations) and structures of domination is effectively precluded. This possibility requires *the elaboration of a non-reductionist understanding of power analysis, focusing upon the autonomy of social struggles and practices understood in relation to immanent communities of interest and recognition.*

As Ball and others have noted, the dominant tradition of power discourse in modernity derives from a Hobbesian perspective of a war against all (Ball 1988: ch. 4; Clegg 1989: esp. ch. 2).[1] Within such a perspective any differences between power and domination must always be matters of degree, as in the possible example of structures of domination being conceived of as institutionalised, reproduced asymmetrical power relations. Against such a background, the question arises as to the possibility of identifying a meaningful and politically significant distinction between power and domination. A useful starting point in such an exercise is the location of the concept of power (to) within an alternative perspective which is much more fruitful in terms of its transformative possibilities. The distinctiveness of this alternative lies in its concern with the *generation* of social power. It is a perspective most significantly elaborated by Hannah Arendt and Jürgen Habermas, whose intellectual legacy from Arendt is little known and certainly less acknowledged.[2]

Arendt and the Power of Inter-est[3]

In pursuing her objective of elaborating political possibilities 'in manifest contradiction' to the fundamental assumptions of Western political theory, Arendt set out 'a new lexicon of politics' (Arendt 1989: 17; Disch 1994: 24). Central to this challenge is the replacement of the fundamental dichotomy of the dominant tradition, that of subject–object, with a distinctively human alternative, that of intersubjectivity or subject–subject. Within the resultant lexicon (social) power is conceptually and *above all politically* distinguished, not by its implication in agency, but above all by its character as *collective action*; that is, power is expressive of 'the human ability not just to act but *to act in concert*' (Arendt 1972: 143, emphasis mine). This dissonant and radical conception of power is rooted above all in the definitive term within Arendt's lexicon: plurality.

Plurality, Arendt argues, is 'the condition – not only the *conditio sine qua non*, but the *conditio per quam* – of all political life' (Arendt 1989: 7).[4] In Arendt's explication of the multiple, cumulative meanings of such plurality, we can find a distillation both of the most basic premises and of the conclusions of her political positioning. Fundamentally, plurality refers to the fact of human multiplicity: 'men, not Man, live on the earth and inhabit the world' (ibid.). Such multiplicity is the basis of diversity ('sameness in difference'), the very foundation of power and politics, which proposes the specification of both humanity and individuality as involving the recognition that 'we are all the same, that is, human, in such a way that nobody is ever the same as anyone else who has ever lived, lives, or will live' (ibid.: 8). It is this diversity which gives rise to both the challenge to and the potential of constructed immanent communities: as Disch notes, 'the possibility of community is never simply given or essential to human beings but *must, rather, be built by speech and action*' (1994: 32, emphasis mine).[5] Diversity, in that political progression which is plurality, gives rise in turn to the definitive characteristic of human interconnectedness, the 'web of human relationships which exists wherever men live together' (Arendt 1989: 184).

Arendt contrasts the power generated through concerted action with the violence which she proposes underpins all forms of domination and which is distinguished by its instrumental character (1972: 145). Thus, her conception of power is distinct from the various exemplifications of power over considered in Chapter 1, elaborated as these are around a model of instrumental action, in which some actors, individual or collective, strive to use or succeed in using others as means to particular ends. Within her general typology, authority, whose 'hallmark is unquestioning obedience by those who are asked to obey', is identified as institutionalised power. Recognising the empirical complexity of political systems, however, Arendt notes that 'nothing is more common than the combination of power and violence' in the securing of outcomes (ibid.: 147–8).

The explanatory and practical possibilities of the Arendtian conception of power can be clarified and expanded by taking account of the dualism identifiable in her work with respect to models of action. Although the extensive secondary literature on Arendt's work offers distinctly conflicting interpretations of these models of action, each interpretation offers constructive possibilities in relation to a positive conceptualisation of power as concerted action. Thus Passerin d'Entreves argues for 'a fundamental tension in her theory between an expressive and a communicative model of action' (1994: 84). While expressive action 'allows for the self-actualisation or the self-realisation of the person, and its norms are the recognition and confirmation of the uniqueness of the self and its capacities by others', communicative action 'is oriented to reaching understanding and is characterised by the norms of reciprocity between subjects who are recognised as equal' (ibid.: 85). Corresponding to these action types are two different models of political action: the first agonal or agonistic model focuses on expressive action as manifested in the initiative of situated, contextually responsive leaders, while the second focuses upon the processes of self-organisation involved in democratic and/or associative politics.[6]

Implicitly suggesting that, in spite of its merits, d'Entreves' explication goes too far in the direction of transforming Arendt into a 'Habermasian' before the fact, Benhabib has offered an alternative reading of the conceptual and political possibilities identifiable in her work. Instead of communicative action, Benhabib proposes that it is more accurate to think in terms of a *narrative* model of action. 'Whereas *communicative action* is oriented to reaching understanding among conversation partners on the basis of validity claims raised in speech acts, *narrative action*, in Arendt's theory, is action embedded in a "web of relationships and enacted stories"' (1996b: 125). This qualification leads Benhabib to juxtapose d'Entreves' distinction, expressive–communicative, her preferred alternative, agonal–narrative. The significance of this alternative lies in the contrasting conceptual possibilities that arise from it: 'whereas action in the agonal model is described through terms such as "the revelation of who one is" and "the making manifest of what is interior", action in the narrative model is characterised through the "telling of a story" and "the weaving of a web of narratives"' (ibid.: 125–6). In a comparison of great political significance, Benhabib argues that '(w)hereas action in the first model is a process of discovery, *action in the second model is a process of invention*. In contemporary terms, we may say that the first model of action is essential *while the second is constructivist*' (ibid.: 126, emphasis mine).[7]

It is important to bear these action possibilities in mind in turning to a second major conceptual/theoretical source for the identification of a non-instrumental conception of power, one which is, in its origins at least, integrally connected with the first. Habermas' concept of communicative action derives, as Benhabib notes, from his crucial distinction between 'labor' and 'interaction' and, as such, 'is deeply indebted to Arendt's critique of Karl Marx in *The Human Condition* and her ... differentiation between work, labor and action' (ibid.: 199). In considering Habermas' contribution to an alternative conceptualisation of power and consequently of the possibilities of a contemporary democratic politics, we must recognise that, whatever their significant reworkings, the analytic and political possibilities – and the limitations – implicated in both its key terms, communicative action and the public sphere, represent appropriations of Arendt's work.

Habermas and the Power of Communicative Action

Habermas proposes as the basis for a non-instrumental conception of power a conception of communicative action understood as a distinctive type of social action oriented not to the successful pursuit and achievement of goals but to reaching understanding (on the basis of validity claims raised in speech acts).[8] Communicative action is thus the proposed Habermasian solution to the possibility of power (to) as concerted action. In a critical explication of the distinctive Arendtian conception of communicative power, Habermas proposes that 'the communicatively produced power of common convictions originates in the fact that those involved are oriented towards reaching agreement and not primarily to their respective individual successes. It is based on the fact that they do not use language "perlocutionarily", [that is] merely to instigate other subjects to a desired behaviour, but "illocutionarily", that is, for the noncoercive establishment of intersubjective relations' (1977: 213).

Where Habermas disagrees with Arendt is with respect to her argument that the concept of power should have *exclusive* reference to relations of concerted action. Noting that Arendt supports this position by equating strategic social action with instrumental action in which the crucial factor is the implication of force and violence as opposed to intersubjectivity, Habermas argues that it is much more useful to conceive of communicative action and strategic action as *alternative* types of social action, both of which are to be contrasted with instrumental action which may be understood as 'nonsocial action that can also be carried out by a solitary subject' (ibid.: 221). The advantage of such a conceptualisation, Habermas argues, is that it retains the distinctiveness of a concept of power (to) focused upon the all-important question of the generation of power while equally recognising the centrality of strategic action in the acquisition, maintenance and exercise of power (over). The centrality of strategic action to definitive structures of modern domination, capitalism and the state, has led to the Hobbesian/Weberian identification of power 'with a potential for successful strategic action' (ibid.). Opposing such a comprehensive identification, Habermas agrees with Arendt's argument that 'strategic contests for political power neither call forth nor maintain those institutions *in which that power is anchored*' (ibid.: 222, emphasis mine).

Habermas' theory of communicative action represented the culmination of an attempt to rescue the project of critical theory from the impasse at which it had arrived with the Frankfurt School's surrender to Weber's reading of modernity as systematic domination over nature and man. Central to this attempt is the key proposition that 'Western modernisation constitutes only a one-sided utilisation of the rationality potential of modernity' (White 1990: 97). A fully adequate account of both the potential and – according to Habermas – the partial reality of the rationality project of modernity involves the recognition of a parallel process to the Weberian theorisation of modernity as the comprehensive subordination of all world phenomena to criteria of purposive-rationality: this parallel process is one in which 'there is a rationalisation of everyday practice ... accessible only from the perspective of action oriented to reaching understanding – a rationalisation of the lifeworld that Weber neglected compared with the rationalisation of action systems like the economy and the state' (Habermas 1984: 340).

In explicating the possibilities and limitations of Arendt's communications concept of power, power is specified by Habermas as a unique social resource, produced through communicative action, understood as action directed towards intersubjective understanding. Power conceived in these terms underpins and provides the only defensible legitimation of collective decisions in a post-traditional world and, as such, may be viewed as central to both social production and social reproduction understood as symbolic processes in a distinctively modern world. If we understand communicative action as a 'principle of sociation' providing the medium through which social integration as a differentiated process of symbolic social reproduction is achieved, then the power (to) of such communicative action becomes central to those processes of social development constitutive of rationalised modernity (ibid.: 337).[9]

The models of both Arendt and Habermas have been of course the subject of wide and continuing critical examination. In some cases, the resultant criticisms are so fundamental and wide-ranging as to amount to outright rejection.[10] Even among many sympathetic critics who acknowledge and appreciate the potential implications of Arendt's argument regarding the specifically human character of the generation of social power as opposed to mechanical force, there is a fundamental questioning of the boundary that she seeks to establish around the political space to the exclusion of what she conceives of as disruptive and ultimately degenerative social intrusions.[11] In advancing what was clearly intended to be a redemptive perspective on the fall of modernity with respect to ancient possibilities of an interest free politics of civic republicanism, her general stance appears to portray an irrecoverable, socially determined erosion of the boundary between public and private necessary for an autonomous, innovative politics.[12] Similarly, those who appreciate the critical and emancipatory intent of the Habermas *oeuvre* nevertheless have expressed a wide range of concerns about problematic aspects of his successive specifications of communicative action and the public sphere. Of particular and chronic concern are Habermas' commitment to a consensual model of political outcomes, his assumption of the givenness of interests and of the unitary character of the public sphere.[13]

Whatever the limitations of their original application and/or conceptual explication, the extent to which the arguments of Arendt and Habermas concerning an alternative, distinctive conception of power contain analytic possibilities for a transformative democratic politics of empowerment in late modernity will be considered in Part II. For the present, it is sufficient to note that in principle at least, these arguments do offer a 'meaning-ful' alternative to the equation of power and domination under modernity,[14] and to the closure of political possibilities that follows from such an equation. In particular, they represent variable but analogous approaches to a distinctive conceptualisation of power (to) as expressing concerted action rooted in the intersubjectivity of historically grounded and situated action. The significance of such a concept of power lies in the purchase it offers in approaching questions and issues which are central to the articulation of a genuinely democratic politics in late modernity. Among such questions are: the relationship between concerted power and community, the determination of interest(s) within community and the relationship of concerted power and community to structures of domination.

Power, Community, Interests and Domination

In their different ways, both Arendt and Habermas recognise the significantly *constructed* character of community under modernity; that is, they mutually propose that truly modern communities may all be subsumed under Benedict Anderson's categorisation of the 'communities' of nationalism: they are all 'imagined communities' (Anderson 1991).[15] As we saw above, for Arendt the possibility of community is only realisable through speech and action, which is to say, through the power (to) that is the concerted action of intersubjectivity. This link between power and community is produced and can only be reproduced by 'publicity', the *sine qua non* of that public space which is the context of political freedom. It seems clear what Arendt wishes to convey by this term: the symbolic creation of 'a common world' through the open discussion of issues which connect, either actually or potentially, those involved in the discussion (see Disch 1994; also Parekh 1981: 92). Both the necessity and the desirability of such open discussion is rooted in the fundamental reality of plurality. Thus, for Arendt, the public space derives from 'the simultaneous presence of innumerable perspectives and aspects in which the common world presents itself and for which no common measurement or denominator can ever be devised' (Arendt 1989: 57). Plurality and that diversity of viewpoints which derives from it provide irreducible elements of the Arendtian public space.

As Disch points out, Arendt's specification of the public space, the '*inter-est*, which lies between people and therefore can relate and bind them together', carries the potential of a significant contribution to discussions of contemporary democratic politics (1994: 35). Crucially for Arendt, the inter-est 'always fulfils the double function of binding men together *and* separating them in an articulate way' (ibid.). This emphasis on both commonality and articulate(d) separation allows one to distinguish a specific Arendtian conception of interest from that of both the liberal and the communitarian models of politics. Whereas the liberal model identifies an irreducible diversity of interests and identities and consequently specifies a procedural model of conflict resolution, the communitarian model proposes an essential common interest expressive of the authentic beings of the diverse members of the political community. In contrast, Arendt's conception of interest juxtaposes the commonality of shared discussion with the irreducible plurality of humanity in a recognition of articulate separation.[16] In the Arendtian perspective what sustains the solidarity of interest is the distance of separation (Disch 1994: 36; cf. Barber 1998).[17]

The analytic possibilities we can therefore identify in Arendt's discussion of these issues concern the specification of concerted power as an immanent community of interest, an interest not externally given or derived but *constructed* through the symbolic commonality of discussion and argumentation, a discussion which nevertheless is not understood as realising a pre-existing essence which would deny the plurality of the public realm.

Similar possibilities are clearly identifiable in the work of Habermas. In particular, the concepts of communicative action and the public sphere have been fundamental to his development of the above all political project of a critical theory. For Habermas, under modernity the very possibility of the symbolic production and reproduction which is the social is increasingly the achievement of that concerted power which is communicative sociation. Upon the power (to) generated by communicative action which is expressed in the production of freedom in and through (immanent) community rest both the preservation of autonomy and the construction of solidarity.[18]

Communicative Action and the Debate about Power

Central to contemporary discussions of the conceptualisation and analysis of power, whether modernist or postmodernist, has been a continuing debate about power and 'interests' (Davis et al. 1991). The potential contribution of Habermas' argument about communicative action to a consideration of empowerment and community in late modernity can be further explored by locating it within that debate. This debate concerns the (disputed) necessity in *any* discussion of power of some reference to a concept of interest. An initial pluralist contribution to discussions of power was clear, even categorical, on this issue: it made an explicit equation of interest with expressed preferences, an equation defended on both epistemological and methodological grounds (see, in particular, Polsby 1980). Various critics argued fiercely against such a position, proposing that it failed to address the extent to which and the ways in which the *shaping* of preferences was an important, indeed crucial, aspect of any structure of domination. These criticisms culminated in the text *Power: A Radical View* which set out Lukes' argument concerning a concept of 'real interests', a concept explicitly contrasted with consciously held preferences.

One major line of criticism of the 'radical' position detailed by Lukes concerned the degree to which its counterfactual referent – the notion of self-ascription of interests under privileged conditions – greatly constrained its practical utility. This limitation is seen as vitiating the degree to which Lukes' argument can provide a solution to the so-called 'paradox of emancipation'; that is, the paradox wherein the emancipation of the dominated can only be achieved by the intervention of an external agent, who must logically become another possible source of domination.[19] Arguing that Lukes' critique was fundamentally constrained by an ultimate effort to identify interests with 'real' wants and preferences, Benton's Gramscian solution to this paradox required the replacement of any reference to interests with a reference to transformative objectives, such objectives being further proposed to be revealed in the symbolic content of practices (Benton 1981: 172). While Benton's counter-critique of Lukes' 'radical' position has been a standard aspect of the genealogy of 'power positions', the analytic possibilities raised by his position have not been developed.

Central to such a solution is the proposition that an adequate methodology of power requires recognition of a meaningful and identifiable distinction between expressions of wants and preferences and the symbolic and immanent meaning of social practices dissonant with the reproduction of structures of domination. Benton proposed that intellectual subordination is easier to achieve and sustain than practical subordination but this might be more coherently expressed in a contrast between intellectual compliance and practical resistance.[20] The theoretical coherence of this distinction requires a necessary further sociological assumption concerning the inherently unstable properties of structures of domination. Thus, for example, in assessing capitalist structures of domination, one could propose that the 'self-reproducing practices and strategies of the ruling class (group) bring about spontaneous practices of resistance on the part of subordinate classes (groups)' (Benton 1981: 173; Giddens 1982b).

The alternative conception of interest and its place in political discourse to which Benton's critique of the conceptualisation of 'interests' gives rise has two implications of particular relevance to a conceptualisation of power in terms of processes of concerted action. The first of these arises from a central feature of the alternative conceptualisation, namely, the specification of *both* the indispensably cognitive *and* evaluative character of interest-ascriptions. This feature presupposes a type of specifically cognitive and causal discourse 'which issues in characterisations of social positions, [social] relations and their future possibilities' (ibid.: 181). The second implication is that the very possibility of social processes of empowerment is dependent upon the existence of 'ideological struggles', *understood as a variety of discourses and related social practices.*[21] For such 'ideological struggles' to take place requires that it 'cannot be the case the mechanisms which operate to produce a pattern of wants, etc. in conformity with the purposes of those who hold power [that is, are superordinates in an overall structure of domination] act without confronting, or even simultaneously producing counter-tendencies. *It is a condition of possibility of "struggle" that opposition of some form exists*' (ibid.: 181, emphasis mine).

Such struggles, as Benton notes, have a dual dimension to them; they are both discursive and formally rational. The former dimension concerns that variety of dissonant forms of action identifiable as the symbolic content of alternative social forms. It seems reasonable to understand such content as involving distinctive substantive values and needs interpretations, that is, a distinctive conception of the good society.[22] Thus, the distinction regarding the content of ideological struggles again raises the question of the relationship between evaluative judgements and normative judgements: that is, between competing conceptions of the good society, on the one hand, and judgements about justice and its implementation, on the other.

Recognising that Habermas' stance on this issue has been the object of considerable critical scrutiny, the theory of communicative action can still make a clear contribution to the formulation of a defensible and utilisable relationship between power (to) (understood as concerted action) and the identification of interests, a relationship moreover which avoids the pitfalls of Benton's 'paradox of emancipation'. Two conditions are central to the communicative model: 'the agent's claim to rationality in disputes about proposed collective arrangements and how that claim makes him/her intersubjectively responsible to others' (White 1990: 88). These conditions require that in generating the power of concerted action, agents cultivate their capacity to think reflexively about their interests and the underlying values and needs from which such interests derive. The coherence of the communicative model (with regard to the clarification of interests) is further maintained by the concept of *generalisable* interest which requires a mutual commitment to (ontological and social) pluralism and a choice among alternatives in terms of such a concept.[23]

The relevance of these possibilities to a distinctive conception of power is further strengthened by a consideration of the relationship between power and interests. As is well known, the central point of methodological contention in the pluralist position concerns the possibility of confining the study of power to the identification and analysis of overt clashes (Bachrach and Baratz 1962; Lukes 1974). To formulate the conditions for deliberation about interests as, above all, a structure of communication is to recognise that very possibility of ideological hegemony (and resistance to it) which Benton, for example, identifies as key to an alternative conception of power; that is, it is to offer both a mechanism whereby the possibility that the absence of overt clashes may express a structure of domination can be identified and a possible procedure whereby the formulation of alternative (generalisable) interests to those implicated in such a structure may be attempted.[24] Moreover, as we shall see shortly, the clarification of the interaction between conceptions of the good society and the just society and the empirical anchoring of the former in terms of symbolic practices and struggles for recognition, strengthens the cognitive aspect of the generation of power through *intersubjective* processes of interest identification and identity formation.

Power and Domination

Central to the analysis of a transformative politics of empowerment in late modernity is the question of the relationship between intersubjective, concerted power and structures of domination. It is here that Habermas' work is arguably least useful. In spite of the discussion of 'new social movements' in *The Theory of Communicative Action* as significant sites of oppositional resistance to pressures of systemic sociation, a clear point of unity between Arendt and Habermas lies in their rejection of social movements as possible 'carriers of new collective identity, capable of institutionalising the positive potentials of modernity ... or of transcending particularistic and expressive politics' (Cohen 1985; see also Cohen and Arato 1992). This limitation is due in significant part to a more fundamental conceptual limitation, a limitation which represents a serious obstacle to Habermas' effective engagement with the possibilities of transformative politics in late modernity. This limitation concerns Habermas' conceptualisation of modernity in terms of system and lifeworld.[25] (See, for example, Mouzelis 1991: Appendix I.)

The system–lifeworld model understands modernity as a process of rationalisation structured around the independent but unequal development of two social systems. These systems are distinguished according to the degree to which purposive-rational action or interaction predominates. Interaction is the mode in terms of which the institutional framework of a society or of the sociocultural lifeworld is structured, whereas purposive-rational action is the mode in terms of which technically oriented subsystems are structured (Habermas 1989b). Within the terms of this distinction, the crisis of modernity is identified in the pathologies that arise from the increasing incursion of purposive-rational subsystems into larger and larger areas of the lifeworld. The corresponding practical task of a critical social theory is to facilitate the achievement and defence of the boundary between the systems of interaction structured around communicatively derived norms and purposive-rational subsystems, above all the economy and the state.

As Honneth notes, the critical consequence of this model is to relegate processes of social domination to a secondary role in the structuring of modernised societies. Specifically, *power or domination that disruptively influences the ... process of will-formation results not from the administrative control of socially privileged groups but also from the pressure for adaption that purposive-rational organisations socially exercise.* To this extent, the basic conflict that distinguishes social evolution does not dwell within the process of social understanding as an opposition between social groups or classes, but is set out in the field of opposition between purposive-rational and communicatively-organised action spheres. (Honneth 1993: 268, emphasis mine)

Systems of interaction and purposive-rationality are therefore proposed by Habermas to coexist but *do so independently of one another*, except for the propensity for the latter increasingly to react destructively upon the former. Neither the content nor the character of processes of interaction is influenced by purposive-rational systems; the only threat is to their integrity. Honneth among others argues for the inadequacy of such a conceptualisation and proposes that its defects can be substantially addressed by a second model of structure and development undeveloped but clearly identifiable in Habermas' work (Honneth 1993: 269 seq. and in general chs. 7–9).[26]

In this second model, derived from the interpretation of Marx offered by Habermas in *Knowledge and Human Interests* (Habermas 1978), the realities of social division (whether of class, gender or race for example) necessitate that social subjects benefit unequally from institutionalised norms. In such circumstances, the process of communicative action must be substantially shaped by struggles between asymmetrically advantaged social groups. Social interaction in this model is conceived of therefore as a struggle between social groups to determine the organisational forms of purposive-rational action. 'Under conditions characterised by an unequal division of burdens and privileges, communicative action assumes the form of a struggle that the concerned subjects conduct over ways of conducting their common praxis' (Honneth 1993: 270). Honneth makes it clear that the conflicts specified in this second model are not to be understood as strategic conflicts over desired goods; rather, the struggles concern 'the legitimacy of existing social norms and the introduction of new ones'. *They are above all struggles over normativity.* Struggles around communicative rationalisation in the form of the change of institutional frameworks must be thought of as 'a process of repression and liberation'. Most importantly from the point of view of understanding the relationship between power to as concerted and situated agency and structures of domination, transformative insights into the limitations of a given structure of social interaction, whether discursive or formal, derive from 'the concrete knowledge of suffered domination and experienced injustice'. As a result, 'the path that leads to the institutionalisation of justified norms is prepared by *the practical struggle of social groups and not by linguistic understanding alone*' (ibid.: 271, emphasis mine).[27]

Certain important consequences for the relationship between power and domination follow from this explication of Habermas' second model of struggle. Structures of domination may be understood as expressions of negotiated but nevertheless contingent compromise in the chronic struggles around the expression of divergent ethical communities. As such, they are, in Benton's terms, sites of 'ideological struggle' and provide contexts with the potential to give rise to manifestations of power as historically situated concerted action. Further, contrary to the premises of the system–lifeworld model, purposive-rational subsystems are just as determined by and expressive of practical-moral viewpoints and consequent power struggles as formal sites of communicative interaction.

An adequate understanding of the relationship between power and domination therefore requires recognition of the unstable character of structures of domination, of the chronic character of ideological struggles in terms of values, norms and practices, and of the consequent contextual generation of concerted action in response to experiences of injustice. The production of power in such a perspective involves action, discursive or formal, which is potentially or actually transformative of structures of domination. Both the generation of power and its strategic employment in the context of 'arenas of struggle' are therefore central aspects of the analysis of the interrelations between power and domination (Hindess 1982: 498–511). The reality of such power struggles requires, as Hindess has emphasised, that we recognise outcomes for what they are: not the functional product of proposed differential capacities, as within the perspective that sees power and domination as conceptual synonyms differentiated only by possible empirical regularity, but as 'produced in the course of the practices of agents which are always subject to definite conditions and obstacles, which often include the practices of other agents' (ibid.: 502). This is not to deny, as Hindess also recognises, that mobilisation may take place 'on the basis of objectives that are given in advance of the struggle in question, or that discourses on "interests", their own or those of others, may play an effective role in the constitution of particular forces' (ibid.: 508).[28] As has been noted above, to the degree that struggles and resistance have a formalised character, such discourses will necessarily take on a more prominent aspect. Equally, however, it has to be recognised that a *sufficient* explanation of resistance and mobilisation cannot be advanced in terms of the stated objectives involved, since 'objectives are not always given independently of particular conditions of struggle but also ... may (change or develop) in the course of struggle' (ibid.: 509).[29]

The important point at issue here is the need to recognise the importance of the contextual character of power and its relation to structures of domination. *Power as concerted action is always historical and situated.* Hindess is right to argue that those differential capacities which provide the contours of structures of domination as reproduced asymmetries should be seen, not as the *givens* of any analysis of struggle and possible transformation but as *contextually conditional elements* within it, the realisation and relevance of which are subject to the deployment of definite means of action. As such, 'they cease to be capacities to secure, to realise or to control, and become at best capacities to act in pursuit of certain objectives ... struggles over divergent objectives [or in Honneth's terms, over norms and their implementation] really are struggles, not the playing out of some pre-ordained script' (ibid.: 507).[30]

If one accepts, *contra* Arendt, that there is always a necessary link between particular structures of domination and the potential for particular productions of power, the question to be clarified concerns the nature of the link. However, the implications of the position developed here are that the meaningful nature of the generation of social power precludes the possibility of a mechanical one-to-one relation between a particular structure of domination and a particular generation of power. The basic reason for this impossibility concerns the multi-dimensional character of empirical processes of domination. In identifying structures of domination, we are identifying pure types which are not found in isolation in processes of struggle.[31]

Domination and Power

Bearing such a qualification in mind, how can we conceive of the relationship between domination (structural 'power over') and power (concerted action)? A useful starting point is offered by Layder's critical analysis of the attempts by Lukes and Giddens to offer an integrated solution of the structural and agentic aspects of social relations (Layder 1985: 131–49). In summation, Layder's various criticisms produce the following propositions:

1 'Power as Agency' and 'Power as Structure' are ontologically and analytically separable, though empirically related, phenomena.
2 Structural power is relatively independent of agency.
3 Agency is always subject to the influence of structural power.
4 Structural power, while being the outcome of human action at specific historical junctures, acts over time as sedimented constraint on future agency.
5 Structural power can be defined as 'a set of (prior) *reproduced asymmetric relations* between groups based on the possession of, and restriction of access to, certain resources' (emphasis mine). (That is, group possession must be conceived of as the property of an historically emergent structure (i.e. a set of reproduced asymmetric relations between groups) and not simply as a property of action or agency as such.)

It will be clear from the previous argument that in the perspective adopted here, the degree of interdependence of structural and agentic elements is regarded as being greater than Layder proposes. Nevertheless, this schema does offer a useful framework to consider the relationship(s) between power and structure. The major conceptual amendment proposed here is the replacement of the term 'structural power' by that of 'domination'. This allows a much needed clarity to be brought to the discussion of power by the adoption of an exclusive focus for its conceptualisation and analysis. The present work conceives of that focus as one of concerted agency, necessarily and simultaneously both individual and collective. Social power is therefore understood as 'power to', the power of concerted agency, inherently interactive and meaningful, which agency is conceived as expressive of communicative interaction and as corresponding to immanent symbolic communities. In contrast, the concept of domination refers to reproduced asymmetric social relations. While such relations are correctly seen as being, in Layder's apposite term, 'obdurate' over time, nevertheless, they are inherently unstable, the contingent manifestation of negotiated compromises within the context of inter-group struggles expressive of strategic action.

Structures of domination are most usefully understood as both indicating the parameters of reproduced asymmetric relations and as specifying sites of ideological struggles, such struggles being invariably practical and, on occasion, intellectual and practical. In identifying possibilities and processes of social transformation, we must distinguish between the ways in which particular types of social agency (including sustainable forms of social conflict over issues of social distribution and social regulation) may contribute to *the reproduction of particular structures of domination* and the ways in which particular types may be understood as expressive – either discursively or formally – of possibilities of alternative immanent communities. Of course, when viewed empirically such types are not invariably or necessarily mutually exclusive; on the contrary. Equally, it would be quite misleading to view all conflicts chronically 'pre-determined' by the structural logic of a particular structure of domination as having any potential or even significance for processes of social transformation.

Obviously, what is central to such considerations is the need to avoid specifying or more accurately asserting collective action via some mechanical reductionism. Taking seriously both the plurality stressed by Arendt and the constructed nature of communicatively generated communities under modernity requires that we take particular care to avoid such reductionism in exploring the relations between (structures of) domination and manifestations of power as concerted action. There is, however, an equal necessity to contextualise the normative and analytic possibilities raised by the conception of power as concerted action in wider social processes whether at the level of social network, workplace, industry, region, national state, supra-national structures or transnational context; all refer to potential arenas of struggle around objectives of domination and transformation. This leads, for example, to the further requirement of a historical specification of struggles for social domination and empowerment with respect to constitutive and functionally rationalised structures of modernity such as capitalism and the international system of states.

Postmodernist perspectives on the character of the social in a denaturalised and therefore socially constituted world frequently evince fundamental scepticism regarding the essentialism of putative structures, whether for example of capitalist modernity or state power, and consequently question the possibility of identifying *any* necessary linkages between positions of super- and subordination and struggles implicating alternative ethical communities. From such a perspective, not only have the meta-narratives of early phases of modernity been shown to be ill-founded, but any possibilities of historically situated transformative politics centred on processes of concerted action have been rendered redundant. To demonstrate that such is not the case requires the identification of an alternative to various forms of social reductionism (of which economic reductionism is only the most familiar example) and to a decontextualised political activism.

A useful starting point in the explication of the complex and significantly contingent linkage between structured asymmetries of

domination and realisations of collective action is offered by Mouzelis'
discussion of the construction of social orders (1990). Mouzelis'
basic argument is that social analysis of the constitution, reproduction and transformation of social orders is most usefully undertaken
from a stance which conceives of such orders as being composed of
distinctive institutional spheres, each with its own technology, appropriation of such technology and specific ideology. These spheres are
those of economic, political and cultural production, respectively, no
sphere being given analytic priority over any other. Consequently,
while one such institutional sphere is clearly that of economic production, the concept of forces or technologies of production does not
have to refer exclusively to economic production: 'there are technologies of political production just as there are technologies of economic
production' (ibid.: 55). Thus, *the political structure of domination,*
for example, may be conceptualised and analysed with respect to
both its internal relations and its relations to other structures of
domination with regard to technology, appropriation and ideology.

In the course of establishing the distinctiveness and analytic autonomy of institutional spheres, while stressing the empirical autonomy of collective agents, Mouzelis formulates the possibilities of
collective agency in terms of the relationship between *locations* in a
structure of domination (whether economic, political or cultural)
and *social practices* seen as reactions to such locations. Explicating
his concept of appropriation, he argues that it is a merit of the
Marxist concept of relations of production that it links class locations and class practices, institutional analysis and an analysis in
terms of strategic conduct: 'the more we focus on how agents *react*
to their locations by trying to maintain or transform their structural
positions *vis-à-vis* the means of production, the more we are concerned with issues of strategic conduct – with issues concerning the
manner in which subjects construct their identities and their views
of what constitutes their interests, how they go about promoting
them, and so on' (ibid.: 61).

Subsequently, Mouzelis proposes that 'class exploitation is a very
special type of "closure", where the resources over which the antagonists are fighting *derive directly from their relationship within the
system of production*' (ibid.: 62, emphasis mine). He concludes: 'class
exploitation is not simply group competition over the distribution of
rewards; *it is a fundamental type of conflict situation, which allows
the establishment of quite precise links between the antagonists and
the overall institutional context in which their conflict is embedded*'
(ibid., emphasis mine).

What is proposed here is a direct link between a particular structure of domination and, at the very least, the notion of social conflict. Such a relationship is one in which the structure of domination does not merely set the parameters indicative of structured antagonisms between dominant and subordinate groups and in relation to which relational practices must be contextualised if any adequate account of the character and possibilities of power relations is to be developed.[32] It is rather one within which, to use Mouzelis' term, practices are to be conceived of as reactions to the structure of domination; that is, practices may be thought of as reactive and not creative. In relation to the analysis of transformative struggles, such reactive practices may be reasonably argued to generally serve to reproduce existing structures of domination. They principally exemplify processes within structures of power over (domination) rather than struggles based in processes of power to.

The limitation of such a perspective concerns the absence of any consideration of the role of normative frameworks framing the absence, presence and form of such conflicts. A helpful possibility in this regard is offered by Paul Edwards' proposal regarding the deployment of different levels of analysis to deal with the identification and analysis of the several meanings of social conflict (Edwards 1986: esp. ch. 2.). Edwards' particular concern is with modes of production but there would appear to be no reason why his argument could not be extended to incorporate other structures of domination, such as state power, gender and race. The most fundamental 'conflictual' level is that of a 'structured antagonism' between dominant and subordinate groups, such antagonism being definitive of the overall structure of domination (Urry 1995: 170–2).[33] Such a structured antagonism may be seen as definitive of a structure of domination but this by no means determines all practices, let alone all or indeed any outcomes, which occur in relation to its general asymmetry. There is, as Edwards notes, considerable variation in the ways in which both conflict and cooperation occur within the parameters of any given structure. A particular advantage of Edwards' formulation in the context of the general discussion of power and domination is that it makes no assumptions regarding either the generation or the identification of privileged or prioritised interests.

Power and Immanent Community

One crucial issue remains to be considered: the question of the immanent communities implicated in power struggles under modernity. As

Honneth notes in his pathbreaking explication of 'the moral grammer of social conflicts', within the sociological literature at the very least, the identification and analysis of counter-hegemonic agency (whether in terms of resistance, protest or rebellion) has been subsumed under categories of 'interest' (Honneth 1996). It is of course within this perspective, whether in political science or political sociology, that the preoccupation with the possibility of establishing coherent link-ages between mobilisation and interests has its location and meaning (Ball 1988: ch. 4; Clegg 1989: ch. 2). Mobilisation in relation to domi-nation is proposed to take place on the basis of interests, conceived of as arising from objective inequalities in the distribution of material rewards and opportunities. Excluded from this schema therefore is any reference to what Honneth terms 'the everyday web of moral feelings' (cf. Moore 1978).

Interests over morality

Proposing that analytic and practical limitations arise from this exclusion of ideas of moral consciousness, Honneth has developed an alternative model of mobilisation focusing on 'a concept of social struggle that takes as its starting point moral feelings of indignation, rather than pre-given interests' (Honneth 1996: 161).[34] Within the terms of this model, transformative social struggles are understood as concerning demands for social recognition of new forms of identity. Of the possible foci of identity distinguished by the model, those expressed through legal rights and social esteem respectively involve forms of recognition which represent *moral* contexts for *societal* conflict, 'if only because they rely on socially generalised criteria in order to function' (ibid.: 162).[35] In Honneth's identity model, there-fore, social struggles are understood as 'practical [i.e. moral and politi-cal] process[es] in which individual experiences of disrespect are read as typical for [sic] an entire group … in such a way that they can moti-vate collective demands for expanded relations of recognition' (ibid.).

Identity politics

The analytic potential of this model is enhanced by a number of characteristics. First, it involves no theoretical pre-commitment regarding the character of resistance. Social groups may use material, symbolic or merely passive force to publicise and seek restitution for the disrespect they identify and experience as typical. Secondly, the conception of struggle requires no distinction as between intentional and unintentional forms of social conflict; that is, actors are not required to be aware of the driving moral motivation of their actions. Thus, Honneth argues, 'one can easily identify cases in which social movements intersubjectively misidentify, as it were, the moral core of their resistance by explicating it in the inappropriate terms of *mere* interest-categories' (ibid.: 163, emphasis mine).[36] This emphasis upon the possibilities of identifying the transformative implications of particular processes of resistance parallels Gramsci's methodological injunction to look beyond the 'borrowed conceptions' of hegemonic language in order to identify the symbolic content of practice (Benton 1981: 172). Thirdly, the concept of identity struggles involves a critical link between the personal and the social, since individual expressions of disrespect can only be articulated in terms of universal ideas and appeals.

If the foregoing characteristics give the 'recognition' model a useful empirical and therefore analytic flexibility, its theoretical content is in contrast quite precise. Whereas utilitarian models of social resistance and social struggle focus upon some concept of interest as the key *explanans* in their various arguments, the recognition model identifies the violation of deeply rooted expectations regarding recognition within the context of moral experiences as the key element in transformative struggles. The relevance of both models to the analysis of social power rests upon the requirement that concerted collective resistance can only occur on the basis of some intersubjective framework which specifies the relevant experience(s) as typical of an entire group; that is to say, both models propose a relationship between social power as collective mobilisation and some conception of immanent community. Both these conceptions are necessarily social but only transformative processes of the most general kind involve projects of change which are societal in scope.[37]

While Honneth's recognition model does have significant potential for the analysis of transformative struggles, its formulation contains a number of limitations which need to be addressed. The first of these concerns the critical issue of general applicability to the relationship between domination, power as concerted action, and immanent community. One category of recognition struggles specified by the model concerns the pursuit of esteem within the framework of an immanent ethical community. The achievement of such esteem is proposed by Honneth to necessitate participation in an intersubjectively shared community of values. However, as Alexander notes, there is an 'unacknowledged ambiguity' in Honneth's discussion of this matter (Alexander and Lara 1996). On the one hand, his argument suggests that the mere fact of symbolic participation in a shared ethical community is sufficient to provide recognition, that is, to provide social affirmation in terms of particular conceptions of 'the good life'. On the other hand, he proposes that, in order for such recognition to be consistent with a framework of justice, it must be capable of reconciliation with the plurality of a wider symbolic community, at least at the level of a legal community.

The immediate difficulty that arises is that, in an age characterised by both the diffusion and intensification of various fundamentalisms, the realisation of many conceptions of 'the good life' has been seen – and pursued through – the potential or actual domination of other communities articulated around different values.[38] In such circumstances, 'demands for recognition that appear subjectively legitimate to [particular groups of] social actors, which emerge, indeed, from their concrete forms of ethical life, are deeply suspect in moral terms' (ibid.: 134). Honneth's attempted resolution of the demands of 'the good life' and justice involves the proposition that the mutual valuation of ethical communities, the foundation of their mutual empowerment, arises from the anthropological force of human need. Thus, he asserts: '"Solidarity" can be understood as an interactive relationship in which subjects mutually sympathise with their various different ways of life because, among themselves, they esteem each other symmetrically' (Honneth 1996: 128). As Alexander rightly comments, this developmental commitment to an anthropological imperative makes Honneth seem overly confident that recognition struggles will necessarily lead to change, both transformative and emancipatory, as opposed to being transformative and dominational, creating and/or strengthening exclusions and subordinations (Alexander and Lara 1996: 134).[39] What is therefore required is a substantial engagement with 'the contingencies of actual historical outcomes' and with 'the complex moral and institutional textures' necessary to realise the 'good and just' life.

As Arendt and Paul Edwards in their very different ways make clear, the relationship between power as concerted action and wider institutional frameworks is mediated and complex.[40] In such mediations, actors play a critical and irreducible role in articulating and thereby mobilising immanent communities of Arendtian inter-est and (partial) identity. Recognition of the distinctiveness of power as concerted action requires analysis of the illocutionary, performative processes implicated in its realisation (Alexander and Lara 1996: 131–2).[41] The consideration of the possibilities offered within the conceptual frameworks of the public sphere, citizenship and new social movements, respectively, for a theorisation of such mobilisations *and* mediations is the central focus of Part II below.

A second limitation in Honneth's formulation of the recognition model concerns the unequivocal weight attached to the development of law as a medium of transformative recognition. Thus,

Honneth proposes that only under modernity does there occur that differentiation in terms of personal relations, legal relations and ethical communities of esteem of such a kind as to make possible the emergence of *distinctive* social struggles (struggles, in effect, of 'difference') embodying the pursuit, at least in the case of law and communities of value, of intersubjective immanent communities of mutual recognition. Here again, *the issue of normativity, its generation and embodiment, is central.* Under modernity, Honneth argues,

> for the first time, we find normative structures built into legal relations (with the *possibilities* for universalisation and de-formalisation ...) and into communities of value (with the *possibilities* for individualisation and equalisation) – normative structures that can become accessible via emotionally laden experiences of disrespect and that can be appealed to in the struggles resulting from these experiences. (Honneth 1996: 170, emphasis mine)

Honneth's proposed resolution of recognition struggles via incorporation into law is both more complicated and more contentious than he recognises. For example, his argument links the self-respect sought in recognition struggles to processes and institutions of social organisation and understands such organisation in modernity principally in terms of the gradual extension of citizenship rights. Advancing a developmental model relating to the gradual abstraction and generalisation of law to the extension of its normative reach, he analyses the role of law in the development of horizontally defined citizen communities. But, legal generality and abstractness do not in themselves tell us anything about recognition of moral autonomy or its diminution (Alexander and Lara 1996: 133). As we shall see in Part II, the analysis of the limitations of legal generality in terms of creating and masking fundamental social exclusions and misrecognitions has become central to contemporary citizenship analysis (Chapter 7 below).

For this reason, it is necessary to build upon Honneth's overly formalistic discussion by identifying power as collective action as central to the recognition struggles of modernity, early, high and late. To conflate the 'simple' fact of legal regulation with the practical/political recognition of moral capacity and consequent ethical restructuring may lead to the neglect of processes of subordination via incorporation and equally to the neglect of critical processes of 'normalisation' (see Chapter 6 below). Such neglect can be addressed by an analysis of the ways in which the 'moral capacity of different groups of actors is crystallised by social movements that intervene in the public sphere in an illocutionary way' (ibid.). Expressing the possibilities inherent in a critical appropriation of Honneth's argument, empowerment in late modernity via the extension of communicative democracy requires that the contingent, fallibilistic specifications of procedural law be chronically challenged in the form of struggles, intellectual and practical, expressive of alternative immanent political communities.[42]

A third problem raised by the recognition model concerns its analytic scope. While elaborating this model, Honneth does refer also to an alternative, utilitarian model in terms of which social struggles may be analysed. Whereas the recognition model identifies as the key element in transformative struggles the violation of deeply rooted expectations regarding recognition within the context of moral experiences, utilitarian models of resistance and struggle focus upon some concept of interest as the key *explanans* in their various arguments. Discussing the possible relationship between the two models, Honneth argues for the necessity of analytic sensitivity to the possibility that conflicts articulated in terms of distribution and control – and therefore explicable within the terms of the utilitarian model – may be expressive of parallel, if not arguably deeper, struggles over the constitution and/or disruption of conceptions of ethical community. Thus, 'the [empirical] investigation of social struggles presupposes an analysis of the moral consensus that unofficially governs, within the context of social cooperation, the distribution of rights and responsibilities between the dominators and the dominated' (Honneth 1996: 167).[43]

This formulation has led some commentators to argue that, while Honneth formally identifies two analytic models for the analysis of struggle and mobilisation, he does in reality propose the recognition model as a comprehensive one, a position which is then contested on the grounds of the necessary theoretical independence of distributive and identity divisions and struggles (Fraser 1997: ch. 1; see also, Young 1990). Such an interpretation finds further support elsewhere in Honneth's work, as in his argument that the recognition paradigm offers a coherent framework within which to articulate a critical theory of capitalist society connecting institutional forms and transformative struggles (1995: ch. 1). Thus, he argues, 'under the economic conditions of capitalism the process of mutual recognition among human beings is interrupted because one social group is deprived of precisely those preconditions necessary to obtain respect' (ibid.: 13).

If we translate this perspective into a lexicon of domination and power, domination is understood as disrespect and misrecognition, socially institutionalised as marginalisation and exclusion; power as collective mobilisation on the basis of consciousness of injustice and transformative struggles as the relation between them. The recognition model appears as a variant of identity politics, albeit a highly sophisticated one, and may appear assimilable to the postmodernist proposition concerning the totally constructed nature of social inclusions/exclusions.[44] For this reason, Fraser, for example, has argued for the necessity of a 'perspectival dualism' involving what she proposes as two analytically distinct paradigms of justice, those of redistribution and recognition respectively. Each paradigm specifies injustice in a distinctive manner and each advances distinctive remedies for such injustices (1997: ch. 1).[45]

Such arguments suggest strongly that Honneth's suggestion that all transformative struggles in modernity can effectively be understood as recognition struggles may be judged as too wide and somewhat misleading, particularly given the centrality of the identity paradigm to postmodernist perspectives. Support for the necessity of recognising the potential for transformative struggles to arise in the context of the structural antagonisms specified by Paul Edwards can be found in other arguments developed by Honneth himself in the context of a critique of the political project of Arendt and Habermas (1995: ch. 2). Both in their different ways respond to what they consider the technicisation of the modern world and its intrusion into/erosion of public life by proposing alternative possibilities for the intersubjective realisation of autonomy and solidarity. Arendt does so in the form of a redemptive critique articulated around a model of politics 'purged' of any elements of modernity. Habermas does so, as will be explicated in Chapter 5 below, by elaborating a dichotomous model of instrumental and communicative action, assigning them to separate spheres and confining all possibilities for intersubjectivity and transformative struggle to the latter. Neither argument therefore, Honneth proposes, theorises any space for transformative struggles arising within the context of the historical variations of capitalism and of the capitalist work process (nor by extension within the context of any other dominant institutional form). Both abstract, for example, from the historical determination of the rationalisation of work processes and of production technology and characterise modernity either as technicisation and reactive fundamentalism (Arendt) or in terms of the problematic integration of mediatically coordinated systems and post-traditional lifeworlds. Both exclude the possibility of analysing the ways in which the transformation of instrumental action generates resistance and struggle, whether in the context of the factory or the 'smart machine'. Arguing that struggles over the work process are critical struggles over the systematic expropriation of autonomous and meaningful activity, Honneth proposes the utility of recognising a third mode of action in addition to the Habermasian dichotomy between instrumental and communicative action. This third mode represents an internal analytic differentiation within the instrumental mode between action which serves to reproduce existing forms of domination and expropriation and action which contests them. Such oppositional practices are conceptualised as cooperative effort by workers to recover control over their own work activity.

> In the broad front of instrumentally oriented action sequences which seek to bring an externally determined work process back within the horizon of an autonomously planned and controlled work activity, working subjects press a claim which is immanent to their activity. (Honneth 1995: 48)

The present chapter has argued for the analytic and political necessity of distinguishing between domination and power and has explicated such a distinction through a conceptualisation of power as intersubjectively generated concerted action derived from a critical appropriation of the conceptualisation of power by Arendt and Habermas. Analysis of the relationship between the resultant conception of power and structures of domination involves the elaboration of a non-reductionist but contextually grounded understanding of power analysis, focusing upon the autonomy of social struggles and practices understood in relation to immanent communities of interest and recognition. Such transformative struggles focusing on projects of self-control and self-government in terms of the power of concerted action have been and continue to be integral to the contestation of forms of domination generated by capitalism and the modern state system respectively. The next two chapters will consider capitalism and the modern state as key sites of domination, struggle and empowerment in modernity, seeking in particular to identify and locate within historical perspective major developments and competing characterisations in late modernity.

Notes

1. Clegg argues for an important distinction between two possible frameworks for modern power analysis, one deriving from Hobbes, the other from Machiavelli. The former, Clegg argues, provides the basis for positivistic treatments of social power, which within this perspective are treated as ultimately homologous to all other natural phenomena. The latter departs from the concern with questions of causality characteristic of the Hobbesian perspective and focuses upon the identification and explication of strategic

issues within contexts of meaning. Clegg identifies and constructively uses an important distinction. However, the key point for the argument presented here is that both these frameworks are equally concerned with questions of power over (Clegg 1989). For a valuable exploration of a plurality of approaches to political relations, see Ball 1987.

2. There is more at stake here than setting the record straight, important though that is. The real significance of Arendt's conceptualisation, whatever the difficulties of the general position, both philosophical and political, of the framework within which it is elaborated, is that it is advanced in the context of a specifically *political* argument about the erosion of political freedom under modernity. On Habermas' debt to Arendt, see Seyla Benhabib 1996b: ch. 6.

3. For an explication of Arendt's very specific and crucial understanding of public space as that of the *inter-est*, see p. 42 below.

4. The following specification of the semantic and political richness of the Arendtian conception of plurality follows Disch's illuminating discussion. See Disch 1994: 32.

5. Both the challenge and the potential are increased under modernity, the challenge due to the subversive powers of capitalism and states, the potential due to the enhanced possibilities for struggle in relation to immanent communities.

6. Honneth's explication of the 'struggle for recognition' effectively combines two modes of action. See Honneth 1996.

7. See the discussion of social movements and framing in Chapter 7 below.

8. Dallmayr argues that ultimately both instrumental and communicative action are goal-oriented, the difference being that the goals involved are different. It is true that Habermas himself argues that teleological structure is fundamental to all types of action. Nevertheless, the practical distinction between the two types of activity seems clear and the implications for distinctive conceptions of power relations meaningful and useful. See Dallmayr 1985; also White 1990: 46–7.

9. See Chapter 5, however, for the way in which Habermas' abandonment of the proposition of group struggles in favour of what McCarthy terms 'the seducements of systems theory' leads him to reconceptualise power in precisely those mediatised Parsonian terms which he had been at pains to reject in his essay on Arendt.

10. On Habermas, for example, see Mouzelis 1991 and Giddens 1985a: 95–121.

11. Cf. Cohen and Arato 1992: 177–200; Honig 1993: 7–125; Isaac 1998: 221, n. 19.

12. While she celebrates the 'glorious and promising' contribution of the workers' movement to the maintenance of radical democratic political initiatives and innovations, Arendt does so at the cost of ignoring both the context of these developments (working class movements' implication and subordination in economic reproduction) and the projective goal of such council-republican political projects (the realisation of an alternative model of control over industrial processes) (Cohen and Arato 1992: 199). Cohen and Arato rightly propose that this fundamental anti-modernism

blinds Arendt to the possibilities for a pluralistic and democratic politics represented by both the causal dynamics and processes of social movements in modernity.

13. See the analysis and critical appropriation of these issues in Chapters 5 and 6 below.

14. The double meaning here is both deliberate and most important.

15. Of course, the degree to which this is the case will (always?) be empirically variable. For Arendt, this is so because the process of construction will always take place within the narrative web provided by the community of memory. For Habermas, although there is an increased tendency under modernity for a reflexive process of 'community construction' to replace 'traditional communities', there are limits to this possibility.

16. In general terms, this may be understood as a contrast and connection between a dialogue of justice and multiple conceptions of the good life. As will be discussed in Chapter 7 below, this contrast has become central to critiques and innovations in the contemporary analysis of citizenship.

17. The importance of this link between difference and solidarity to an analysis of contemporary political debate and practice will become clear in Part II. See especially Chapter 7. Note that the proposed reciprocal link here between the autonomy of individualisation and the immanence of social commonality anticipates Honneth's argument about the relationship between the personal and the social in structures of recognition. See Honneth 1995.

18. Two points should be noted here. The first concerns the question of limits to the determination of modernised lifeworlds by rational normative judgements; the second concerns the question of limits to the possible subversion of modern lifeworlds by alternative modes of mediatised sociation associated, in Habermas' fullest statement of his theory, with the dominant functional systems of modernisation, namely money and administrative power (over). Regarding the first of these points, Dallmayr has registered the concern that Habermas' account points to the possibility of the loss of integrity of the lifeworld in the face of an increasingly pervasive rationalisation, albeit of a communicative as against instrumental variety. (See Dallmayr 1985: 245.) Stephen White, however, argues against such a conclusion, emphasising that, within Habermas' discussion, evaluative arguments (embodying a concern with both substantive values and need interpretations, that is, a concern with the articulation of the good society) are not subsumed under normative arguments about justice. White does concede that the account offered by Habermas of the relationship between rational normative judgements and evaluative judgements – that is, his account of the relationship between conceptions of the good society and the just society – may not be adequate, a reservation which, as we shall see later, is made more emphatically by Benhabib among others (see White 1990: 103; Benhabib 1992: ch. 3, 104–13).

On the question of the possible limits to the subversion of even modernised lifeworlds by modes of mediatised sociation within Habermas' argument, White makes the important point that Habermas' categorical assertion that communicative sociation 'cannot be replaced' by sociation through money or (administrative) power must be seen, *not as an empirical proposition*, but rather as a specification of the conceptual parameters of the Habermasian lifeworld, given his research programme's conceptualisation of the human subject. The argument does offer an account of the generation of resistance to processes of colonisation, but the long-term viability of meaningful resistance and consequently of communicative action to the reproduction of social and cultural life does and must remain an open question. As White notes, 'While [the] theoretical interpretation [deriving from Habermas' research programme] must, of course, be shown to "fit the facts" of contemporary social life in some sense, it nevertheless has an ineradicably *practical* – that is, moral and political – dimension. What is "really" at stake in the changes Habermas emphasises cannot be totally divorced from actors' decisions about what kinds of beings they take themselves to be' (White 1990: 111).

19. The link between such arguments and the Foucauldian perspective discussed in Chapter 1 will be obvious.

20. See the discussion in the following chapter of computerisation as an arena of struggle.

21. It is worthwhile indicating Benton's specification of the implications of his characterisation of 'interests' in full: '[The] features of [my alternative] concept of 'interests' fit it to play a multiplicity of roles in a variety of discourses and related social practices in which identities are formed and transformed, in which conflicts of loyalty are resolved, in which specific courses of action are urged or opposed, and in which exercises of power are legitimated' (1981: 181).

22. Such a conception might be understood in terms of Dallmayr's specification of the 'strong' view of the lifeworld. See Dallmayr 1985: 243–4.

23. For a critical analysis of the political viability of this proposition in a context of the mobilisation of difference see Part II below.

24. Cf. Arendt's discussion of the methodology of Jaspers and its implications in *Men in Dark Times* (1995). Flyvbjerg interprets his impressive case study as demonstrating the superiority of a Foucauldian over a Habermasian perspective on the relationship between power and rationality. However, his demonstration of the way in which strategic action, particularly with regard to the manipulation of public perception, erodes an agreed public interest, in fact supports the Habermasian model. That is, what Flyvberg demonstrates is not 'subjectless power' but systematically distorted communication. See Flyvbjerg 1998.

25. See Chapter 5 below for a larger discussion of the difficulties raised for Habermas' analysis by his commitment to a systems-theoretic approach.

26. For an outstanding discussion of the way in which Habermas' 'de-utopian' turn is reflected in the manner in which he appropriates psychoanalysis, see Whitebook 1996: 75–89. As Whitebook notes, Habermas' move away from psychoanalysis is integrally bound up with his recognition of the ambiguity in the concept of self-reflection in psychoanalysis. Self-reflection can refer to the traditional Kantian reconstruction of the presuppositions of knowledge and action; on the other hand, it can mean, as in psychoanalysis, 'the practical (and affective) reflection by a subject, *and struggle against*, the ossified blockages to insight and development that have occurred in the self-formation process' (1996: 82, emphasis mine). With Habermas' rejection of the second possibility and embrace of the first comes

a move away from psychoanalysis and a focus on a systems-theoretical approach and an impersonal learning process to the exclusion of the integral contribution of social struggle.

27. For an interesting and important exploration of the implications of this position in relation to the issue of civil disobedience, see Frankenberg 1992. Note Frankenberg's proposition that 'in action-theoretic terms, civil disobedience actualises the idea of *democratically constituted political institutions and procedures* as a plurality of public forums or "transactional milieus" in which numerous agreements concerning collective goods such as peace, ecological balance, or biological security are "constantly made renewed, tested, revoked and revised"' (26, emphasis mine). The quotations in this sentence are taken from another relevant contribution to this discussion, McCarthy 1985. See also Hannah Arendt 1972: 49–102. See below, Chapter 4, for a consideration of such arguments in the context of resistance to state domination and Part II for an analysis of current possibilities for political empowerment.

This proposition – and the limitation in Habermas' perspective it involves – has increased in importance with the growing conservatism of Habermas' position. See Chapter 5 below.

28. For an analytically insightful and historically informed discussion of the role played in such struggles by frames of injustice, see Moore 1978.

29. A classic modern example, in both senses of that term, is the emergence of second wave feminism in the US in the context of male-dominated struggles against the military-industrial complex.

30. For a comparative informed discussion of the ways in which 'contextually conditional elements' have both shaped and been shaped by such struggles producing the major national variations of organised capitalism, see Lash and Urry 1987 and Urry 1995.

31. See, for example, the substantial not to say voluminous literature on the relationship between capitalism and gender stratification. See Walby 1993 for a useful restatement of the empirical complexity of the constitution of inequality. Mann's *Sources of Social Power* represents a thematic specification and analysis of the empirical entwinings and crystallisations of the historical variability of power over ('cagings').

32. On 'structured antagonisms', see P.K. Edwards 1986: esp. ch. 2.

33. Urry is at pains to emphasise the critical analytic importance of identifying the distinction between the necessary and contingent elements in persistent and enduring structures such as capitalist relations. Further, such structures must be recognised as having clear limits with regard to their capacity to produce events and conditions of reproduction. Consequently, 'it is necessary to investigate the conditions under which [the] causal powers [inhering in structures] are in fact realised. [The] fundamental *inter*dependence of such entities means that the causal powers of some … constitute the conditions necessary for the realisation of the powers of others' (1995: 170). See the discussion of the political constitution of capitalism and of the Economic Polity in Chapters 3 and 4 below.

34. Moore speaks of the 'consciousness of injustice' (Moore 1978), a conception which, as Honneth also expresses it, 'is intended to bring out the idea that the social ethic of the suppressed masses contains no idea of a total moral order or projections of a just society abstracted from particular

situations, but is … a highly senitive sensor for injuries to intuitively recognised moral claims' (1995: 209).

35. The parallel with the role of generalisability in Habermas' specification of communicative sociation is obvious and non-accidental.

36. In arguing thus, Honneth is clearly adopting a parallel methodological and epistemological stance to that adopted by Benton; that is, Honneth's stance requires the possibility that we can juxtapose self-ascribed communities and objectively identified communities and propose the superiority of the latter. Thus, we may substitute 'moral resistance mobilised by experiences of injustice' for 'interests' in Benton's argument and express Honneth's position as follows: moral resistance mobilised by experiences of injustice can be objectively ascribed 'on the basis of principles and standards of general applicability; in that such ascriptions are corrigible; and in that the basis of ascription … [is] independent of the identity of the ascriber' (see Benton 1981: 170). See also Moore 1978.

37. Given both the strong propensity to identify the boundaries of the societal with the circumscribed territoriality of states and (to state the position minimally) possible tendencies toward the de-territorialisation of political processes in late modernity, such projects are by no means exclusively or even primarily national in character. See the discussions of citizenship and social movements below.

38. For illuminating discussions of the relationship between particularism and universalism in the current epoch, see Barber 1996 and 1998.

39. While both strongly commending the originality of Honneth's project of bridging theorisations of 'the just society' and 'the good life' – or in shorthand terms, of linking the liberals and the communitarians respectively – and positively evaluating the realisation of that project, Alexander is specifically critical of the degree to which Honneth's argument is limited by this implicit commitment to an anthropological (in the philosophical and not the disciplinary sense) evolutionary perspective on social transformation. Given Honneth's earlier critique of Habermas, one should note a certain irony in the fact of Alexander's accusation that Honneth's evolutionism leads to an underestimation, even a neglect, of the critical illocutionary role of actors.

40. Alexander and Lara (1996) in their sympathetic but critical discussion of Honneth's recognition argument also emphasise the importance of mediation in the determination of social outcomes.

41. As noted above, Hindess rightly emphasises this contingent dimension in proposing 'struggles are just that, struggles' (Hindess 1982).

42. Isaac stresses that such a complementarity was central to the articulation of Arendt's position (Isaac 1998: ch. 5). 'Outbreaks of radical democracy' must be seen therefore as occurring within the broader framework of law. Only Arendt's unsustainable abstraction of the political from the social would preclude the possibility of legal reform arising from such 'outbreaks'.

43. Honneth notes the critical stimulus given to the empirical exploration of questions of 'moral economy' by the work of Edward Thompson and Barrington Moore respectively. See, for example, Thompson 1963 and Moore 1978.

44. This would be an inaccurate reading, given Honneth's emphasis, as far as socially generated moral conflicts are concerned, upon the necessary

structural linkage between institutionalised forms of disrespect and the generation of recognition struggles.

45. She is at pains to emphasise that the distinction is analytic, recognising that empirically the two are intertwined. Thus, 'the most material economic institutions have a constitutive, irreducible cultural dimension. *They are shot through with significations and norms.* Conversely, even the most discursive cultural practices have a constitutive, irreducible political-economic dimension' (1997: 15).

3

Capitalism and Struggle: From the Factory to the Smart Machine

That was the real mystery: Why did global commerce, with all of its supposed modernity and wondrous technologies, restore the old barbarisms that had long ago been forbidden by law? If the information age has enabled multinational corporations to manage production and marketing spread across continents, why were their managers unable – or unwilling – to organise such mundane matters as fire prevention?

The short answer, of course, was profits, but the deeper answer was about power: Firms behaved this way because they could, because nobody would stop them. (Greider 1998: 341)

The central argument here concerns the importance, both analytically and politically, of distinguishing between domination (power over) and power (to). The previous chapter added the further stipulation that all structures of domination are inherently unstable. In the modern world, the most generalised and integrated structures of domination, both spatially and temporally, are those of capitalism.[1] This chapter identifies and explores the principal characteristics of capitalist modernity, particularly those definitive of the present phase of capitalist structuring, while noting the patterns and processes of resistance to such domination.

A useful starting point in understanding the nature of capitalist structures of domination is Offe's argument concerning 'matrices of social power' (Offe 1984: 159–61; 1985: 1). Such matrices are not attributes of social actors but of modes of interaction. The concept of a matrix of social power stipulates therefore a *systematic* advantage arising from a *dominant* mode of interaction. Developing the analytic possibilities, we can reserve the conceptual referent 'power' for practices through which power as a social creation is generated, while treating social matrices within which systematic advantage arises from a dominant mode of interaction as those of domination. In exploring capitalism as a cluster of structures of systematic domination, we are therefore considering the ways in which capitalism as an internally differentiated system of political economy (a system, that is, of both social and societal reproduction) has a dynamic which produces – if unopposed – systematic differential advantage and disadvantage. Similarly, in exemplifying patterns of resistance to such domination in terms of alternative realisations of social power and manifestations of social struggle, we consider the generation of alternative manifestations of social power within the context of capitalist domination.[2]

It is important to grasp at the outset that capitalism is not a thing, a system, a model but, first and foremost, *a process*. Debates about the origins of this process – debates which are far from being of mere academic interest but involve clear and definite political implications and conclusions – are extensive and continuing (Hilton 1978; Holton 1985; Wallerstein 1974). These debates do not concern us directly here but the necessity of grasping the dynamic and historically grounded character of the process of capitalist modernisation does. While emphasising the importance of the historically changing character of successive phases of capitalist modernisation, it is possible nevertheless to identify certain general characteristics which are central to the structuring both of particular phases and of the forms of domination characteristic of each phase.[3]

Viewed historically, capitalist modernisation has meant the subordination of social forms to the pursuit of a single goal, that of the private appropriation of profit or the accumulation of capital.[4] This has involved a wide variety of possibilities and strategies both determined and limited by the specifics of diverse contexts (Chase-Dunn 1989; Arrighi 1994). Certain elements, however, have been of central importance. These are commodity production, market exchange, wage labour and a highly organised technical and social division of labour, among which wage labour has been crucial in securing the possibility of profit-seeking as '*the* basic way for social life to be reproduced' (Harvey 1989: 103). The variable institutionalisation of capitalist modernisation, as we shall see, has arguably involved the social realisation of all these elements as structures of domination (that is, as necessary matrices of asymmetry and systematic disadvantage).

The process of capitalist production has been argued by Arrighi to have taken the form historically of successive cycles of expansion within each of which expansion has been fuelled by the realisation of new opportunities for profitability, as specified in Marx's formula $M{\rightarrow}C{\rightarrow}M'$ (Money→commodities→more money) (Arrighi 1994: esp. ch. 2). In time, the overall characteristics definitive of the particular cycle come to represent limits to further expansion, leading to destabilisation, crisis and a fundamental restructuring, marking the historical realisation of a new cycle. What drives the process of capitalist modernity is the endless and – within the terms of capitalism understood as a distinctive logic of power – inescapable pursuit of profit.

Although as we shall see, the identification of the overall character-istics of a particular cycle or period of historical capitalism is essen-tial to an adequate specification of the major modes of domination to be found within that period, it is possible to indicate the principal sites of struggle within capitalist modernity in general. These are markets, the organisation of production (of commodities) and politi-cal organisation.

The Labour Market as a Matrix of Social Domination

Both conceptually and historically, capitalist modernity has been identified with three sets of market arrangements: the labour market, the money or credit market and the commodity market, of which conceptually the most significant and irreducible is the labour market. The existence and viability of modern capitalism as a system of pro-duction is crucially dependent upon the existence of wage labour as the essential complement to the existence of money and the acquisi-tion of raw commodities. Upon this proposition both Marx and Weber, for example, are in agreement, the former making it central to his conceptualisation of both the nature and the dynamic of capi-talist modernity:

> In themselves money and commodities are no more capital than the means of production and subsistence. They want transforming into capi-tal. But this transformation itself can only take place under certain circum-stances that centre in this: namely, that two very different kinds of commodity-possessors must come face to face into contact: on the one hand, the owners of money, means of production, means of subsistence, who are eager to increase the sum of values they possess, by buying other people's labour-power; on the other hand, free labourers, the sellers of their own labour-power, and therefore the sellers of labour.... With this polarisation of the market for commodities, the fundamental conditions of capitalist production are given. (Marx 1970, Vol. I: 714)

Modern capitalism is not therefore simply a variation on earlier examples of the pursuit of profit through exchange relations. Its *sine qua non* is the embeddedness of such pursuit in the exploitation of 'abstract labour power'. This view is reiterated in Polanyi's classic argument concerning 'the great transformation': the creation of national markets as a result of deliberate mercantilist state policy was, Polanyi proposes, a necessary condition for the historical development of capitalism but not a sufficient one (Polanyi 1957).[5] The sufficient condition is to be found in the creation of 'fictive commodities': labour, land and money. The world historical significance of the great transformation, Polanyi notes, lay in the subordination of all social relations to economic relations, which subordination was achieved, both conceptually and practically, through the process of commodification.

> labour, land and money are obviously *not* commodities; the postulate that anything that is bought and sold must have been produced for sale is emphatically untrue in regard to them.... Labour is only another name for a human activity which goes with life itself, which in its turn is not produced for sale but for entirely different reasons, nor can that activity be detached from the rest of life itself, be stored or mobilised; land is only another name for nature, which is not produced by man; actually money ... is merely a token of purchasing power which, as a rule, is not produced at all, but comes into being through the mechanism of banking or state finance. None of them is produced for sale. The commodity description of land, labour and money is entirely fictitious. (Polanyi 1957: 72)[6]

To adapt Arrighi's terminology, therefore, the logic of domination that is capitalist modernity *requires* the process of commodification, including the commodification of a thereby dehumanised activity as 'abstract labour power'. This process critically depends upon the subordination of labour to the domination of capital through the suppression and subsequent exclusion of any and all possibilities of decommodification.[7] This underlying logic is continuous from the genetic developments of early modern capitalisms to its endorsement in much discussion and policy implementation regarding strategies for economic development in the contemporary Second World.

Offe specifies three main reasons why labour power must be considered a fictive commodity (Offe 1985: 56–7). First, there are severe limits upon the degree to which the labour markets themselves determine the availability of labour power. Whereas genuine commodities are produced according to their expected saleability in the market, labour power is not. A range of social sites other than purely market-oriented enterprises – notably the family – provide the key loci for decisions to produce those human beings in relation to whom the fictive commodity labour power is created. Given that the operative motivations are largely distinct from the question of marketability, fluctuations in the labour market do not meet with an instant response in terms of the production of labour power.

Secondly, there is the critical fact of the contingency involved in the transformation of labour power into labour actually performed. All employment contracts necessarily contain a degree of indeterminacy, in effect a gap between the precise specification of pay on the one hand and a relatively underdefined specification of concrete work tasks on the other.[8] The key function of managerial authority is to close this gap in any given situation – but not to eliminate it since it is the essential basis of the 'flexibility of labour'. Both the existence and the maintenance of the gap allow the variable use of labour power, both qualitatively and quantitatively (ibid.: 57).[9]

Thirdly, labour power is marked out as a fictive commodity by its embeddedness in its owner. By comparison with that legal transfer of titles which otherwise characterises market exchange, the purchase of labour is a relatively indeterminate affair (Offe 1985: 57). Buyers of labour power must rely on the participation and therefore control of the worker since they cannot exclusively control the purchased commodity and, in addition, the use of labour power requires the cooperation of its owners.

The fictive commodification of labour power serves as the basis, both conceptually and historically, for the complex institutionalisation of the labour market as *the* basis of capitalist modernity. In explicating the nature of the labour market as a matrix of social domination, it is first of all necessary to consider its distinctiveness in relation to other markets. Shared characteristics are those of opposition and competition. The labour market organises production and distribution as an exchange relationship of wages and labour and, consequently, as in all other markets, suppliers and buyers stand opposed. Similarly, suppliers and buyers compete with other suppliers and buyers with respect to demands and offers. As Offe points out, this competition generates specific strategies of supply and demand (Offe 1985: 14). For labour, such strategies require the specification of the type, quantity, location and timing of the labour inputs offered, in addition to the basic strategy of adjusting the actual level of wage demanded. For management, on the other hand, the aim is to reduce the specificity of their demands for the type and quantity of labour needed or, failing that, to raise the wage offer to such a level that demand can be satisfied from the available supply. In addition to these strategies, both suppliers and buyers share, in common with other potential power relationships, the common adaptive strategy of seeking to free themselves from dependency on the other by finding substitute sources for the satisfaction of need.

The range of strategic possibilities implicated in the arena of labour market relations is further extended by those strategies adopted, not in direct pursuance of competition with the other party, but rather in order to minimise the level of competition on one's own side. Offe identifies such strategies as those of coalition formation and exclusion. In the former case, for example, workers may come to an agreement to establish maximum limits for the supply of services or minimum limits for price/wage demands and by this means may avoid the twin possibilities of either outbidding each other (with respect to supply) or underbidding each other (with respect to demand). In the case of the strategy of exclusion, the central purpose is to prevent access to the market by those potential suppliers who would either be prepared or compelled to accept one or other – or both – of these twin possibilities. Such competitive strategies may be increased in principle by attempts to intensify the level of competition on the other side of the exchange. Thus, for example, buyers of labour may actively pursue strategies intended to prevent or undermine attempts at coalition building on the supply side.[10]

Strategic interaction is of course a necessary implication of market exchange. The historical structuring of capitalism as a matrix of social domination depends upon the extent to which both buyers *and* sellers can actually make use of this 'in principle' symmetrical list of market strategies. Offe identifies five main obstacles to autonomous interaction arising from the market situation of labour, representing a systematic differential of disadvantage which allows us to speak of an 'in principle' relationship of domination (Offe 1985: 16 seq.).

- Due to its fictive character, the formal availability of labour power in the market is determined as we have seen not by market forces but by extra-market factors.
- In social structural terms of necessity historical in character, the availability of labour power is determined by all those socio-economic processes which create 'labour power' by the elimination of all those social conditions which would allow social communities to maintain themselves, *other than by the sale of labour power through the market*. (That is, the availability of labour power is chronically dependent upon the institutionalisation of the outcome of social struggles focused on the process of commodification.)
- In the market situation, labour is constrained by temporal constraints upon its availability. In simple terms, labour power cannot

afford to wait. This situation arises from labour power's definitive non-ownership of the natural or manufactured means of production. A supply of labour power that does not meet a demand upon whatever terms is literally 'worthless'. This market dependency of labour power is reinforced by the need of labour for a continuous supply of 'adequate' subsistence.

- Sellers as opposed to the buyers of labour are more dependent upon market-derived resources. Through technological change, production may very well be maintained even with a fall in labour input per unit of output, but the reproduction of labour power cannot be maintained at the same level with a fall of income per household.
- The final obstacle is difference in the qualitative potential for adaptation of the demand and supply sides of the market, respectively. Of decisive importance here is the greater degree of qualitative 'liquidity' of capital in comparison with labour. Over the short or long term, every unit of capital passes through a phase of 'liquidity' – that is, of translation into money. Unlike capital, the labour capacity that suppliers of labour have to offer does not pass through a phase of 'liquidity' in which it could rid itself of an all-qualitative determination.

In sum, therefore, the supply side of the market is subject to a number of objective determinants arising from the social reality of labour power as a fictive commodity: temporal constraint, dependency upon the market for subsistence and very limited capacity for qualitative adaptation. These objective determinants together create a power differential in favour of the demand side of the labour market and to the disadvantage of the supply side. Individual sellers of labour power – or workers' organisations – must compensate for their lack of autonomy with respect to market strategies by reducing the rate of pay demanded for labour power. The formal domination and exploitation of labour arises from the asymmetrical strategic capacity of supply and demand, thereby structuring the labour market, the central institutional mechanism of capitalism as a matrix of social domination.

Regimes of Accumulation

In order to illuminate structures of domination and possibilities for empowerment in the current epoch of modernity, it is necessary to place these formal considerations about the labour market as a matrix of domination within the context of the periodisation of capitalist modernity in general and of the contemporary phase of that modernity in particular. In doing so, we can draw upon the possibilities generated by periodising capitalist development into distinctive regimes of accumulation and associated modes of social and political regulation (Aglietta 1979; Lipietz 1986). In Lipietz' formulation, a regime of accumulation 'describes the stabilisation over a long period of the allocation of the net product between consumption and accumulation; it implies some correspondence between the transformation of both the conditions of production and the conditions of reproduction of wage earners'. The achievement and relative stability of this correspondence depends upon a wide range of complex and contingent social factors:

> norms, habits, laws, regulating networks and so on that ensure the unity of the process, i.e. the appropriate consistency of individual behaviours with the schema of reproduction. This body of interiorised rules and social processes is called the *mode of regulation* (Lipietz 1986: 19; quoted in Harvey 1989: 122; see also Urry 1995)

The analytic significance of these interrelated concepts is that they direct our attention to the complexity of the social relations required by the historical realisation of capitalist modernity. Their conceptual referent is to 'the complex interrelations, habits, political practices, and cultural forms that allow a highly dynamic, and consequently unstable, capitalist system to acquire a sufficient semblance of order to function coherently at least for a certain period of time' (Harvey 1989: 122).

Thus, the 'mode of regulation' is a useful way to conceptualise 'how the problems of organising labour power for the purposes of capital accumulation are worked out in particular places and times' (ibid.: 124). There is general agreement that the history of twentieth-century capitalism can be divided between two main regimes of accumulation/modes of regulation: the first of these is most usually referred to as 'Fordism' but, in order to emphasise the general *societal* dimensions involved, I shall follow Harvey's usage and adopt the term 'Fordist-Keynesian'. For reasons upon which there is no general agreement, this regime is now seen as having become substantially de-institutionalised (chronologically the decline is usually identified with the 1970s). Various labels have been attached to the subsequent arrangements – disorganised capitalism, post-Fordism, the regime of flexible accumulation – the diversity being much more than semantic but associated with significantly competing specifications of the changes occurring, of the reasons for such changes and of the likely consequences (Castells 1993, 1996; Hall and Jacques 1989; Hollingsworth and Boyer 1997a; Hollingsworth et al. 1994; Lash and Urry 1987; Offe 1985; Piore and Sabel 1984; Sayer and Walker 1992; T. Smith 1994; Swyngedouw 1986; Tolliday and Zeitlin 1991; Womack et al. 1990).[11]

Given the nature of the labour market as the key institutional mechanism of capitalist modernity, it is important to identify the major outlines of labour market relations in the Fordist-Keynesian regime of accumulation. The Keynesian dimension of this regime represented a demand side solution to the crisis of overproduction and competition brought about by the prior Fordist dimension. The integration of both these dimensions in the long boom of the 'golden age of capitalism' – identified by Harvey as the apogee of this regime – involved a distinctive historical stabilisation of the formal labour market politics outlined above (Marglin and Schor 1989). This stabilisation rested above all upon a particular containment of the domination tendencies inherent within capitalist modernity, a containment which may reasonably be seen as a trade-off in which metropolitan capitalism accepted certain accommodations facilitating mass consumption as an integral part of the Fordist-Keynesian regime while generally – and critically from the point of view of an assessment of domination and empowerment – extending dominance with respect to enhanced control over production processes.

The continued viability of this trade-off depended upon a successful channelling of the power of organised labour into issues of allocation and not control.[12] The possibility of such an accumulation/regulation strategy and thereby of the overall stability of the Fordist-Keynesian power equation was further dependent upon the historical realisation of two other institutional complexes: first, the dominance of the corporation and, second, the welfare state, the latter being understood as referring not merely as in conventional usage to the public provision of collective social need but in the widest possible terms to all the modes and mechanisms of state intervention identifiable in the most advanced centres of capitalist modernity in the three decades after 1945.[13]

In addition to being the key site for the direct subordination and containment of organised labour (see below), the corporation provided the institutional framework for the four key elements of growth and consequent profitability definitive of the Fordist-Keynesian regime: 'a … commitment to steady but powerful processes of technological change, mass fixed capital investment, growth of managerial expertise in both production and marketing, the mobilisation of economies of scale through the standardisation of product.... Scientific management of all facets of corporate activity ... became the hallmark of bureaucratic corporate rationality.' As a consequence, the 'decisions of corporations became hegemonic in defining the paths of mass consumption growth' (Harvey 1989: 134).

As has been the case for capitalist modernity throughout its history, the coherence of the specific Fordist-Keynesian regime of accumulation was dependent upon a particular complex of political mechanisms and modes of intervention.[14] The foundation of the regime in a cycle of high growth–high consumption–profitability required that this complex be geared to enlarging and sustaining mass consumption. This was the purpose of Keynesian economic management with respect to fiscal and monetary policy. But, in addition, political compromise and the need to facilitate the availability of labour power for the critical core corporate sector of the economy was manifested in the comparative variations both of welfare statism and of interventions in relation to the respective rights and therefore powers of capital and labour. In the not so longer term, these variations on the institutional provision of the fictive commodity 'labour power' led to a significant decommodification of labour (see, for example, Offe 1984). The coherence of Fordism-Keynesianism as a regime of accumulation was further undermined when, as the technological innovations and corporate rationalisations (including those of labour power) which had fuelled the long boom began to produce diminishing returns, the historical trade-off between allocation and control deteriorated into a struggle over both (Crouch and Pizzorno 1978; Goldthorpe 1984). Before considering the characteristics of capitalist modernity which emerged as a result of that struggle, it will be helpful to consider the second site of struggle in capitalist modernity: the organisation of production.

The Organisation of Production: Edwards' 'contested terrain'

The limitations upon the contractual specification of the precise activities in which 'abstract labour power' was to be realised in production processes were always (and increasingly) severe and, consequently, until the age of information technology at least, the examples of such specification were fairly limited (Edwards 1979). Exploration of the degree to which returns upon investment in labour costs are sought through strategies of control over the organisation of production have been an illuminating, if contentious, area of analysis for the study of capitalist domination.[15]

There has been extensive analysis and debate concerning the historical variable forms of labour control in relation to the organisation of production in successive phases of capitalist modernity. In the most far-reaching version of the labour control hypothesis, which prioritised power issues over those of economic efficiency, Marglin proposed that the primary rationale of the factory system itself is not the efficient coordination of production factors but the establishment and maintenance of capital's control over labour (Marglin 1974, 1991). Although even sympathetic discussants have found Marglin's formulation of this argument unsustainable, the general argument does have the merit of highlighting important questions concerning the social processes involved in the institutionalisation of capitalist production.[16]

Edwards offered a more nuanced, not to say documented, and now classic account of the history of labour control under capitalist modernity as exemplified in the case of the United States.[17] This account is structured around the identification of successive forms of labour control, each form being proposed as a reciprocal learning response to the overall limits of an existing dominant mode, particularly as these limits are made manifest in the dialectical pattern of the ceaseless search for profitability on the one hand and the fact of worker resistance on the other (Giddens 1982b).[18] In an important indication of the specificity of such identifiable patterns, Edwards' account emphasised that this pattern of successive substitution only occurred in the core of the differentiated political economy, where the increasingly social character of production under an emergent new form, corporate capitalism, provided the impetus for new forms of labour control – and new forms of worker resistance. Capitalist modernity has been and remains chronically characterised by such configurations involving the coexistence and interdependence of a wide variety of modes of labour control, the realisation of which has not been primarily historically linear but significantly functional.

What emerges quite clearly from Edwards' discussion is the complex, contingent character of the domination–resistance dialectic under capitalist modernity but also and critically, the interweaving of the interactions definitive of that dialectic with other conflicts possessing independent dynamics of their own.[19] More generally, we have a clear indication of the necessity of understanding both the structure and the dynamics of capitalist modernity in terms of a political economy; that is to say, an adequate analysis of capitalist modernity requires a consideration of both the differentiation of processes of social production into economic and political spheres, and of the necessary interdependence and interaction of such spheres. Of course, the comparative historical forms of such differentiation and interdependence/interaction are significantly different (Lash and Urry 1987; Mann 1993: chs. 15–19). Thus, for example, Edwards makes clear the way in which labour's attempt to establish collective control over the labour process in the United States was defeated through the direct repression of labour, *frequently and substantially through coercion*. Such a strategy – involving direct coercive conflict in terms of private violence – was only possible with the compliance, not to say the possible collusion, of the public authority.[20]

In laying particular emphasis upon the learning, processual nature of the strategies of both capital and labour, Edwards highlights the limitations of purely systemic, deterministic accounts of the history of capitalist modernity. The latter perspectives, outstanding amongst which is Braverman's seminal text of the labour process literature, *Labor and Monopoly Capital*, reduce the question of domination and struggle under capitalist modernity to functional responses to determinate laws of capitalist development.[21] Such perspectives entirely exclude the interactive perspective necessary to understanding the dynamics of power *as a relational phenomenon* and thereby preclude a meaningful analysis of the historically situated relations between capitalist domination and diverse resistance struggles.

In abstract terms, identifiable in Edwards' analysis is a succession of attempts to solve capital's perennial problem of translating labour power into labour; that is, a series of historically situated interactions expressive of struggles to establish capitalist domination on the one hand and the historically variable mobilisation of resistance, centring on projects of self-control discussed in Chapter 2 above and therefore including projects to realise a transformative politics, on the other (Honneth 1995: ch. 12). As has been indicated above, from the point of view of capitalist domination, this problem is a dual one, involving new combinations of technology and labour power required by the pursuit of profitability and a more intense and consistent level of control over labour. Thus, technical control, too narrowly identified by Edwards as epitomising Fordism, 'involves designing machinery and planning the flow of work to minimise the problem of transforming labour power into labour as well as to maximise the purely physically based possibilities for achieving efficiencies' (Edwards 1979: 112). Within the terms of Edwards' account, the attempt to institutionalise systems of technical control in turn generates fresh possibilities for worker resistance. In due course, such resistance generates the impetus to develop and institutionalise the final system of labour control identified by Edwards, that of bureaucratic control. Both are inherently social and organised around what Paul Edwards identifies as 'structured antagonisms' (Edwards 1986). There is, however, a major distinction between them which is of great importance in an explication of the historical variability of capitalist domination. *Whereas technical control rests upon the physical and technological aspects of production, bureaucratic control rests upon the social and organisational structure of the plant.* If technical control seeks subordination through technique, the bureaucratic system seeks subordination through rules.

In the contrast between the two different systems of structural control analysed in Edwards' discussion, we can identify two distinct possibilities of domination. In the case of technical control, the principal strategy of domination is *externally coercive* in that the intended goal is the coordination, and thereby subordination, of the worker with and to the available technology. In the case of bureaucratic control, on the other hand, the principal strategy of domination is *internally coercive* in that the intended goal is not merely to produce a given level of performance but also and equally to 'produce' the behaviour necessary to make the bureaucratic system work, to 'produce', if you will, the 'bureaucratic worker' (Edwards 1979: 148 seq.). The intention therefore is to institutionalise a mode of regulation in the sense discussed above. The Foucauldian parallels are obvious and are reinforced by Edwards' further argument that the characteristics associated with this variant of structural control generate their own form of worker resistance, which resistance is argued to stem from the very rule-oriented strategy definitive of bureaucratic control. The inculcation of such rules is only possible given fairly high levels of job security; in turn, the successful production of bureaucratic workers leads to above average levels of plant identification. In combination, these two factors lead, Edwards argues, to increased levels of demand for participation in the making and interpretation of rules. Thus, a dialectic of domination–resistance is continued.

The complexities of the historically variable relationships of domination and power under capitalist modernity are illuminated in the arguments deriving from a critical appropriation of Edwards' account.[22] Apart from wide-ranging questions of historical detail, which cumulatively represent a clear challenge to the coherence and utility of Edwards' typology of labour process control, the most direct and comprehensive critique has concerned the adequacy of the 'capitalist control versus worker resistance' model itself.[23] This critique centred on the argument that any adequate understanding of the complexities of control in relation to the labour process has to take account of relations of cooperation between labour and capital equally as much as relations of direct resistance.[24] Thus, Burawoy, who in a series of projects has developed what is in effect an alternative model of the labour process and its historically variable character as a mechanism of surplus extraction, argued that the term adaptation is preferable to resistance because workers' actions incorporate 'ideological mechanisms through which the workers are sucked into accepting what is as natural and inevitable' (Burawoy 1978: 274 n.).

Building upon this proposition, Burawoy developed a contrast between two forms of labour control, despotic and hegemonic, corresponding to successive phases of capitalist development, competitive capitalism and monopoly capitalism, respectively. According to Burawoy's analysis, the greater effectiveness of the hegemonic system may be seen to lie in a classic strategy of social domination – divide and rule: that is, the achievement of the stabilisation of overall capitalist domination depended upon the working of a series of interrelated mechanisms. These were the acceptance by workers of the rules in terms of which the labour process was organised, *rules which individualised reward at the expense of collective solidarity*; a complementary mechanism of the internal labour market which institutionalised individual advancement as against collective struggle and, finally, the 'internal state', which provided and promoted individual rights and constrained managerial discretion but simultaneously inscribed, in practice as well as principle, managerial control over the labour process (and, one might add, all other aspects of company policy).

The implications of Burawoy's argument concerning the institutionalisation of a hegemonic system for the analysis of the relationship between domination and power can be further explicated by reference to Honneth's discussion of the structuring of the moral grammar of social struggles (1995: ch. 12). Honneth proposes that it is possible to demonstrate in the case of socially subordinate strata that 'the ideas of justice according to which social groups morally evaluate and judge a social order are more likely to be found in typical perceptions of injustice than in positively formulated principles of value' (ibid.: 212). However, the opportunities both to formulate perceptions of injustice and to bring them into the public sphere are limited and controlled by state and/or institutional processes. 'These techniques of control … represent strategies for the maintenance of cultural hegemony of the socially dominant class by latently narrowing the possibilities of articulating experiences of injustice' (ibid.: 213). In particular, Honneth identifies two sets of processes which act as mechanisms of normative class dominance: first, there are processes of cultural exclusion which limit the possibilities of articulating class-specific experiences of injustice by systematically withholding the appropriate linguistic and symbolic means for their expression. These strategies operate through public education, the media of the culture industry or forums of political publicity.[25] Secondly, there are processes of institutionalised individualisation, strategies encouraged by the state and other institutional orders which effectively counteract possibilities of communicative agreement and mobilisation around group- and class-specific experiences of injustice by either requiring or facilitating support for individualistic action orientations. Such strategies of individualisation are, Honneth notes, 'exceedingly complex. They extend from social and political rewards for individualistic risk-taking, to the administratively ordered destruction of neighbourhood living environments, to the establishment of competitive labour markets within the factory or office' (ibid.: 214).[26] One might tentatively advance the hypothesis that with the decline of traditional forms of authority, the role of the second complex of processes of individualisation has increased, whether with respect to the diffusion of performance related pay schemes, the mediatisation of 'celebrities' from 'ordinary backgrounds' or 'get-rich-quick' lotteries or television games.

Domination and Power in Capitalist Modernity

Debates concerning the labour process raise a number of key issues for the analysis of domination and power in capitalist modernity. On the question of hierarchy, Marglin quite clearly adopted the unequivocal stance that, in capitalist modernity, such hierarchy is purely a function of labour control and in no way connected with the generation of surplus *per se*. His critics reject this stance, arguing that the two are in fact interconnected. A second question concerns the interrelatedness as against the relative autonomy of different potential sites of domination and struggle, such as labour markets and the labour process. Edwards argued in favour of such interrelatedness, proposing for the case of the United States at least, that segmented labour markets and the variability of power differentials in each of such markets are directly related to the sectoral location of the segment of labour involved.[27] Burawoy, on the other hand, in spite of proposing a correlation between market conditions and type of factory regime, nevertheless argued for the 'relative autonomy' of labour process relations from other aspects of society. In the case of his discussion of hegemonic arrangements, this stance, however, leads to an unbalanced picture of the degree to which capitalist domination remains unopposed within the sphere of production. Crucially, his discussion omits any reference to struggles between capital and labour not merely over the precise content of the effort bargain but, much more importantly from the point of view of the question of domination, resistance and transformation, over the conditions which govern such individual bargains (Edwards 1986: 51).

This last point goes to the very heart of the argument developed here concerning the necessity of maintaining a viable distinction between the concepts of domination and power. It requires the recognition that, while the theorisation of capitalist modernity must incorporate those structural elements which implicate modes of interaction embodying such systematic disadvantage between capital and labour as to make it possible to speak of matrices of social domination, the historical realisation of any configuration of capitalist modernity always involves both *complexity and contingency*. In spite of the realities of structural domination of capitalist modernity, the power of domination is never comprehensive nor without tension and contradiction. Nor should the identification of those struggles relevant to the analysis of transformative politics be in any way confined to merely *reactive* processes of resistance which, as Paul Edwards and others rightly argue, may in fact, when placed in context, be seen in reality as generally facilitative of the overall process of class subordination.

From this perspective, accounts such as those advanced by Braverman (certainly), Richard Edwards and Burawoy all tend to overemphasise the extent to which the systematic disadvantages of capital in both labour markets and labour processes are translatable into an unconstrained and therefore unilateral structure of domination. Burawoy's account of hegemonic regimes is deficient to the extent that it omits organised forms of factory struggles. The discussions of Taylorism by Edwards – and others – are equally deficient to the extent that they neglect the evidence indicating that Taylorism was not merely one of a succession of strategies intended to establish more effective control over labour and the labour process in pursuance of a more efficient surplus extraction (that is, was a pro-active strategy of domination), but was developed in response to the realities of an already established collective solidarity of labour (that is, is best comprehended within a framework of struggle) (Johansson 1991: 302 seq.).

Political Organisation: the Third Site of Struggle

One possibility above all emerges clearly from the preceding discussions of the various sites of struggle definitive of capitalist modernity: whatever their heuristic value in illuminating particular aspects of capitalist modernity, typologies are of limited value in explicating the differentiated complexities of regional, national and international capitalisms over several centuries. While, as we shall see shortly, it is both necessary and important to recognise the vital role played by successive hegemonic states in successive phases of capitalist expansion, it is equally important to accept the necessity of viewing capitalist modernity as the referent of a distinctive logic of power, quite distinct from all forms expressive of an alternative logic, that of a *territorialist* logic of power. The driving force of this distinctive logic is the accumulation of capital; the consequent means, the ceaseless search for profitability. Given that the continued institutionalisation of capitalist modernisation is dependent therefore upon the continuing accumulation of capital, two factors are of particular importance in driving the expansionary tendencies of a given phase forward; the (if unmodified) 'coercive laws' of market competition and the class struggle generally endemic to capitalism (that is, the variable potential for resistance on the part of the subordinates specified by the matrices of social domination definitive of a particular phase of capitalist modernisation). The chronic innovation consequent upon the need to combat falling profits, however, merely leads to a vicious circle of 'creative destruction' which renders individuals, families, communities, regions and states historically redundant and superfluous to the next round of capitalist expansion.

> The struggle to maintain profitability sends capitalists racing off to explore all kinds of other possibilities. New product lines are opened and that means the creation of new wants and needs.... The result is to exacerbate insecurity and instability, as masses of capital and workers shift

from one line of production to another, leaving whole sectors devastated, while the perpetual flux in consumer wants, tastes and needs becomes a permanent locus of uncertainty and struggle.... The drive to relocate to more advantageous places (the geographical movement of both capital and labour) periodically revolutionises the international and territorial division of labour, adding a vital geographical dimension to the insecurity. The resultant transformation in the experience of place and space is matched by revolutions in the time dimension, as capitalists strive to reduce the turnover time of their capital to 'the twinkling of an eye'. (Harvey 1989: 106)

Historical capitalism therefore must be understood in processual terms as involving the chronic revolutionising of existing structures of production and thereby of all existing social forms, that is, the accelerating destruction and creation of old and new configurations of space and time (ibid.: Part III). It is important, however, to recognise that the chronic revolutionising of the international and territorial division of labour not only permits but actually requires the coexistence of a *diversity* of both labour markets and organisational forms of production. It is a mistake and a distraction to become fixated upon the search for dominant modes of control over the labour process.[28] Surveying the political/economic scene which has emerged in recent decades, Harvey notes:

the way in which new production technologies and co-ordinating forms of organisation have permitted the revival of domestic, familial, and paternalistic labour systems, which Marx tended to assume would either be driven out of business or reduced to such conditions of gross exploitation and dehumanising toil as to be intolerable under advanced capitalism. The revival of the sweatshops in New York and Los Angeles, of home work and 'telecommuting', as well as the burgeoning growth of informal sector labour practices throughout the advanced capitalist world, does indeed represent a rather sobering vision of capitalism's supposedly progressive history.... *Under conditions of flexible accumulation, it seems as if alternative labour systems can exist side by side within the same space in such a way as to enable capitalist entrepreneurs to choose at will between them.* (1989: 187, emphasis mine)

Relationships of domination and power within capitalist modernity therefore have to be contextualised and the relevant context must be one which addresses the underlying dynamic of capitalist modernity. Here two such possibilities present themselves: the first of these focuses on the possible transition from one regime of accumulation to another; in the historical conjuncture of the most recent restructuring of capitalism, the transition from the Fordist-Keynesian regime of accumulation to another which Harvey, for example, has labelled, somewhat tentatively, the regime of flexible accumulation (ibid.: ch. 9). The second possibility, by no means incompatible in conception, if differing in focus, detail and interpretation from the first, is that developed by Arrighi in his argument concerning 'the long twentieth century' (Arrighi 1994).

Issues of domination and power derivative from the contingent realisation of historical capitalism are central to Harvey's analysis of the crisis of the Fordist-Keynesian regime and of the possible transition to a subsequent regime (1989: chs. 8–10). According to this account, it was above all the rigidities deriving from the major strategic settlements definitive of the Fordist mode of regulation, particularly rigidities in labour markets, labour allocation and labour contracts, which undermined that regime of accumulation as rates of profit began to fall. Attempts to remove these rigidities, that is, to renegotiate and restabilise the 'wages in return for control' trade-off which had been central to the stabilisation of Fordist-Keynesianism, were fiercely resisted, a process greatly influenced by the balance of forces created by large-scale production. As Goldthorpe argued, the much vaunted pluralism which its proponents had seen as the critical refutation of radical arguments concerning the systematic differentials of power under capitalist modernity viewed as a whole now came to be seen as a disruptive force threatening the viability of economy and society (1984: 315–44).

Parallel rigidities became increasingly obvious in another area of the Fordist-Keynesian regime, as the political entitlements embodied in the social citizenship of welfare statism encountered the limitations of a static, if not declining fiscal base. 'Behind all these … rigidities lay a rather unwieldy and seemingly fixed configuration of political power and reciprocal relations that bound big labour, big capital and big government into what increasingly appeared as a dysfunctional embrace of such narrowly defined vested interests as to undermine rather than secure capital accumulation' (Harvey 1989: 142).

It is the comprehensive attempt to transcend these rigidities that gives rise to that aggregate state of affairs which Harvey labels flexible accumulation. This state of affairs he characterises as follows:

> It rests on flexibility with respect to labour processes, labour markets, products and patterns of consumption … is characterised by the emergence of entirely new sectors of production, new ways of providing financial services, new markets, and, above all, greatly intensified rates of commercial, echnological, and organisational innovation … has entrained rapid shifts in the patterning of uneven development, both between sectors and between geographical regions … [and] has entailed

a new round of ... 'time-space compression' in the capitalist world – the time horizons of both private and public decision-making have shrunk, while satellite communication and declining transport costs have made it increasingly possible to spread those decisions immediately over an ever wider and variegated space. (ibid.: 147)

As with the Fordist-Keynesian regime, the diverse processes required to realise the contours of a new distinctive configuration necessitated extensive struggles. These struggles, articulated in terms of a distinctive ideological project, and the subsequent outcome have conventionally become identified with the political project of the New Right as embodied in the Reagan and Thatcher governments, although a more accurate analysis might emphasise culmination rather than initiation. Of central importance in institutionalising the 'regime' of flexible accumulation was a substantial intervention in relation to the matrix of social power discussed above: the removal of substantially all the constraints upon the operation of labour market forces and – partly as a consequence of that development and partly as a result of the qualitative suppression of organised labour solidarity in the form of trade union organisation – of much of the power of labour resistance in the workplace. The consequences were such as to render characterisations in the mid-1990s of the interactions typical of labour markets in the decades post-Second World War, in Robert Kuttner's graphic phrase, 'like archaeological descriptions of a lost continent' (1997: 74).

The new 'Jurassic Park' of flexible accumulation combines enhanced profitability and greater domination. Typical corporate strategy is to convert as large a portion of the workforce as possible from permanent staff to contingent employees on short-term contracts of variable length and condition. Although competitive pressures to avoid payroll taxes (or their comparative national equivalent) and fringe benefits provide part of the rationale for such developments, the principal motivating factor is cost-cutting and flexibility, in which is necessarily embodied a greater vulnerability of labour. A significant facilitating factor in this reassertion of the labour market advantage of capital over labour is the possibilities provided by new information technology. Contracting-out, whether in regard to specialised expertise such as stock analysts or computer experts or more routine but periodically required services available through subcontractors and temp agencies, has become an integral part of the capital–labour equation under the new flexible regime.

The aggregate effect of all the processes of deregulation, deunionisation and flexibilisation has been a new and historically novel commodification of labour; in effect, a 'production' of labour which much more closely approximates to Polanyi's fictive commodity than was previously the case. Kuttner proposes that there are ultimately only two ways to think about this development. Either one adopts the stance that there is something about the new information economy which makes it imperative, efficient and above all 'natural' to treat labour more like any other commodity or *one accepts that these developments reflect shifts in power rather than any economic imperatives dictated by new technologies.* Surveying both alternative conceptualisations, Kuttner reaches the following conclusion. While it is certainly the case that the current global economy is far more marketised in general than that of the Fordist era, a transformation which has encompassed labour markets, the underlying cause has much less to do with a spontaneous explosion of *laissez-faire* in response to the information economy and a great deal more to do with the erosion of 'the two great stewards of the mixed economy – organised labour and the state –' and an increase in 'the relative power of business to evade tacit contracts with its employees' (Kuttner 1997: 80). To reiterate the quotation at the head of this chapter: 'the deeper answer was about power: Firms behaved this way because they could, because nobody would stop them' (Greider 1998: 341). In this perspective, deregulation in its diverse aspects is not about a technology-driven pursuit of economic efficiency but about a qualitative shift in that matrix of power which is capitalism.

While the preceding discussion has indicated the limits of the social contract which defined the Fordist-Keynesian regime, we must bear in mind the degree to which that regime was grounded not only in a particular worldwide structure of capital accumulation but also in a *particular accommodation of struggles* between capitalist domination and labour power. As Kuttner notes:

> there was nothing inherent in the old mass-production economy that dictated unionisation, wage-and-hour legislation, limits on laissez-faire trade, or the custom of lifetime employment.... That they existed at mid [20th] century was more the fruit of political struggle than of economic determinism. The factory economy was perhaps somewhat more amenable to unionisation, because it agglomerated thousands of workers in the same physical location, which promoted class consciousness and in turn mobilised a political constituency for a mixed economy with constraints on the ability of private capital to treat labour as a commodity. (Kuttner 1997: 80)

The rise of the regime of flexible accumulation saw a very substantial shift towards the commodification of labour; that is, towards the institutionalisation of largely unconstrained capitalist domination. This has been achieved in two main ways: first, by the spatial and, on the basis of new forms of informational technology, concomitant temporal extension of integrated capitalist activity into areas possessing fewer institutional constraints upon the asymmetrical power of capital both in the labour market and in the organisation of production; secondly, by the systematic erosion of the interventionist capacities of both organised labour and the state in relation to the dominating potential of capital. The principal mechanisms whereby the latter project has been pursued and achieved have been the weakening of wage regulation, privatisation and/or deregulation (above all of capital mobility) and a general assault on union power (ibid.: 96–101).[29]

The Restructuring of Capitalism and the 'Informational Age'

In the era of flexible accumulation, the dual aspects of capitalist modernity – the ceaseless search for profitability and the concomitant pursuit of surplus extraction – chronically realised in a variable fusion of technology and hierarchy have found further expression in the explosion of information technology. As Castells notes in his outstanding study of 'the information age', 'the current technological revolution ... originated and diffused, not by accident, in a historical period of the global restructuring of capitalism, for which it was an essential tool' (1996: 13; see also Shaiken 1986).[30] By the 1990s, Castells argues, the information technology revolution had effectively transformed the work process, introducing new forms of social and technical division of labour. However, an adequate understanding of the complex dynamic of this development in different settings can only be arrived at by placing it in a wider context in which management decisions, industrial relations systems, cultural and institutional environments and government policies all play key roles.

What clearly emerges from studies concerning both the potential and the implementation of the new technologies is the tension which exists between that potential with respect to both recognition and creative performance (that is, a qualitatively enhanced *power to*) and a variety of countervailing constraints predominant among which are the valorisation of profit and the strategic defence of managerial prerogative (*power over* and its attempted institutionalisation as domination) (Adler 1992; Shaiken 1986, 1993; Zuboff 1988).[31] As we have seen with earlier technologies, the information age offers new possibilities for domination but also new possibilities for resistance and transformation (Edwards 1979). The new informational technology is Janus-faced in its implications for domination and empowerment. This ambivalence follows directly from the reality that, once again,

> the design of technology is not only a question of machines and systems but of *power and political choice*. Computers and microelectronics lay the basis for highly productive manufacturing systems that fully utilise the capabilities humans have to offer and, consequently, enhance the work environment. *A more participatory technology, however, requires a broad public awareness and democratic involvement in defining goals for designing automation*. (Shaiken 1986: 15, emphasis mine)

Of course, in any given instance, whether the capital–labour relation is such as to realise a matrix of domination as against a matrix of power requires specific exploration in relation to a wider pattern of institutional and cultural resources.[32] What is clear is the degree to which the implementation of technology is driven by the *fusion* of profit-seeking and the attempt to enhance domination. In the capitalist restructuring of the 1980s, 'more often than not technologies were introduced, first of all, to save labor, to subdue unions, and to trim costs, rather than to improve quality or to enhance productivity by means other than downsizing' (Castells 1996: 249).[33]

With respect to the enhancement of domination, it should be emphasised that, in relation to both profit-seeking and control, computerisation possesses a flexibility that was absent from the earlier forms of technical control. With the new technology, a change in the production process does not require a redesigning of the relevant machinery, only a rewriting of the relevant program. And the implications of the 'smart machine' for the relations between capital and labour in diverse contexts are far reaching.[34] Not only has computerisation transformed, in some ways transcended, previous constraints of space and time as far as the coordination of production and access to low wage pools of labour are concerned, but it has also created possibilities for much more precise processes of labour control.[35] Computer-based controls not only extend the direction of work activities by technical means; they also incorporate feedback systems which contribute a novel element to technical control. The novelty lies in the fact that these systems do not merely send out instructions but also receive back information upon the basis of which work performed may be evaluated and monitored.

Computerisation has thus enhanced the possibilities for greater control on the part of capital both in the form of the surveillance and monitoring of labour activity and in the form of the coordination of that enormous diversity of economic activities in widely differing spatial and temporal environments typical of the transnational corporation, a diversification which is significantly motivated by the search for political environments where capital can operate without the constraints of organised labour or political intervention.[36] At the same time, the dehumanisation of labour inherent in the dystopias of the totally computerised organisation of work generates inevitable alienation and resistance.

Finance Capital

In addition to the specific changes occasioned in the capital/wage labour relation by the developments of the information age, the new technologies are also integrally involved in, indeed are the *sine qua non* of, the outstanding characteristic feature of the current phase of capitalist modernity: the dominance of finance capital.

Harvey, for example, concludes his discussion of the extent to which a variety of political/economic developments in recent decades amount in combination to the emergence of a new regime of (flexible) accumulation by noting that the key mechanism of the coordination of the diverse processes of spatial and temporal flexibility has been an 'explosion of new financial instruments and markets, coupled with the rise of highly sophisticated systems of financial coordination on a global scale' (1989: 194). The scale of these financial developments is of such a magnitude as to suggest the possibility of 'the flexibility achieved in production, labour markets, and consumption [being] more ... an outcome of the search for financial solutions to the crisis-tendencies of capitalism, rather than the other way round'. Such a possibility prompts the further conclusion that 'the financial system has achieved a degree of autonomy from real production unprecedented in capitalism's history' (ibid.).

In a similar vein, Castells, evaluating the significance and determinative power of the network society which he sees as having arisen from the qualitative changes of 'the informational revolution', proposes that the current phase of capitalist development is

> profoundly different from its historical predecessors. [As such] it has two fundamental distinctive features: it is global, and it is structured to a large extent, around a network of financial flows. Capital works globally as a unit in real time; and it is realised, invested, and accumulated mainly in the sphere of circulation, that is as financial capital. (Castells 1996: 471)

While there is general agreement concerning the dominance of financial markets in the present phase of capitalist modernity, this agreement does not involve a consensus on the novelty of this autonomy. An alternative position is identified within a second possibility for the historical contextualisation of questions of domination and power referred to above, namely, Arrighi's argument concerning the 'long twentieth century' and the broader framework within which its analysis must be located. Arrighi specifies this context as cyclical rather than linear: the successive cycles of expansion, stagnation, destabilisation, crisis, restructuring and further expansion which have characterised historical capitalism as a whole. An attempt to address the fundamental relationships of domination and power within the contemporary phase of capitalist modernity may be usefully located within the conceptual framework of such a cyclical periodisation.

Arrighi's central contention is that the present period (characterised here as late modernity) is one of fundamental transformation within capitalist modernity. A full understanding of the nature and dynamics of this transformation, however, requires analysis in relation to the long-term cyclical development of Western capitalism since the fourteenth century (Pollin 1996). Within such a perspective, the present period of financial ascendancy is not totally unprecedented but represents yet another of those periods of financial expansion which are the 'autumn' of an existing configuration of capitalist modernity as it slowly gives way to another new order.[37]

The dominance of finance capital is not merely that of predominance but literally one of domination; that is, the activity of financial markets is expressive of such a degree of practical autonomy as to represent the subordination of any and all alternative configurations of organisational power such as corporate capital and national states (although see below for the interpenetration of financial and corporate capital). Financial assets are growing in value faster than any other economic resource. According to Greider, the total stock of financial assets from advanced nations expanded in value by 6 per cent a year from 1980 to 1992, more than twice as fast as the underlying economies were growing (1998: 232). By 1992, the financial assets of the OECD countries totalled some $35 trillion, which represented double the total economic output of those countries (see also Castells 1996: 471 seq.; Kapstein 1996).

Financial markets and institutions exist to meet a basic need under capitalist modernity, the need for flexibility (or liquidity) in capital's pursuit of profit. This 'enables capitalists to maximise their profit opportunities without having to commit themselves to any particular line of business' (and, incidentally, as we have seen above, makes any particular form of the organisation of production a matter of contingency) (Pollin 1996: 114). Flexibility thus creates the potential for financial expansion when a given regime of accumulation has reached its limits.

The correlation between declining profitability and financial expansion gives rise to a key question: where do the profits deriving from financial transactions come from if not from production and exchange of commodities (Pollin 1996: 115)? Pollin suggests three answers to this question: (1) profits may represent a redistribution within the capitalist class as a whole; in such a case, what is actually involved in expansion is a redistribution of existing profits; (2) concomitant to the process of financial dealings, the capitalist class as a whole is able to achieve a redistribution of wealth and income in its favour; such is the case with corporate takeovers when new owners force down wages and tax payments to creditors of outstanding public debts; and (3) financial deals may be profitable on a sustained basis if they allow the transfer of funds from less profitable to more profitable areas of production and exchange (ibid.: 115–16).

If we consider some of the detail of the recent explosion of global financial assets, we can identify manifestations of each of these possibilities. Both the fastest and the largest element in the growth of these assets is debt, above all government debt (Greider 1998: 232). From 1980 to 1992, government debt in the OECD countries grew at 9 per cent a year, three times faster than economic output. (There are elements of Pollin's answers 1 and 2 in this situation.) Greider indicates that this accelerating burden of governmental debt is one of the three main sources of inter-state competition for capital which in their complex interrelations have enormously enhanced the autonomous power of a globalised financial capital to a position of domination.[38] Moreover, from the point of view of an assessment of the potential for domination of financial capital in the present era of capitalist modernity, the critical mechanism is neither speed nor volume but price.[39] As the cost of servicing existing debts steadily mounts, economies have to run faster and faster in order to stay in the same place (Greider 1998: 234).

The implication of the agency of financial capital in a complex pattern of differential power relations clearly involves a situation of such systematic advantage. That this situation amounts to one of substantial domination may be illustrated in a number of ways. The first of these concerns the way in which the structural relationship between the continued viability of elected governments and the continued viability of commercial banks (and of course their myriad investors, large and increasingly relatively small) has required the management of recurrent debt reflations through the basically simple expedient of transferring potentially catastrophic private debt into public rescue operations. In the shadow of the collapse of the Soviet Union and, with it, of the state socialist project, there is more than a little irony in the reality that 'a kind of remnant socialism still exists on behalf of financial institutions and investors, who are rescued from their own mistakes by governments that discreetly spread the costs among other citizens' (ibid.: 237).[40]

The dominance of finance capital is further, and arguably more starkly, revealed in its structural capacity to condition and, on occasion, directly determine the course of governmental action.[41] Historically, apart from the literal defence of territorial integrity up to and including war-making, probably the greatest priority of states has been the maintenance of sound money, affecting as it does so many aspects of social activity. Other than in a purely defensive, constrained and anticipatory fashion, contemporary governments effectively have lost that capacity. The recommendation of an earlier age to 'walk softly and carry a big stick' has been replaced by the starker warning: 'You can't buck the markets!'[42]

The rule of finance capital over governments and peoples graphically expresses the domination embodied in (unfettered) capitalist modernity, a domination in which a technologically empowered capital mobility provides the ultimate expression of globalisation. In the context of a consideration of the possibilities for political empowerment in late modernity, it is all the more significant that this most social embodiment of chaos theory should apparently be out of control. Contrary to the impression frequently conveyed of a seamless web of globalised activity, the historical reality of the current phase of capitalist modernity is one of extreme fragmentation, which carries an unquestionable capacity to implode in the absence of international regulation. Consequently, 'the real question involved in stabilising the globalised financial system is about *political power*: "Who shall govern these important matters, governments or private markets?"' (ibid.: 256, emphasis mine)[43] or, in an alternative formulation, the proposition is advanced that 'the central struggle of our time is that between laissez-faire-capitalism, which represents ... financial interest, and social democracy, which represents democratic control of the economy in the interests of ordinary people' (Elliott and Atkinson 1998: vii).

Posing the issue in such a way immediately gives rise to a further question: leaving aside the question of political will, do the dominant political agents of modernity, national states, have the capacity to confront and contain the power of capital? State interventionism has been a prominent characteristic of modernity: at the height of the Fordist-Keynesian regime, welfare statism was seen as an integral and irreversible aspect of the relationship between capitalist and democratic modernity. Subsequently, this element has been subject to fundamental critique, both intellectual and practical. In addition, the viability of states in an epoch of globalisation has constantly come into question. These issues, central to the analysis of domination and empowerment in late modernity, provide the subject of the next chapter.

Notes

1. Note that the proposition refers to *generalised* structures. Of course, other social dimensions have provided and continue to provide the basis for general structures of domination, notably gender and ethnicity, but, while undoubtedly possessing important international features, neither gender nor ethnicity has historically manifested the generalised structures characteristic of contemporary capitalism.

2. It is important to bear in mind that structures of domination are pure types not found as such empirically.

3. The following account draws upon David Harvey's discussion in *The Condition of Postmodernity*. Apart from its inherent lucidity, it forms a helpful backdrop to his consideration of the transition between regimes of accumulation which I shall refer to later. Harvey 1989: esp. ch. 5.

4. Note that 'private' here has a necessarily residual and relational meaning: that which is fundamentally not subject to public scrutiny and control, however the latter is understood. Such an understanding would therefore not preclude instances of state capitalism as examples of private capitals.

5. Polanyi's account has the advantage of making clear the implication, either positively or negatively, of political processes in capitalist development.

6. On the relationship between state development, state action and the creation of the preconditions for commodification, see Giddens 1985b: ch. 6.

7. That is, the process is critically dependent upon coordinated political mechanisms, most notably those of the state which can carry forward processes of commodification by means of the ultimate sanction of violence. See, for example, Giddens 1985b.

8. This has been an important dimension in the computerisation of work.

9. Offe takes an over-structural and therefore restricted view of the causes operative in this relationship. While the question of the efficiency gap is a key factor in the determination of managerial strategy, so also is the wish to maintain or extend total control over the work situation. See Susanna Zuboff's illuminating discussion of the ways in which the implementation of automation and the accompanying process of legitimation in terms of technical necessity reflect the pursuit by management of the goal of elite

control. This situation Zuboff contrasts with the empowering possibilities potentially involved in the implementation of 'informating', in which process all participants in the production process are viewed as creative agents rather than objects to be dominated and directed (Zuboff 1988). Of course, to be generally successful such a collaborative process has ultimately to be durable in the face of the pursuit of profit. See also Howard 1986.

10. See the discussion in the previous chapter of Honneth's arguments concerning strategies of domination intended to subvert possibilities of empowerment.

11. As Hollingsworth and Boyer note, both the Fordist and the flexible system of production are ideal types and, as such, subject to the usual strengths and weaknesses of that methodological device. 'Neither type ever existed alone in space and time. Even where standardised mass production [a hallmark of Fordism] was the dominant technological paradigm, there were always firms – or even entire industries – that were organised on opposite principles. The two organising principles were complementary with one another. Mass production tended to respond to the stable component of demand, while batch or medium-size production systems tended to cope with the variable part of the same demand. So coexisting forms of production broadly shared the same short-run flexibility and long-run performance.... [Nevertheless] though flexible systems of production both pre- and postdate Fordist systems of production, we must recognise that in recent years flexible systems have become further differentiated into various subtypes' (Hollingsworth and Boyer 1997b: 20–1). For an interesting consideration of the extent to which the conceptualisation of the new global production system as 'the flexible production model' can be characterised by what Paul Edwards terms the 'fundamental structural antagonism' of the capital/wage-labour relationship, see T. Smith 1994. In exploring the ways in which the single-union plants characteristic of the flexible production system can actively reproduce divisions in the workforce reminiscent of the era of multiple unions, Smith implicitly illustrates several of Offe's propositions regarding the importance in the matrix of domination between capital and labour of divisions within labour itself. See ibid.: 56.

12. As Armstrong et al., Matthews and others have noted, this process, beginning with the variable containment of labour in the post-Second World War world, was never entirely successful, varying according to a number of comparative contingencies, including national location within the overall capitalist world system and the possibilities and constraints conferred by comparative national institutional configuration (Armstrong et al. 1984; Matthews 1989).

13. For a discussion of dominant perspectives on the current situation of welfare statism, see Chapter 4.

14. There is no intention of endorsing a teleological functionalist argument here. To recognise that governmental policy in the Fordist-Keynesian regime was geared to a certain set of priorities is not of course to reduce either policies or institutional forms to systemic logic or elite autonomy: that there is a chronic tension between structures of modern domination, including those of capitalist modernity, and processes of political modernity is a central theme of the present work. As will have been clear from the

discussion of Honneth's critical analysis of the perspective advanced by Habermas, a central argument of the present work is that systemic totality may be an aspiration but nevertheless remains a social and political myth, albeit a powerful and significant one.

15. For a useful survey of the various positions within the labour process debate, their relationship and significant incompatibilities, see Rowlinson and Hassard 1994.

16. In a substantially critical discussion of the specifics of Marglin's arguments concerning capitalist hierarchy, Maxine Berg argues that 'fundamental to our understanding of the origins of capitalist hierarchy is not the form of work organisation or the type of technical change, *since multiple alternatives and combinations of these were a permanent feature of industrial society.* Priority must go to understanding the context of accumulation, the limitations on it or the opportunities for bringing into play one or other technical and work combination.' So, just as 'the rise of the putting-out system in seventeenth century Europe can be explained by the proclivity of capital to seek out cheap labour, [so] the recent decentralisation of production processes evident in the new international division of labour aided by the new technology is equally a reaction to the barriers created in the centralisation of industry – notably the collective worker. Dispersal mystifies and complicates the capital–labour relationship; it weakens organised labour and exploits a cheap labour force, especially women.' In spite of this emphasis upon the crucial causal role played by the search for profit, Berg nevertheless argues for the critical importance of the 'autonomy' of technology in the achievement of both increased productivity gains and labour control (Berg 1991: 191, emphasis mine). Other attempts to identify a single focus for the extraction of economic surplus in capitalist modernity have given rise to similar criticisms.

17. While Edwards' account is concerned with only a single case, albeit that of the national capitalism which was clearly hegemonic in the post-Second World War 'golden age of capitalism', it seems reasonable to argue that the general possibilities to which his account points, such as the importance of a learning process on the part of both capital and labour and the determination of forms of labour control by the search for profitability and struggles expressive of worker resistance, are suggestive beyond the contours of the US example. See, for example, Harvey's discussion of the quite distinct timing of the institutionalisation of Fordism in Europe (1989: 128).

18. The relevant types are: personal control, cooptation and scientific control and structural control, this last being differentiated into two sub-types, technical control and bureaucratic control. So the direct imposition of personal entrepreneurial control – and the conflicts and instabilities to which it gives rise – was replaced by the quasi-impersonalism of supervisory control as competitive capitalism was succeeded by a more differentiated political economy of which the most dynamic sector was oligopolistic.

19. See, for example, his account of the practically interdependent but causally independent struggles focused upon the role of supervisor in the second phase of personalised control (Edwards 1979: ch. 4). An emphasis upon the empirically complex character of diverse comparative crystallisations of power is of course central to Mann's argument concerning power (over) (1986, 1993).

20. Mann rightly emphasises US exceptionalism in the degree to which violence was a major factor in the determination of capitalist/wage labour relations (1993: ch. 18).

21. This deficiency is not ameliorated by Braverman's conflation of structure and agency in his account, so that the 'agency' of the capitalist class appears unconstrained in its realisation of capitalist totality. See Wood 1982.

22. This applies not only to the criticisms of Edwards' argument in *Contested Terrain*, but also to those directed at his subsequent, collaborative work with Gordon and Reich. See David Gordon et al. 1982.

23. For a useful summary of some of the major criticisms, see Edwards 1986: 42–6.

24. These criticisms exaggerate the extent to which Edwards' account fails and/or is unable to incorporate those dimensions of both capitalist and worker agency which must be subsumed under the heading of cooperation or accommodation as against resistance. It seems entirely accurate and meaningful to assimilate Edwards' discussion of the production of the 'bureaucratic worker' to Foucault's discussion of the characteristic dynamics of modern power with its central emphasis upon securing subjective involvement in processes and therefore structures of domination. Of course, the fact of such a parallel does not say anything about the validity of the argument being advanced in these terms. As we saw in Chapter 1, Foucault's argument mistakenly forecloses on the possibility that other modes of modernity may provide the source for relations of power and resistance operating independently of those arising within the framework of capitalist modernity.

25. Cf. Moore 1978: ch. 14.

26. On the role of state action in the marginalisation and diffusion of collective experiences of injustice, see the discussion of Wolin's conceptualisation of Welfare Statism in the following.

27. A systematic analysis of the possible variations in such relationships would require the type of comparative analysis advanced by Lash and Urry 1987. In relation to the analysis of capitalism in late modernity, the important general point raised by Edwards' characterisation of the US position under Fordism concerns its spatial diffusion; that is, the segmentation of labour markets and the corresponding question of the variability of power relations within particular markets now has greater salience with respect to international and/or transnational considerations.

28. As Geller notes, even as early as the 1920s, it is possible to identify within the ambit of a single firm (Ford's) the juxtaposition of all three of Edwards' modes of labour control (Geller 1979–80: 39–46). Similarly, the contemporary phase of international and territorial 'restructuring' has resulted in the temporal coexistence of sweatshops in, for example, India and the United States. Edwards discusses a number of other arguments making the same general point. See Edwards 1986: 41.

29. The empirical, comparative picture is more complicated than these brief statements might suggest. Struggles continue and arise in what seem the most inauspicious of circumstances. The European Union represents one key arena within which organised resistance to the unilateral determination of interactions between capital and labour, let alone between capital and

consumers and capital and citizens, has been and continues to be the occasion of struggle. Nevertheless, if we wish to relate shifts within the various power equations within which capital is implicated to the general dynamic of historical capitalism, the closing three decades of the twentieth century have undoubtedly seen a major shift in the direction of capitalist domination and massively increased social inequality both national and international.

30. While being greatly impressive in its sheer scope and documentation and constantly stimulating in its interrogation of the social landscape of the present, Castells' stance on the causal status of 'the informational revolution' is equivocal, to say the least. We find three distinctive positions on the issue in the opening pages of the first volume of *The Information Age*:

> the information technology revolution has been instrumental in allowing the implementation of a fundamental process of restructuring of the capitalist system from the 1980s onwards. In the process, this technological revolution was itself shaped, in its development and manifestations, by the logic and interests of advanced capitalism, *without being reducible to the expression of such interests*. (1996: 13)
>
> Technological innovation and organisational change, focusing on flexibility and adaptability, were absolutely critical in ensuring the speed and efficiency of restructuring. It can be argued that without new information technology global capitalism would have been a much-limited reality, flexible management would have been reduced to labour trimming, and the new round of spending in both capital goods and new consumer products would not have been sufficient to compensate for the reduction of public spending. (ibid.: 19)
>
> The term informational indicates the attribute of a specific form of social organisation in which information generation, processing, and transmission *become the fundamental sources of productivity and power*, because of new technological conditions emerging in this historical period. (ibid.: 21, emphasis mine)

This last proposition seems difficult to reconcile with Castells' equally emphatic statement that the new techno-economic system can be adequately characterised as *informational capitalism*. The parallels with the debate between Marglin and his critics and earlier arguments such as Galbraith's concerning the techno-structure are obvious. Castells is formally quite clear about his wish to avoid what he sees as the 'meaninglessness' of technological determinism, arguing that the social and the technological are inseparably fused. At the same time, however, the general air of 'informational functionalism' permeates much of the general argument ('the power of flows takes precedence over the flows of power') in a way that is difficult, if not impossible, to reconcile with his equal recognition that the social organisation of technology is politically structured. Thus, 'trends do not stem from the structural logic of the informational paradigm, but are the result of the current restructuring of capital–labour relationships, helped by the powerful tools provided by new information technologies, and facilitated by a new organisational form, the network enterprise' (ibid.: 273).

31. See, in particular, Zuboff's valuable distinction between and consequent analysis of automation and informating, the former emphasising enhanced domination through the incorporation of the worker into the heteronomy of the 'smart machine', the latter emphasising the potential for collaborative agency and enhanced individual creativity (Zuboff 1988). Clearly, in the absence of an institutionalised structure of rights meaningfully constraining the unilateral autonomy of capital, even an 'informating' strategy must ultimately fail to affect the matrix of domination while providing the basis for resistance struggles. See Kuttner 1997.

32. This is graphically illustrated in Watanabe's study of the comparative impact of the introduction of robots in the automobile industry in Japan, the United States, France and Italy (Watanabe 1986).

33. For excellent case studies, see Parsons 1987 and Appelbaum 1984.

34. For a sustained and optimistic argument concerning the revolutionary extent and consequences of the changes involved, see Piore and Sabel 1984.

35. Castells emphasises that it is not low cost alone which drives the spatial relocation of production but the combination of low cost and automation. See Castells 1993: 31, 37.

36. In addition to Shaiken, on the ambiguous potential of the 'smart machine' for the organisation of work, see Zuboff 1988. On the rationale underlying the globalisation of capitalist modernity in the late twentieth century, see Barnet and Cavanagh 1994; Greider 1998; Mander and Goldsmith 1996.

37. Seen in this way, the present decline of US hegemony within capitalist modernity is comparable to three previous 'long centuries': those of the Genoese sixteenth century, the Dutch seventeenth century and the British nineteenth century.

38. Greider proposes that the two other main sources are the emerging markets of Asia and the rising volume of capital that multinationals require to compete effectively in technologically advanced sectors of the world economy. See Greider 1998: 233–4. See also Korten 1995: Part IV and Kuttner 1997: ch. 5.

39. This reality tends to be obscured in the current fascination with the speed and extensiveness of capital flows in the current era.

40. This is all the more the case given the extent to which the dominant political agenda has become structured, both rhetorically and practically, around the replacement of debilitating public subsidy by the stimulating rigours of private independence.

41. As in the case of the United Kingdom's withdrawal from the Exchange Rate Mechanism as the result of the agency of the financier, George Soros.

42. Consequently, the maintenance of sound money now involves the pursuit of market-dictated deflationary policies, at the centre of which lies the 'crisis of welfare statism', on which see Chapter 4 below.

43. For an alternative, much more sanguine, view of inter-governmental collaboration and response to the challenge of capital mobility, see Kapstein 1996.

4

States: Domination or Empowerment?

Both conceptually and substantively, the modern state is overwhelmingly associated with relations of domination. Indeed, in this context, modern frequently carries the connotation of a qualitatively enhanced effectiveness in the achievement of domination. The more modern the state, the greater its degree of identifiable penetration and regulation of any and all social processes within the territory to which it lays claim.[1] Of all the characteristics associated with the modern state, the most fundamental, definitive and inescapable is that of force. Just as it appears possible to chart the development of the modern state in terms of its degree of success in suppressing all other autonomous jurisdictions, in imposing a universal and codified pattern of rule(s) upon a previously heterogeneous and particularised patchwork of social practices and in regulating relations with external peers and competitors through the systematised mobilisation and judicious use of force, so also does the coherence of the cluster of attributes – succinct or extended – primarily associated with the modern state not merely require the inclusion of force but, in both argument and *realpolitik*, appears to definitively depend upon force.[2]

It is this apparent intimate and integral association of the modern state with force, with the structuring of domination, which appears to make it an inauspicious focus for the analysis of any possibilities in regard to a transformative politics of empowerment. Such a conclusion underlies the pessimism which characterises a wide variety of responses towards the meaningful scope of political possibilities in the present phase of modernity, whether evidenced in declining rates of electoral participation, opinion poll data regarding popular evaluations of the general social character of politicians and the possible human contributions of political structures and processes or the intellectual disenchantment with traditional political models which motivates the attempted identification of 'third ways' and other attempts at secular transcendence. Such disenchantment with any variant of state interventionism, at least as far as arguments concerning the possibility/ desirability of restraining and/or compensatory actions in relation to the mobility of capital or the flexibility of labour are concerned, has been an integral part of the neo-liberal agenda. But there has been an equal disenchantment with what Offe has characterised as 'the left's central project ... a collectivist-etatist version of industrialism' (Offe 1996: 158). As he further notes, the source of such disenchantment is accurately expressed in Przeworski and Wallerstein's argument that

> historical experience indicates that governments cannot be trusted with precisely those alternatives that would make a difference, those that require large doses of state intervention. The dilemma of the Left is that the only way to improve material conditions of workers and poor people under capitalism is through rather massive state intervention, and the state does not seem to be a reliable mechanism of intervention. The patient is sick, the drugs are available, but the doctor is a hack. (quoted ibid.)

The extent of such disenchantment with the efficacy of models and projects of social transformation focused upon statist intervention is a major indication of the historical centrality of such intervention to the process of societal rationalisation under modernity. As Poggi, Giddens and Mann among others have demonstrated, the modern state and the modern state system have been an integral part of the modernisation process (Giddens 1985b; Mann 1993; Poggi 1978). The historical institutionalisation of formal rationality was achieved through the circumscription and organisation of space. Through the media of territoriality and centripetal force, whether unicameral or federal in form, and with the elaboration of an historically distinctive theory of sovereignty, the European states system developed out of the crucible of warfare to become the dominant form of world political organisation (Tilly 1975, 1990).

Whatever its variants and complicated individual trajectories, therefore, the modern state system has been *the* modern system of rule *sans pareil*. The most distinctive feature of this system, as Ruggie emphasises, has been the differentiation of the subjects of rule into 'territorially defined, fixed, and mutually exclusive spaces of legitimate domination' (Ruggie 1993: 151). From this reality has flowed the recurrent contradiction specified by Arrighi as the motor of modernity, a contradiction between 'an "endless" accumulation of capital and a comparatively stable organisation of political space', the transient resolution of which he proposes as the *historical* process of making and remaking the modern world system under successive hegemonic state powers (Arrighi 1994: 33). Viewed conceptually, Arrighi proposes, this contradiction can be specified in terms of a tension between 'capitalism' and 'territorialism' as opposite modes of rule or logics of power (ibid.).[3] Thus, the logic of 'territorialism' is the logic of controlled and coordinated space, in relation to which logic capital is a means and/or a by-product. The logic of 'capitalism', in contrast, is the maximisation of flexibility in the pursuit of accumulation in relation to which territorial acquisition in its turn is means and by-product.[4]

Using this distinction, we can identify alternative strategies of state formation (and by extension, state reproduction). In a territorialist strategy, control over territory and population is the primary objective and control over mobile capital the means. In a capitalist strategy, on the other hand, this relationship is reversed, with control over mobile capital being the primary objective and control over territory and population the means. Arrighi is at pains to stress that such a distinction 'implies nothing concerning the intensity of coercion employed in the pursuit of power through either strategy'(ibid.: 34). Thus, for example, the Venetian republic, the first hegemonic state of the modern political economy, singlemindedly pursued both a capitalist logic of power and a coercion-intensive path to state formation.

The origins and epochal restructuring of the modern inter-state system, of which the dynamic of the modern state has been both a significant cause and an equally significant expression, is proposed by Arrighi therefore to lie in the opposition between capitalist and territorialist logics of power. Thus, the dynamic of the modern world political economy was set in motion by the emergence in the mid-fifteenth century of a regional subsystem of capitalist city-states in northern Italy (Arrighi 1994: 36 seq.). All the main elements of modern capitalist rule are anticipated by this configuration: the site of 'an extraordinary concentration of wealth and power' arising from the complementarity of the accumulation of capital from long-distance trade and high finance, the management of the balance of power, the commercialisation of war and the development of residential diplomacy and the first expression of a vital element in modern realisations of power and domination, the gathering of and the control over information (cf. Giddens 1985b: esp. chs 6, 7 and 9).

Recurrent attempts by territorialist rulers to either incorporate this concentration of capitalist power within their domains or, alternatively, to prevent such incorporation by any of their rivals led in the following two centuries to the complete disintegration of the medieval system of rule, culminating in that system-wide threat to the existing structure of rule through a combination of peasant and urban revolts which characterised the first half of the seventeenth century (Arrighi 1994: 41; see also Anderson 1974). Out of this systemic chaos and the purposive agency of the first truly modern hegemonic state, the United Provinces, there arose 'a new anarchic order', famously embodied in the Peace of Westphalia.[5] In the crucible of this new world order, the critical parameters of the modern state as both the agent and the expression of a reorganisation of political space of world historical significance were clearly spelled out:

> Rights of private property and rights of public government become absolute and discrete; political jurisdictions become exclusive and are clearly demarcated by boundaries; the mobility of ruling elites across political jurisdictions slows down and eventually ceases; law, religion and custom become 'national', that is, subject to no political authority other than that of the sovereign. (Arrighi 1994: 31; cf. Ruggie 1993)[6]

In Arrighi's depiction of the subsequent history of the modern political economy, the historically situated mutual determination and interpenetration of the logics of capitalism and territorialism finds expression in successive reorganisations of world political-economic space under a leading capitalist state.[7] These successive reorganisations have been the very historical stuff of the processes of societal rationalisation, the changing terrain of recurrent struggles around orders of domination and communities of resistance. Throughout these reorganisations, however, one element has remained constant: 'the distinctive signature of the modern ... variant of structuring territorial space ... [as expressed in] the familiar world of territorially disjoint, mutually exclusive, functionally similar, sovereign states' (Ruggie 1993: 151).[8]

The classic calligraphy of the signature of these modern states, equally influential across all the disciplines concerned with the explication and the exploration of political modernity, has been that of Max Weber.[9] Weber defined the modern state as 'a human community that successfully claims the monopoly of the legitimate use of physical force within a given territory' (Gerth and Mills 1946: 78). Domination is obviously fundamental to this definition, as indeed it is to Weber's conception of politics in general. Moreover, as Hoffman argues, within this definition force is not only one attribute among several contributing to a coherent definition, but is in fact 'the dimension which gives the Weberian definition its *structure*' (1995: 36). Thus, while the attributes of territory, monopoly and legitimacy are specified as necessarily coexisting with force in a mutually determining pattern, so that in their absence force alone cannot take a statist form, nevertheless it is force alone that 'provides the conceptual "glue" which renders the interrelated attributes coherent' (ibid.: 37).

It is a commonplace criticism of Weber's definition of the state that it is *de facto* a definition which backprojects the dominant characteristics of this modern phenomenon into the pre-modern world. What connects the modern and the pre-modern, both conceptually and empirically, is a shared emphasis upon domination. In itself, the proposition that the differences between pre-modern and modern states as political phenomena are differences of degree and not differences of kind (and therefore permit useful comparative categorisation) may give rise to meaningful conceptual and empirical debate.[10] *What is not meaningful, either conceptually or politically, is Weber's argument that all politics is ultimately an expression of strategic domination.* The central purpose of the present text is to develop a critique of precisely this proposition, a proposition which must treat domination and power as conceptual synonyms and views all political processes and outcomes as manifestations of strategic action.

If, on the other hand, domination and power are treated as is proposed here as conceptual antonyms, it is possible to conceive of a politics of empowerment as distinct from a politics of domination. On the basis of such a dichotomy, it then becomes possible, as Hoffman persuasively and forcefully argues, to affirm the specificity of Weber's definition of the state with its emphasis upon the centrality of force (the modern exemplar of the politics of domination) while recognising the conceptual distinctiveness of politics in general (a politics of sociability and therefore mutual empowerment) (1995: ch. 3; cf. Linklater 1998).

Of central importance in establishing and maintaining this distinction is an engagement with the implications of the anthropological literature on stateless societies.[11] The major conceptual import of this literature is to specify and empirically underpin a concept of 'government' as a political mode quite distinct from the state. The main characteristic of government as a distinctive political form is the absence of that force which fundamentally defines stateness. In contradistinction to the state, what is decisive about government is not force but discussion, persuasion and negotiation with a view to reconciliation. Unlike the judicial processes which take place in state-centred societies, here there are no winners or losers: all feel they have gained something and customary rules are loosely and flexibly interpreted. Force is not the ultimate incentive towards compliance with socially accepted rules: while there are sanctions which 'enforce' rules, these are 'quite the opposite' of what we normally understand as force (Hoffman 1995: 40).

This is not in any way to argue that what emerges from the anthropological literature is a picture of societies without force. It would be more accurate to say that in general terms most of these societies recognise physical conflict as a legitimate way of obtaining redress for wrongs experienced or perceived. However, the critical point is that 'force ... is not concentrated into specialised agencies' (Hoffman 1995: 41). As opposed to the situation of state-centred societies in which concentrated and hierarchically organised force is the ultimate sanction for the maintenance of order, in stateless societies 'force is seen as *threatening to governmental processes*' (ibid., emphasis mine). As Hoffman concludes:

> If force is decisive in defining the state, order, community and co-operation are central in identifying government. What is decisive and essential in the case of one is incidental and contingent in the case of the other. Government ... is a process of regulating social behaviour ... and ... force is at best incidental [to it]. (ibid.: 42)

Consideration of 'the anthropological argument' makes such a conclusion unavoidable. While empirically there may be an argument that in modernised societies which have undergone substantial processes of societal rationalisation, the resultant disparities of power may be of such magnitude as to require that monopolistic and territorially focused activity pursuing exclusive legitimacy be based upon force, this does not provide any warranty for the argument that political processes in general (law-making, judging and administering) *logically* entail such force.[12]

Central to Hoffman's critique of Weber's comprehensive subsumption of *both states and politics* under the rubric of force is the cogent argument that the very rationale of the modern state lies in an inevitable failure to achieve that goal which defines its existence. No state, as Hoffman proposes, is ever fully successful in its claim to the monopoly of the legitimate use of violence in a given territorial area. Were it to be so, there would no longer be a necessity for it to exist. There is always resistance, whether from the criminal, the rebel or the civil dissident. Moreover, in the world of modernity with its plurality of contexts of agency and identity, there are always competing legitimations.

The challenge to the conceptual and empirical domination of states therefore lies in the empowerment potential of government, the potential for a non-statist politics 'which is *not* monopolistic and territorially exclusive and therefore does not require underpinning from coercive agencies like the army and the police' (Hoffman 1995: 44).

The Continuing Implication
of the State in Modernity

If it is recognised, therefore, that the modern state system has been the expression of a distinctive world historical epoch in the political organisation of space, the question might reasonably be asked as to whether a combination of factors, including those discussed in the previous chapter, is not so eroding (even has not so eroded) the conditions of existence of such modern states as to amount to an epochal shift in that very spatial organisation. That such is indeed the case is the by now commonplace central proposition of much argument concerning the reality and meaning of 'globalisation'. The main import of such argument is that changes in the density and dynamic of both spatial extent and rapidity of transactions in real time have qualitatively transformed the processual, identificatory and even causal significance of the state system. We shall consider the validity of such claims in due course.

Of equal importance, however, in any contemporary assessment of how to situate the modern state within a general matrix of domination and power is an engagement with the 'internal' characteristics and dynamics of modern states.[13] Two main questions form the basis of this 'internalist' interrogation of the character of state agency in late modernity. The first of these concerns the extent to which the proposed erosion of autonomous state capacity in an era of putative economic globalisation has been associated with a growth in both the quality and quantity of state action, with regard to the 'non-economic' dimensions of civil society, and the further extent to which it may be reasonable to propose a direct relationship between economic liberalisation and the growth of such a 'surveillance state'.[14] The second question, the exploration of which certainly overlaps at points with the first, concerns the political significance and possible transformation of the dominant state form associated with the institutionalisation of inclusionary regimes of democratic modernity, welfare states (Offe 1984: *passim*).[15]

To the very real extent that welfare statism has been and continues to be identified with the most developed forms of collective, as opposed to individual, mobilisation and provision, the identification of significantly divergent perspectives on the fundamental political rationale of such welfare statism offers important possibilities for the analysis of domination and empowerment in late modernity. These possibilities can be usefully approached by distinguishing three main arguments concerning the possible transformation of those modes and mechanisms of state agency encompassed by the welfare state. The first of these proposes that there has been such a transformation and that the only important question concerns the cause(s) involved, their possible consequences and the implications of both for the structuring of social relations of domination and power in late modernity. The second argument is that to equate the unquestionable political and administrative changes associated with the ascendancy of the neo-liberal political project with a transformation of the fundamental reality and above all political significance of the welfare state as an epochal mode of political domination involves a fundamental misunderstanding of the political parameters of modern state rule under modernity. The third perspective argues that the true political significance of the erosion of welfare statism as a specific ensemble of discourses and practices expressive of a distinctive political rationality is to be found in the recognition that this erosion and the emergence of an alternative complex of discourses and practices amounts to 'the death of the social' as a political signifier of both discourse and practice oriented towards a conception of *universalisation*, and its replacement by discourses and practices oriented towards difference and differentiated community which collectively comprehend a wholly distinctive political rationality.

The Social and Political Erosion of Welfare Statism

The first of these possibilities has found its most coherent and developed expression in the work of Claus Offe (1984, 1985, 1996). Within the broad conceptual perspective on the welfare state indicated above, namely as a 'multi-functional and heterogeneous set of political and administrative institutions', Offe offered an initial theoretical mapping focused on the proposition that the general purpose of welfare states could and should be defined by the goal of 'crisis management'. The pursuit of this goal is expressed above all in the regulation of processes of socialisation and capital accumulation. Such regulation is exemplified, Keane suggests, in the various ways in which welfare states have sought to guarantee the survival of privately controlled exchange processes by minimising their self-paralysing tendencies.

> This economic strategy ... depended upon the formal recognition of the actual power of trade unions in the process of collective bargaining and public-policy making and administration. [In a complementary fashion,]

> welfare state administrations have ... sought to ... regulate the processes
> of socialisation through ... legal transfers of resources to various groups
> whose life chances had been damaged systematically by market exchange
> processes. (Keane in Offe 1984: 13)

In the 'golden age of capitalism', the two decades after the Second
World War, both the effectiveness and the general political legitimacy
of welfare state regulation derived, Offe argued, from their multi-
functional character and varied interventionist techniques. Over time,
however, these apparent strengths were seen as the source of conflict
and instability within both the political and administrative dimensions
of the welfare state. In effect, welfare state systems were increasingly
proposed to generate more problems than they could solve. In
Prewzorski and Hechter's graphic phrase, 'the doctor is a hack'
(quoted in Offe 1996: 158).

According to Offe, the source of the widely mooted failures of welfare statism lay in particular in the fact that welfare states must pursue two ultimately incompatible goals in relation to the capitalist
economy (1984: 147–61). On the one hand, the private character of
capital and labour power under capitalism significantly precludes the
possibility of the organisation of the production process according to
political criteria. In addition to these fundamental legal and practical
constraints, other pressures produce the subordination of welfare
state policies to processes of capital accumulation: the general legitimacy of modern states derived from the effectiveness of the economies in whose management in the era of Fordist-Keynesianism they
both presented themselves and were perceived as being centrally
involved. Moreover, under capitalist modernity, states are dependent
for the fact and the extent of their revenues upon the success of
the economies in which they are implicated (e.g. in terms of direct
and indirect taxation, tariffs and levels of financial borrowing).
In general, therefore, welfare states are necessarily in the business
of promoting the successful operation of processes of commodification, whether with respect to the production of goods or labour
power.

On the other hand, Offe argued in his initial explication, the very
raison d'être of welfare states requires that they constantly intervene
in the prerogatives of capital and labour power in order to pursue the
crucial task of the promotion of commodification. In so doing, they
must necessarily resort to a range of policies of decommodification
which contradict, at least in principle, the spontaneous operation and
therefore the concomitant legitimacy of capitalist economy. In such
circumstances,

the maintenance and generalisation of 'private' exchange relationships depends upon decommodified (i.e. non-market, state) policies which effectively and efficiently promote the investment of capital and the saleability of labour power through public infrastructure investment, mandatory schemes of joint decision-making and social policy, and the application of various administrative regulations and incentives. *In a word, welfare state policies are required to do the impossible: they are forced to reorganise and restrict the mechanisms of capitalist accumulation in order to allow those mechanisms to spontaneously take care of themselves.* (1984: 16, emphasis mine)

There is no doubt that Offe's assessment of the overall consequences of the contradictory effects of welfare state interventionism was that it represented a fundamental shift in the structure of domination between capital and wage-labour (see in particular Offe 1984: chs 4 and 6). The general effect of the welfare state was argued to increase the capacity for resistance on the part of social groups vulnerable to the dominating effects of capital. In schematic terms, a relationship of domination became somewhat more a relationship of power, albeit one still powerfully characterised by different logics of collective action. Formulated in this unqualified way, such a claim may reasonably be regarded with considerable reservation and seen at best as an overstated evaluation, at worst a roseate and misleading caricature of the emancipatory consequences of welfare statism, arising above all from Offe's commitment to a systemic mode of analysis.[16] As Keane noted, 'Second-class citizenship and "poverty traps" … have always been an endemic feature of the post-war extension of "citizenship rights." … Offe understates the degree to which legal-bureaucratic and professional forms of state intervention *weaken* clients' capacity for self-help by continually redefining and monitoring their "needs"' (Keane in Offe 1984: 17).[17] In addition, in the 1980s and 1990s the electoral success and subsequent political projects of parties representing deregulatory neo-liberal, anti-statist approaches to welfare provision, including re-branded parties of the centre-left, has seen the historical questioning if not refutation of Offe's implicit claim that in late modernity public (as opposed to private) delivery of welfare provision is inescapable and irreversible.[18]

Offe himself has recognised this and consequently advanced an explanation of these developments, an explanation involving a significant questioning of the systemic determination and therefore historical durability of welfare statism as crisis management. He proposes that, as a result of social change, there has developed a fundamental tension between the specific goals maximised by the generality of advanced liberal democracies and the maintenance of welfare statism (1996: ch. 8). Central to the relevant processes of change has been a 'destructuration of collectivities', a development which, Offe argues, has eroded those self-conscious interest communities which had previously provided the cultural and normative underpinnings of the welfare state (ibid.: 173). A combination of factors has led to the de-legitimation of *both the goals and the means* (bureaucratic and professional interventionism) of welfare statism.[19]

In addition to his central argument concerning the contradictory character of welfare statism, Offe's original specification of the dynamics of such a political form identified three further reasons for its chronic instability: (1) chronic fiscal problems, arising from the tendency for state expenditures to persistently outrun state revenues;[20] (2) a marked tendency for welfare statism to be characterised over time by an excess of planning failures, arising from two sources in particular: first, various forms of organised reactive resistance to the political rationalities of state domination and, second, a lack of coordination between various state bureaucracies;[21] and (3) finally, a chronic problem of legitimation, arising from the erosion of 'traditional' norms and their contexts of generation by processes of commodification and the inability of the welfare state system to successfully meet the multiplicity of demands that it constantly generates.

Taken together with what Offe proposed to be the fundamentally contradictory character of welfare statism, these further sources of instability, whether individually or in combination, led to the general argument that consequent 'crises of crisis management' were simply endemic to welfare statism as a political order. Such a stance did not preclude the specification and analysis of a number of alternative possibilities which were increasingly identifiable aspects of the Western political scene in the closing decades of the twentieth century and beyond. Offe's analysis focused in particular on the viability of the New Right neo-liberal political project, central to which was a commitment to the substantial recommodification of social life in liberal democratic regimes (1984: 147–61). History did not deal kindly with Offe's considerable, even extreme, scepticism concerning the potential of the New Right, a scepticism which was a direct consequence of his argument that the advanced capitalism of late modernity unavoidably required welfare statist intervention. Any attempt to abandon such a requirement would, he argued, meet with failure.[22]

Given such a stance, it was hardly surprising that Offe made a somewhat more positive evaluation of the potential for stabilisation involved in his second alternative to welfare statism, namely, corporatist solutions of one kind or another, in which the 'anarchy' of social processes under welfare statism was somewhat constrained by tripartite arrangements between state actors and representatives of key sectors of capital and labour (Crook et al. 1992: ch. 3; Schmitter 1974; Schmitter and Lembruch 1979). However, if he doubted the ability of the New Right political project to be translated into a coherent and sustainable governmental project, Offe's assessment of the long-term viability of the established comparative variations of corporatism was equally bleak. He argued that the exclusionary nature of corporatist arrangements and their marked tendency to generate inequitable and de-legitimising patterns of social distribution, especially as far as those sections of wage labour engaged in the public sector were concerned, made it difficult, if not impossible, to maintain such arrangements as a means of containing the crises of welfare statism.[23]

If Offe's initial engagement with welfare statism as a political form placed a central emphasis on the structured inevitability of such a form under the conditions of liberal democratic capitalist societies of late modernity, his later work departs totally from any such premise (Offe 1996: esp. Part III). Rather, it proposes an almost universal stagnation, if not regression, of welfare statism, amounting to 'a turning point in the development of the Western democracies'. A variety of explanations are identified for this development, and these explore the political terrain of 'the core substance of democratic politics' as defined by 'the question to what extent market outcomes must be accepted (in the name of efficiency) or corrected (in the name of equity and justice)' (ibid.: x).

The explanations identified by Offe for the stasis of welfare statism can be classified as those of historical conjuncture, institutional constraint and social structural change. With reference to the conjunctural factor, he advances a version of the globalisation thesis to the extent that he proposes that, following the oil crisis of the early 1970s, there developed, in relation to markets for goods, capital and raw materials, a widening gap between 'what *affects* individual states and what those states *can achieve as* individual states' (Offe 1996: 106). There is a similar effectiveness deficit with regard to threats to the ecological balance and other general threats to human living conditions and survival in contemporary 'risk societies' (Beck 1992, 1999). The overall result can be seen in 'the nation-state's *regulatory competence* retreating hopelessly into the background in the face of a supranational *state of nature* made up of technical, economic, military, and ecological interdependencies and long-range effects' (Offe 1996: 106; Beck 1992). In sum, the interventionist national states have proved increasingly inadequate in dealing with a proliferating global agenda.[24]

If this conjunctural panorama leads to pessimistic conclusions concerning the diminishing efficacy of the 'active state', a consideration of the condition of the internal sovereignty of contemporary welfare states provides no greater grounds for optimism. After an initial phase in which the welfare, interventionist state seemed equal to any and all tasks of economic management and social integration (a more or less universal stance in the Fordist-Keynesian era), the implication of 'the steering state' in the dominant structures of contemporary capitalism so constrained its powers of action and consequent authority as to seriously undermine its capacity to play a coherent coordinating role (Offe 1996: 107).[25]

It appears that a combination of conjunctural factors and institutional constraints has led to a loss of confidence in the *étatist* social-democratic model as a political form and, consequently, to a major shift in the general Western political spectrum. However, while accepting that 'the spheres of state competence and responsibility have shrunk', Offe ultimately questions the validity of these proposed explanations, labelling them as economic determinist. As an alternative, he hypothesises that the strength – or weakness – of state power derives not from environmental factors, whether national or international, nor from the plausibility of competing theoretical explanations, but rather from 'conflictual processes of sociopolitical interpretation and will formation' (ibid.: 113). *The key to successful political mobilisation in relation to strong, interventionist states lies therefore in political struggles.* However, such struggles are necessarily contextualised by relevant social structural conditions: it is in relation to these conditions that Offe proposes his preferred explanation for the stagnation of welfare statism as a political form. Strong states, he argues, can be shown to be positively correlated with the capacity for organisation and action manifested in intermediate associations in the state's environment. Elaborating this proposition, Offe suggests both the causes and consequences of this weakened 'associability' in industrially developed capitalist democracies.

> For a number of years ... a standard topos of empirical and theoretical research into social structure has been the finding (and its interpretation) that 'modern' social structures tend toward the dissolution of large-scale uniformities of social position and social milieu, and the replacement of these by atomised, pluralised, and rapidly changing social and cultural formations ill-suited to association. (ibid.: 114)

This erosion of the autonomous associability of civil society with its consequential effects on the capacity of states to engage in decisive intervention is paradoxically reinforced by the tendency for collective actors, such as churches, professional associations and political parties, to respond to the erosion of their various constituencies by seeking compensatory organisational assistance and resources from the state. Such a development, while superficially comprehensible as a strategy to enhance the civic dynamism of the relevant societies (most obviously in the case of political parties but also more widely), nevertheless threatens the long term political and social stability of liberal democracies in two ways in particular: first, it widens the patronage powers of states by making them in effect the paymasters of an increasingly only nominally autonomous civil society and, secondly, it increases the alienation of those who are outside the charmed circle of those in receipt of state subsidies.

The central thrust of Offe's most recent discussion of welfare statism is that, contrary to his initial theorisation, a combination of reinforcing developments has rendered both its theory and practice static and embattled. Sophisticated and insightful analyses regarding the potential for welfare statism to produce more just, equitable and therefore stable societies continue to be developed, but against a background of a declining, if not entirely evaporated, belief in both the desirability and capacity of welfare statism to function as a framework for an emancipatory politics. On this account, welfare statism has significantly ceased to be an independent variable in the analysis of liberal democratic capitalist societies and discussions centring on the concept have become increasingly programmatic as opposed to analytic.

Welfare Statism and the Economic Polity

This is certainly not the case with a second perspective on welfare statism offered by Sheldon Wolin. Indeed, rather the opposite is true: for Wolin, so central is welfare statism to relations of domination in late modernity that he contends that 'a principal task of democratic theory ... is to establish a democratic critique of the welfare state' (Wolin 1987: 470).[26] Specifying the conception of democracy which underpins this critique, Wolin argues in a manner highly congruent with the position set out in Chapter 2 above:

> Democracy involves more than participation in political processes. *It is a way of constituting power.* Democracy is committed to the claim that experience with, and access to, power is essential to the development of

the capacities of ordinary persons because it is crucial to human dignity and realisation. *Power is not merely something to be 'shared', but something to be used collaboratively in order to initiate, to invent, to bring about.* A democratic critique of the welfare state is a critique of a political arrangement that denies this conception of democracy as political action in the most fundamental sense of using power to constitute a collaborative world. (ibid., emphasis mine)

How are we then to characterise this 'political arrangement' and its implication in domination in modernity? Wolin suggests that in naming this formation 'it is important to retain Marx's emphasis upon the primacy of economic organisation and its class character, but at the same time to recognise that "the economy" represents the ontological principle of modernising ideologies, not a neutral construct for describing the organisation of production and distribution of material goods' (ibid.: 471). It is this ontological principle which connects the ideology of 'the economy' and the positive role of the state in advanced capitalist societies and involves both in 'a common tendency toward the depoliticisation of society; ... both are not only opposed to the redemocratisation of society, they are committed to reshaping the attenuated remains of democratic practices to accord with the needs of a corporate vision of politics' (ibid.).

Wolin proposes that the term 'Economic Polity' most adequately conveys the ontological/ideological assumption of an underlying reality upon which ideally both social and societal life should be focused. Such a formation has the following characteristics: it is positively committed to a conception of an unlimited expansion of power; it is the product of specifically late-modern forms of power generated by the application of scientific knowledge; it is both unique and in principle endlessly reproducible; and finally, *'the ideology of the Economic Polity, like its sources of power, envisions endless expansion but its imperialism tends to be nonterritorial, degrounded, projecting its influence throughout the world, while militarising the emptiness of space'* (ibid., emphasis mine).

Contrary to the perspective which would consider the welfare state as an evolution of political modernity representing a counterweight to capitalist modernity as a structure of domination, Wolin proposes that we should most appropriately regard welfare as a function within the modern state, the latter being defined in Weberian terms as 'a relation of men dominating men, a relation supported by means of legitimate, that is, to be considered legitimate, violence' (Gerth and Mills 1946: 78; quoted in Wolin 1987: 473). That is, the real *political* meaning of welfarism is to be understood only within the context of the modern state as a distinctive structure of domination. Welfarism as a political strategy is both a product of and a response to dominant characteristics of modernity; in particular, 'centralised power, perfected technologies of coercion, disintegrated populations that express their incoherence in a search for lost roots of "identity", and the consociation of economy and polity' (ibid.: 474).

Wheareas the *social* interpretation of welfare statism understands it above all as an institutional response to and containment of the social dislocation and potential human damage produced by capitalist modernity, Wolin's alternative *political* appropriation focuses upon the role played by welfare in the enhancement and maintenance of modern state domination. In particular, his interpretation emphasises the political meaning and importance of the widely recognised arbitrariness of the administrative decisions which generate the various categories of welfare recipient. Considered from a perspective of democratic empowerment, the complex web of political decisions that embodies welfare statism represents an enormous structure of 'exploitable relationship(s) to state power'.

Thus, within the framework of the Economic Polity as *the* modern structure of domination, 'exploitation is as much political as economic in its objectives' (Wolin 1987: 474). As discussed in Chapter 3, the 'creative destruction' that is an endemic feature of capitalist modernity increasingly involves a dialectic between the availability and the disposability of wholesale social groups, even on occasion virtual populations, in relation to the various commodity relationships of the market. But this process requires the containment and stifling of resistance. In these circumstances, 'the objective [of campaigns, both rhetorical and administrative, against the welfare culture] is not simply to free the welfare dependent from the web of governmental power so that he or she can then be inserted into the disciplinary web of the market, but to break the political culture, and thence the power, of the poor' (ibid.: 475).

In the broader perspective of the domination/empowerment distinction proposed here, the legitimacy of modern state domination (in terms of both beliefs and practices) is contested in the struggles that domination generates. Consequently, to understand welfare policy as the pursuit of state domination requires an understanding of the implications of this policy for such struggles. The purposive structuring of domination in such struggles is expressed above all in that variability of welfare processes which Wolin identifies as a central characteristic of their political significance. 'Variability', he argues, 'is the condition that makes possible two complementary phenomena: a certain kind of flexible power and a certain kind of pliable citizen.' Significantly, he adds: 'power depends upon the receptivity of the object, its willingness to support, obey, or, at least, to acquiesce' (ibid.: 477).[27]

Lenin ?

Simply expressed, continued state domination crucially depends upon the neutralisation of potential sources of resistance. Whereas in the social interpretation of welfare statism, marginal populations provide the *explanandum* of state policy, in the political interpretation such populations provide the *explanans*. 'This is because their status of pariah, as defined by the actions and rhetoric of public officials and politicians and disseminated by the media, represents the legitimation of an extension of state power' (ibid.). In a conclusion which links the role of marginality in the modern political formation with the contemporary realities of capitalist modernity discussed in the previous chapter, Wolin notes that

> marginality is a means of expanding a particular kind of state power, one less hedged by ordinary rules (due process), one freer to respond in accordance with the 'objective situation'. 'The guest worker' and 'wetback', the foreigner who cannot find work in his native country are the symbol of marginality on the plane of the international political economy, the ideal 'citizen' of the Economic Polity: mobile and vulnerable. (ibid.)

The significance of this interpretation in an epoch of growing mass migration can hardly be overstated (Roche and van Berkel 1997: esp. Parts II and IV). It is above all the political regulation of marginal populations which provides the central rationale of the welfare state as *the* modern political formation. Any democratic critique of that formation must begin by engaging with both the goals and means of such regulation. The political significance of welfare programmes lies primarily not in their financial details and implications but in their role in the political construction and management of the 'human *materia* of state power'. Wolin designates such *materia* as a distinct category, the virtueless citizen.

The virtueless citizen has no *a priori* claim not to be shaped in accordance with the rational requirements of state power. This lack of a claim is registered above all in the fact that he or she has no control over the conditions of personal empowerment. Or, more strongly, because these conditions may be taken away or even increased, they are not forms of power at all (Wolin 1987: 479).

Enmeshed in a complicated network of administrative regulations which, while promoted under the slogan of 'flexibility', serve to enhance the discretionary power of the state, welfare recipients on typical workfare schemes are caught between the constraint and stigma of 'state handouts' and the less than total 'autonomy' of 'free wage-labour'. In Wolin's graphic phrase, 'the virtueless citizen is the dangling man' (ibid.).

Welfare statism is thus the Reason of State of the modern state. Further, it is essential to the full import of that perspective that the contours of the modern state be seen in a wholly new light. Historical modernity has involved the steady porousness of old boundaries, particularly between state and economy, and the consequent development of a new political formation, a new structure of domination. Bureaucratic rationalisation and the transmutation of the state through the consociation of polity and economy into the Economic Polity have led to a qualitatively transformed system of domination, both intensively and extensively, which Wolin sees as totalising in aspiration and potential.[28] Central to this steady totalisation of power in late modernity is the private colonisation of the public sector. This colonisation includes 'the expansion of private education, private hospitals, the assumption [by the private sector] of various welfare programmes, corporate subsidies of the arts ... the operation of, prisons, and recruitment of large security forces' (ibid.: 491).[29] A consistently 'economising' rhetoric, proposing that 'the private sector' can more effectively deliver both goods and services due to its greater responsiveness to profit motives and market forces, serves to obscure the political rationality which fulfils the disciplinary needs of the Economic Polity.[30]

Wolin concludes his distinctively political theorisation of welfare statism by noting that the true context of the new *realpolitik* is that of the international political economy. The real new world order of contemporary capitalism requires a New Machiavellianism or statecraftiness in which the political rationality of institutionalised bureaucratic arbitrariness, expressive of welfare statism as a structure of domination, plays a vital role in neutralising opposition and constructing legitimacy. Central to the achievement of such rationality is the ideology of systems-talk, at the heart of which is 'the non-suppressive extinction of difference'. Wolin's explication of such system-thinking illustrates a key aspect of state domination in late modernity:

> System-thinking extinguishes difference not by suppression but by a combination of translation and abandonment: social phenomena are renamed 'inputs' or treated as 'cost/benefits' and absorbed into those categories. What cannot be accommodated/co-opted doesn't 'count' and can be ignored. (Wolin 1987: 497)

Welfare Statism and 'the Death of the Social'

If the social interpretation of welfare statism and its stasis adopts a perspective of blocked empowerment, the theorisation of welfare statism as the contemporary Reason of State sees such state interventionism as a key cornerstone of political *domination* in the era of the Economic Polity. A third perspective on welfare statism combines elements from both these earlier perspectives. In elaborating his thesis concerning 'the death of the social', Nikolas Rose agrees with Offe that 'in almost all advanced industrial countries ... the old certainties of "the welfare state" are under attack, and welfare systems are undergoing transformation' (Rose 1996: 327). However, rather than seeing this development as representing a more or less straightforward shift in the balance between capital and organised political intervention in a parallel perspective to that adopted by Offe, Rose adopts a distinctive variant on the political rationality position set out by Wolin, arguing that the decline of the welfare state is most adequately understood 'at the level of "governmentality"'. This governmentality is conceived 'as ... the emergence of a range of rationalities and techniques that seek to govern without governing *society*, to govern through regulated choices made by discrete and autonomous actors in the context of their particular commitments to families and communities' (ibid.: 328).[31]

This third perspective on welfare statism therefore is a Foucauldian interpretation of a range of changes in social thinking and practice associated with the reconfiguration of welfare statism as a political formation, a reconfiguration which Rose and his fellow Anglo-Foucauldians identify with the 'history' (in Foucault's use of that term) of 'advanced liberalism' (Rose 1999: ch. 4).[32] This interpretation fails to specify or engage with the problems and inconsistencies of Foucault's discussion of the inevitability of power as domination.

In what may reasonably be seen as typical Foucauldian mode, Rose contextualises his argument by proposing the important historicity of 'the social':

> 'the social' ... does not represent an eternal existential sphere of human sociality. Rather, within a limited geographical and temporal field, it set the terms for the way in which human intellectual, political and moral authorities, in certain places and contexts, thought about and acted upon their collective experience. This novel plane of territorialisation existed within, across, in tension with other spatialisations: blood and territory; race and religion; town, region and nation. (1996: 329)

As the twentieth century progressed, a range of political rationalities, otherwise divided over many fundamental issues, agreed on the necessity of conceiving government theory and practice in relation to 'the social'.[33] It is this *a priori* of political thought which has, Rose proposes, been undergoing 'a mutation' in recent decades. By way of explanation, he identifies two causes in particular, one a matter of supposed material development, the other involving a variety of cross-cutting political conflicts and ideological debates. First of all, the idea of a national economy which had provided a key factor in the delineation of 'the social' as an object of governance has been increasingly called into question by sectoral economic relationships which cut across national populations (cf. Hollingsworth and Boyer 1997a: ch. 14). Secondly, welfare statism as the political model of 'social' governance was subject to a veritable barrage of criticism across the political spectrum with respect to both its costs and endemic injustices and the political deficiencies of its unaccountable and arbitrary bureaucratic discretion (Hirschman 1991; Rose 1993).[34]

The combined impact of the conceptual revisionism emanating from these sources has been such, Rose argues, as to erode the coherence of 'the social' as a signifier of both discourse and practice. In its place we can identify a new conceptual focus: that of 'the community'. In the variegated sub-discourses of community care, risk communities, multiculturalism and ethical and religious pluralism, Rose detects a 'profound, if uncertain', mutation in ways of thinking and acting. This mutation is expressed in the 'new political languages … embodied in the ways in which a whole series of issues are problematised – made amenable to authoritative action' (1996: 331). In another typically Foucauldian *aperçu*, historically insightful but resonant with political fatalism, Rose briefly but significantly notes the historical transformation of discourse in terms of 'community' from its deployment as part of a language of resistance to an increasingly remote and bureaucratised society to a discourse of expertise. Within this discourse:

> Communities became zones to be investigated, mapped, classified, documented, interpreted, their vectors explained to enlightened professionals-to-be in countless college courses and to be taken into account in numberless encounters between professionals and their clients, whose individual conduct is now to be made intelligible in terms of the beliefs and values of 'their community'. (ibid.: 332)[35]

In other words, a language – and practices – of empowerment is appropriated into a discourse of domination. The distinctiveness of that alternative complex of discourses articulated around 'the community' can be illuminated by contrasting it with that associated with 'the social' (Rose 1999: ch. 5). The first contrast is spatial: whereas Wolin interprets a wide range of contemporary developments as involving a movement towards totality, both at the level of political and economic interconnectedness and at the level of purposive political domination, Rose proposes that the rise of 'the community' is powerfully associated with 'de-totalisation'. While

> government 'from the social point of view' posited a single matrix of solidarity, a relation between an organically interconnected society and all the individuals contained therein, given a politico-ethical form in the notion of social citizenship, ... today ... a diversity of 'communities' is thought to, actually or potentially, command our allegiance: moral communities ... lifestyle communities ... communities of commitment .... (1996: 333)

Although much 'community'-based discourse relates communities to some wider collectivity, the nature of this collectivity is frequently seen as problematic.

A second contrast concerns the ethical character of 'the social' and 'the community' respectively. The social was above all 'an order of collective being and collective responsibility'; 'the community', in contrast, expresses 'a new ethical perception of the individualised and autonomised actor, each of whom has unique, localised and specific ties to their particular family and to a particular moral community' (ibid.: 333–4; 1999: 176–7). Differences with respect to spatial imaginary and ethical character are further reinforced by difference with regard to identification. While the discourses of 'the social' and 'the community' both involve processes of identification, their configuration is quite distinctive. At the centre of such processes in the discourse of 'the social' is the socially identified citizen, 'a member of a single integrated national society', whereas in the discourse of 'the community', communities are 'those networks of allegiance with which one identifies existentially, traditionally, emotionally or spontaneously' (1996: 334). Within the latter discourse, Rose argues, 'communities' are both 'given' (gay men, AIDS sufferers, people with a disability, etc.) and immanent ('to be achieved').

Although, as we have seen, arguments regarding the stasis of welfare statism are both descriptive (fiscal crises, the loss of territorial autonomy within the technologically driven intensification of international political economy) and normative (dependency culture, processes of anti-democratic disempowerment), in relation to which alternatives such as those focused on 'community' tend to carry a high presumptive level of improvement, liberation, emancipation and so forth, Rose is concerned to map out the ways in which 'the community' is becoming (or even has become) the new discourse of government, involving 'a variety of strategies for inventing and instrumentalising these dimensions of allegiance between individuals and communities in the service of projects of regulation, reform or mobilisation' (ibid.: 334). Thus, just as Wolin argues that the administrative identification and regulation of marginal populations is an integral aspect of modern state activity, so Rose proposes that 'community is not simply the territory of government, but a *means* of government' (ibid.: 335).[36] It is a means of 'governing through community' (1999: 176). Exploring the example of the health promotion programmes around HIV and AIDS, he notes that

> Government through community, even when it works upon pre-existing bonds of allegiance, transforms them, invests them with new values, affiliates them to expertise and re-configures relations of exclusion. This does not make 'communities' in some sense false. But it should alert us to the work entailed in the construction of community, and the implications of the logics of inclusion and exclusion, of responsibilisation and autonomisation, that they inescapably entail. (1996: 336)

The decline of 'the social' and the rise of 'the community' as the dominant focus for contemporary governability has been accompanied by parallel and reinforcing developments in relation to other aspects of contemporary social life. Rose highlights three of these. First, the de-socialisation of economic life, 'in which techniques for the maximisation of social welfare no longer appear necessary to secure economic well-being in a market constituted largely by private enterprises' (ibid.: 337). Within the context of the gradual replacement of government of the social in the name of a national economy (Miller and Rose 1990, 1995) by government of particular zones, a fundamental shift is proposed in the rationalities governing employment and unemployment, a shift involving a central emphasis upon the individual as an active agent in their own economic governance (cf. Leadbetter 1999). Secondly, the subjects of government are specified in new ways, central to which is a redefinition of inclusion/exclusion involving the displacement of discourses of prudentialism focusing on mutuality and solidarity by those emphasising the autonomised competence of individuals and families. Whereas under regimes of welfare statism, 'social technologies were to civilise individuals, render them as citizens with obligations to conduct themselves with prudence in exchange for certain guarantees against uncertainty ... in the new prudential regimes, individuals, educated through the mechanisms of marketing and the pedagogies of consumption and lifestyle, are to gain access to previously "social" benefits such as educational advantage, health status and contentment in old age through purchase in the competitive market' (Rose 1996: 343).

Wolin's discussion of the importance of the regulation of marginal populations to the institutionalisation and maintenance of the new Economic Polity is powerfully echoed in Rose's exploration of the new styles of thought and practice associated with the social management of such marginal populations. While recognising the need not to over-emphasise the novelty of the practical and moral divisions between the included and the excluded, Rose proposes nevertheless that there is a 'new territory ... emerging, after the welfare state, for the management of an array of micro-sectors, comprised of those who are unable or unwilling to enterprise their own lives or manage their own risk, incapable of exercising responsible self-government, attached to no moral community or to a community of anti-morality' (ibid.: 347). In this new territory, oppositional forces are widely transformed into service providers and the gap created by policies which seek to reduce welfare expenditure in the name of competitive tax regimes is filled by 'new logics of competition, market segmentation and service management' (ibid.).

The third development which Rose sees as characterising the political rationality that has replaced social welfarism involves a qualitative shift in the relationship between expertise and politics. 'Social government', Rose notes, 'was expert government.' As such, it raised major, and largely unresolved, questions of political accountability. With the erosion of welfare statism, a wide variety of strategies is now being deployed in order to address these deficiencies of accountability, *united only by their detachment from the procedures of democratic politics*. Rose cites statutory regulation leading to struggles over the regulation of expertise rather than enhanced responsiveness to social need, the replacement of professional norms by the criteria of accountancy and the pervasiveness of social audits as examples of such strategies.

The Foucauldian interpretation of the statis of welfare statism and the rise of 'community' regulation exemplifies the intended critical refutation of the central organising concepts of modern political theory that we examined in Chapter 2. Central to this critique is a rejection of the relevance, indeed analytic coherence, of taking the dichotomies of state and civil society and public and private as the continued focus of contemporary political analysis. On this view, states in modernity are merely one among many examples of governmentality (Curtis 1995; Rose and Miller 1992). Wolin, on the other hand, makes clear his continued belief in the desirability of seeing the modern state as the central focus of any democratic political critique of relations of domination in the contemporary advanced world, while arguing for the necessity of contextualising such analysis in a wider Economic Polity. Equally, while exploring the reasons for the stagnation of the welfare state political project, Offe sees states as critical collective actors in the consequent political scene. These differing appropriations of the relationship of welfare statism to the modern state provide an important context for a discussion in Part II of the possibilities for a politics of empowerment.

However, in exploring such possibilities at the opening of the twenty-first century, it is obviously necessary to consider the extent to which states remain as central to struggle and transformative politics. That they may have ceased to be so provides a key aspect of discussions of 'globalisation'.

The Powerless State in Late Modernity?

In their simplest terms, arguments concerning the globalisation of capitalism and its political consequences propose that capitalist restructuring over the last two decades has created both a real and a virtual system of interrelated networks of circulation and production – the outstanding examples being provided by the various money markets and the integrated activities of the multinationals – the combined effect of which is to qualitatively reduce the capacity of states, either individually or collectively, to significantly regulate either 'national economies' or autonomous markets (Holton 1998; Horsman and Marshall 1994; Ohmae 1990; Perraton et al. 1997; Reich 1992).[37] In this scenario, for good or ill, states are increasingly ceasing to be 'real players' in the new world disorder and, as a result, novel power circuits are to be found either at the supra-national level of new trading blocs or at the sub-national level of various regionalisms, whether economic or political (Castells 1993, 1996, 1997; Hollingsworth and Boyer 1997a).

Both Hirst and Thompson and Alan Scott have pointed to the political significance of the use of the term 'globalisation'. They note the 'mythical' status occupied by the typical usage of 'globalisation' to invoke *chaotic or irresistible social forces* and convey a powerful sense of uncontestable – because 'naturalised' – political fatalism (Hirst and Thompson 1996: 1–17; Scott 1997: 16. See also Bauman 1998).[38] The significance of such social myths in relation to political struggles is highlighted by Scott's suggestion that one may usefully view the notion of globalisation as being 'ideological' in Mannheim's sense of an idea whose purpose is to assist or resist social change. Thus, just as 'globalisation' was initially a codeword for both the prescriptions and achievements of the New Right agenda of the 1980s, subsequently it becomes the focus of critique and resistance.[39] Bearing in mind, therefore, the necessity of not falling into the trap of assuming that the globalisation *explanans* of the globalisation-state power relationship can be taken for granted, it nevertheless remains possible to evaluate the globalisation thesis that there has been a major transformation of states as sites of social determination and social struggle.

Such a case is strongly advanced by Castells who, in arguing for the 'systematic erosion' of the power of nation-states, proposes: 'the instrumental capacity of the nation-state is decisively undermined by globalisation of core economic activities, by globalisation of media and electronic communication, and by globalisation of crime' (Castells 1997: 244). This proposition is supported by an impressively wide range of evidence. The territorial integrity of states is seen as undermined by unintended consequences with respect to their own defensive efforts in terms of establishing supra-state structures and by the sub-national perception of state shrinkage and by consequent and diverse political mobilisations and potential political and territorial fragmentations (ibid.: 262–99).

It is common ground between the proponents of such a 'global' view and those who take a substantially different – or wholly opposed – view that there has been a significant increase in the degree of interconnectedness of dominant aspects of the world economy over the last twenty years. The issue then becomes whether or not this interconnectedness, particularly to the extent that it is seen as being rooted in a technological revolution, marks the emergence of a novel transnational system, involving a necessary downgrading of state power in the way that Castells and others propose. A major difficulty with this position is that it may well involve an exaggeration of the coherence of the relationship between the various networks proposed. While Castells, for example, certainly acknowledges that the network society is a brutal arena in terms of winners and losers and is moreover so structured as to institutionalise chronic exclusion for those millions outside the network orbit, he does not appear to consider the possibility of what Scott identifies as the Polanyian perspective; namely, the mobilisation of resistance and the generation of institutions embodying a non-market dominated conception of social order (Scott 1997: 14).

Quite apart from the strongly functionalist overtones of his argument, the evidence does not support the 'strong globalisation' thesis advanced by Castells and others. Both Hirst and Thompson and Weiss have contested 'the myth of the powerless state', the latter quite emphatically. With the single exception of money markets, they argue, it is much more accurate to speak of internationalisation as against globalisation.[40] Weiss, in particular, surveying trade, production and investment, concludes that it is incontrovertible that national and regional networks play a vital role in contemporary economic processes (see also Carnoy 1993).[41] Pressing home her case, she further suggests that the comparative evidence, rather than indicating that fundamental erosion of state power proposed by the globalists, clearly shows a pattern of state adaptability and differentiation rather than loss of power.

On this view, then, states continue to be important as both actors and arenas. Has nothing changed? Here there is apparent agreement that something has, but disagreement over its significance. The agreement concerns a reconstitution of power relations in the closing decades of this century. The disagreement concerns the scope and significance of such a reconstitution. All are agreed that states are still very much part of the historical and analytic scene but differ as to why this is the case. In an account such as is offered by Castells, while states have lost their presumed former capacities in relation to economic activity, they are assuming greater significance as *containers of identity*, particularly the identities of resurgent nationalism (Castells 1997: 305–6). Weiss, as we have seen, implicitly rejects such a view. At the same time, however, she also speaks of a reconstitution of power relations but in a way which emphasises the normality of such a development when seen in historical perspective.[42]

While the arguments advanced by Weiss and others provide a clear corrective to the exaggerations of the 'uniqueness' version of the globalisation thesis, they do carry the danger of downplaying the historical significance of that 'autonomisation' of money markets discussed in the previous chapter.[43] Even accepting the argument that it is much more consonant with the evidence to speak of internationalisation than globalisation, the scale of economic devastation occasioned by capital flows may be enormous.[44] There is, however, a more important reservation to be expressed about Weiss' argument in the present context. This concerns the implicit perspective within which her argument is located, a perspective wholly consistent with what Wolin describes as the ideology of the Economic Polity. Thus, Weiss' conception of 'transformative state capacity' relates exclusively to 'domestic strategies for industrial change' (Weiss 1998: 15). An emphasis upon transformative change is combined with a prioritising of a particular conception of such change which valorises economic competition over democratic empowerment. States are shown – very effectively – to matter because above all they have an important role to play in economic development. The powerful suggestion, explicitly analytic, implicitly normative, is that states not only can be legitimised because they may deliver economic growth but that they should be.

This stance is reinforced by the lack of consideration of the possibility that any conceivable advantages could flow from a diminution of state autonomy. In this vein, Weiss is quite dismissive of Hirst and Thompson's argument that, although economic and other forms of internationalisation have produced a situation in which 'nation-states are now simply one class of powers and political agencies in a complex system of power from world to local levels', states remain as a key source of legitimacy and accountability in relation to powers above and below the national level (Hirst and Thompson 1996: 190 seq.; Weiss 1998: 194; see also Held 1991). Elaborating the point, Weiss argues that if the characterisation of the general future of states were true (which she clearly does not accept), 'it is hard to see what kinds of substantive power the state will retain *if it is no longer where the action is*' (Weiss 1998: 195, emphasis mine). In the context of a consideration of state capacities in relation to power and domination, the obvious question is: *action for whom, over whom?*

This relates directly to a central problem in this area if one is concerned with power and domination and the relationship of the modern state to both. In identifying a mechanism whereby the destructive and dominating tendencies of unconstrained capitalism may be confronted, states have appeared as the obvious, indeed the only, candidate. But to conclude from that any alternative arrangement is unthinkable is to adopt the same TINA logic ('there is no alternative') that characterises the extreme globalist position (Held 1996). It is not self-evident that in the circumstances of late modernity, mobilisation in terms of collective power(s) has to take the form of state (as opposed to governmental) crystallisations with the accompanying characteristics of univocal sovereignty, territoriality and coercion.

Clearly, the empirical situation is both complex and fluid. Within that situation, it is equally clear that states will continue as major sites of social reproduction, struggle and collective agency well into the twenty-first century and probably beyond.[45] If one adopts the position taken up by Weiss that questions concerning the appropriate goals and capacities of political organisations are significantly politically constructed, then it seems entirely reasonable to pursue the strategy adopted by Hirst and Thompson and explore possible lines of development for state powers. In essence, these possibilities concern the future development of states 'as a crucial relay between the international levels of governance and the articulate publics of the developed world' (Hirst and Thompson 1996: 191; Held 1996). This relay function finds its critical expression in the processes of 'public governance', which in turn find expression in the generation and (attempted) enforcement of those general rules that 'regulate and guide action in a relatively consistent way, providing minimum standards of conduct and reliefs from harms' (ibid.: 193). Holton reaches a similar conclusion in his consideration of whether or not the nation-state is finished (1998). Against the stark proposition of 'extreme' globalisers such as Ohmae (1996) that traditional nation-states are 'coming apart at the seams', Holton argues that 'borders still matter'. Not because there can be, if there ever was, anything approaching absolute state sovereignty but because 'most global economic actors have so far felt the need for some kind of stabilising framework of rules and public support structures beyond the networks generated through market transactions. Even in an age of deregulation, most actors continue to look to states to provide or underwrite such supports' (1998: 108). Yet states are becoming 'increasingly implicated in wider sets of relationships with other nations, MNEs, and global NGOs operating across political boundaries' (ibid.).

While it seems entirely reasonable and necessary to recognise the importance of the changing context of rule generation and enforcement, we must equally address the question as to the ways in which it is meaningful and/or desirable that such an activity should be assigned to 'modern states' to the extent that such entities are conceived of as structures of territorially delimited domination, seeking (successfully or not) to impose 'their rules' in terms of legitimacy, territoriality and, ultimately, coercion. There is a reasoned and empirically grounded case for replacing a coercive (and arguably, in a multipolar world with respect to structures, forms and processes, increasingly unrealistic) conception of political process expressed and legitimised in the concept of the modern state with that of government (Hoffman 1995). Such a development would involve a restructuring and decentralisation of processes of public normativity, not a ceding of the significance of a negotiable division between public and private. Indeed, an important implication of the Hirst/Thompson argument concerns the *increased* importance of specifically *public* governance in a modern world characterised by differentiation and plural identity. This argument concerning the specific and irreducible nature of public government as rule-generating and negotiating speaks powerfully against the Foucauldian assertion of the dissolution, as against necessary and chronic problematisation, of the public–private distinction under modernity. Rather, it strongly suggests the importance of recognising the significance of the public domain for a politics of empowerment.

At the beginning of the twenty-first century, what Arendt poses as an ontological reality – the irreducible plurality of the world – is widely recognised as a sociological reality. As political arenas are increasingly constituted by complex regional, national, international and transnational networks, the political structuring of the world in terms of the territorial differentiation characteristic of earlier phases of modernity seems increasingly problematic (Connolly 1991). In such circumstances, there is 'a growing asymmetry between the global and transnational scale of contemporary social life and the territorial organisation [i.e. statisation] of liberal democratic governance' (McGrew 1997: 236). The consequence is a growing intellectual and political challenge to both the effectiveness and the legitimacy of the still substantially hierarchical institutional forms of states as structures of legitimate domination (Held 1995). Just as the struggles for recognition identifiable in earlier phases of modernity were the determinate if contingent expression of the relationship between processes of domination and processes of empowerment, so in the contemporary world such struggles can only be meaningfully contextualised in international and transnational arenas. If the general goal of a transformative modern politics remains the pursuit of universal possibilities of justice, a necessary element in such a project is clearly a critical interrogation of the validity and desirability of privileging states as both arenas and collective actors in late modernity. Within the terms of the present argument, this requires a consideration of the possibilities for a politics of power rather than a politics of domination. That is, it requires consideration of alternative forms of social, political, cultural and global collective action simultaneously constitutive of and expressive of generated political communities. In such forms, processes of self-government are recognised to be as important as – indeed, an essential component of – outcomes. Arising from the identification of and experience of inequality, injustice and exclusion, particularly with respect to self-determination, immanent political communities are not equated with the 'imagined communities' of elite strategy and unintended consequence, but represent the fallibilistic, contingent and therefore amendable outcome of processes of deliberative (or, as I shall argue below, communicative) democracy.[46]

Within the context of such challenges to the democratic limitations of states, we can approach the discussion of the politics of empowerment through a systematic consideration of three main possibilities which have been identified as critical foci and/or agents of change in late modernity. These are the public sphere, citizenship and social movements respectively. In Part II, each of these possibilities will be considered in turn.

Notes

1. This is the fundamental proposition involved in Mann's distinction between the despotic and infrastructural power of states. In a stance which follows logically from his effective privileging of power over, Mann clearly sees modern states as more 'power-full' than pre-modern states in that their capacity to successfully dominate, that is, their capacity to comprehensively structure the social processes which they claim to legitimately regulate, is qualitatively greater (see Mann 1993: ch. 3). Of course, technological innovation and capacity is of great significance in this development but of greater importance, it is argued here, is the aspiration to – and the justification of – higher and higher levels of social regulation (which is to say a specifically *political* regulation, provided it is recognised that these developments can only have their meaning within the framework of a politics of domination. For a discussion of the generation of administrative power in the context of modern states, see Giddens 1985b: ch. 7). A key dilemma of modernity has transpired to be that the modern state, the proposed agent of empowerment in relation to those inequalities identified and generated by societal rationalisation as obstacles to further rationalisation, has itself been identified as a key agent and/or focus of domination. See below for an exploration of this issue.

2. Weber's definition is both the most formally succinct and the most frequently cited. Hall and Ikenberry offer a more comprehensive list but their cluster is still dependent upon not merely the empirical test of force but, more importantly in the present context, upon a conceptualisation in terms of the superior application of force, that is, domination. See Hall and Ikenberry 1989. For a sophisticated and salutary warning against the over-extension of the concept of the state, see Nettl 1967–8.

3. See also Mann 1984 for an emphasis on the territoriality of the state.

4. Arrighi notes that the difference between the two logics can also be usefully expressed by means of Giddens' metaphor which defines states as 'containers of power'. Whereas territorialist rulers tend to increase power by expanding the size of their container, capitalist rulers tend to increase

power by the accumulation of wealth within a small container. See Arrighi 1994: 33 and Giddens 1985b: 13–14.

5. As Arrighi cogently argues, 'chaos' is not the same thing as 'anarchy'. 'Anarchy' designates 'absence of central rule'. Thus, the modern system of sovereign states as well as the system of rule of medieval Europe out of which the latter emerged both qualify as anarchic systems, each having principles, norms, rules and procedures which allow reference to 'anarchic orders'. 'Chaos' and 'systemic chaos', on the other hand, refer to a situation of 'total and apparently irremediable lack of organisation'. See Arrighi 1994: 30. cf. Bull 1977.

6. In *The Empire of Civil Society*, Justin Rosenberg advances a different interpretation in terms of which the Westphalian settlement by its institutionalisation of an 'absolutist' logic of territorialism is not the facilitator of but *an obstacle to* the development of capitalism. The first example of real 'modern' state sovereignty, the political form that was in the longer term to become general throughout Europe and ultimately the world, was to be found in the development of the English state as the public 'political' corollary of an emergent 'economic' mode of surplus extraction. See Rosenberg 1994: 137.

7. Although Arrighi's immediate inspiration is the work of Ferdinand Braudel, the general thrust of his argument concerning the chronic political structuring of capitalist modernity finds a powerful and common echo in a much larger body of work. Thus, Karl Polanyi makes the contribution of states to the process of capitalist development central to his account of 'the great transformation', Christopher Chase-Dunn emphasises the importance attached by Weber to the inter-state system in accounting for the unique development and continued viability of 'the capitalism of the West', Linda Weiss and John Hobson argue the case for both the historical and contemporaneous significance of 'strong states' in the determination of economic (that is, capitalist) development and Weiss has sought to refute the proposition that processes of (market) globalisation are making states increasingly redundant as sources of and foci for economic development (Braudel 1981–84; Chase-Dunn 1989; Weiss 1998; Weiss and Hobson 1995).

8. Of course, in the early phases of this process, the long-term outcome should not by any means be taken as a foregone conclusion. Tilly provides the most systematic discussion of the alternative possibilities of which it is necessary to take account in order to avoid the fallacy of retrospective determinism as far as the succession to the medieval system of rule is concerned. Recognising that there were alternative and viable outcomes is of particular importance at the contemporary juncture of modernity when there is a marked tendency to argue as if processes of large (and not so large) scale social change involved very limited and easily identifiable configurational outcomes. See Tilly 1975: 3–83. See also Ruggie's discussion of the important work of Spruyt in Ruggie 1993: 156. Rosenberg argues, not necessarily teleologically, that capitalism required the territorial segmentation of space, a position not dissimilar to that of Weber, who emphasised that only with a non-imperial organisation of space could capitalism have developed and continued to function (Rosenberg 1994; Chase-Dunn 1989). With regard to the current phase of expansionary states, Arrighi does propose the historical

possibility that, with the disparity between the United States' military superiority and declining economic power, a logic of territorialism will reassert itself (Arrighi 1994: 300 seq.).

9. See, for example, Dahl 1984; Giddens 1985b: ch. 1; Hall and Ikenberry 1989; Mann 1993.

10. Following Ruggie, Arrighi for example subscribes to the view that the modern system of rule, the inter-state system and the modern states which provide its agents and its expression, is a wholly novel epochal phenomenon. From this perspective, one simply cannot grasp the qualitative difference between, for example, the medieval system of rule with its overlapping jurisdictions and mobile elites and the modern system of territorial exclusiveness, caged social processes and largely 'nationalised' elites, if one fails to recognise the distinctiveness of the modern state system and the wholly distinctive social epistemes which give it comprehensive meaning (see Arrighi 1994 and Ruggie 1993). Hoffman (1995), on the other hand, makes a spirited case for the argument that there are indeed pre-modern and modern states, the differences being ones of degree and the crucial common factor being that of force. The issue of sovereignty and of a single public realm of domination are obviously central to the discussion of this issue. For a good example of the convolutions which can arise from the attempt to use the concept of the state on either side of the medieval/modern divide, see Weiss and Hobson 1995.

11. See in particular Clastres 1987, Mair 1962, Nicholson 1984, Roberts 1979 and Schapera 1956.

12. The question as to the desirable or even actual future scope of such activity must be a matter of debate and empirically informed projection. Certainly, with the rise of 'cosmopolitan governance', the possibilities that the scope is and/or ought to be narrowing are obviously enhanced. See Held 1995. See the discussion below of the proposal by Hirst and Thompson (1996) concerning the narrowing of scope due to international developments and the critical response by Weiss (1998).

13. As I hope will be clear, the quotation marks here refer to the definitive interconnectedness of the 'internal' and 'external' aspects of the multiple 'crystallisations' of modernity of which spaces-of-places (for example states) and spaces-of-flows (for example financial capital) are an outstanding example, other examples being ethnicity, patriarchy and state-centred citizenship.

14. For reasons of space, I shall not examine this issue here but see, for example, Lyon 1994.

15. As will become clear, the term 'Welfare State' does not refer here to a narrow and conventional understanding focused upon the provision of social services. Rather, the reference is to 'a multi-functional and heterogeneous set of political and administrative institutions whose purpose is to manage the [general] structures of socialisation and the capitalist economy' (John Keane in Offe 1984: 13). The fact that it might be reasonably objected that such an understanding relates to too narrow a range of the dominant crystallisations institutionalised in modern states – structures of patriarchy being an outstanding example – does not basically affect the force of the main proposition being advanced in terms of this broad conceptualisation of the welfare state: namely, that the historical stabilisation of the

Fordist-Keynesian regime involved modern states in a major coordinating role in relation to the whole subject society.

16. See below, Chapter 5, for a critical analysis of the shortcomings arising from Habermas' commitment to a systems theory approach to political analysis under modernity. Habermas was certainly Offe's theoretical role-model over this issue.

17. Examples of macro- and micro-perspectives on welfare states and domination are to be found in Wilensky 1975 and Stone 1984 respectively. On the gendering of such domination in welfare statism, see Hernes 1987. See Chapter 7 for a discussion of a welfare-state-centred conception of citizenship.

18. The success of such a project should not however be exaggerated, thereby contributing to a self-fulfilling 'mythology' which has to a significant extent already become part of the general political agenda. Comparatively speaking, the assault on the welfare state, both theoretically and practically, has become most marked in the United States. Elsewhere, such as in the United Kingdom, the practical situation would give much more support to Offe's contention about the intractability of welfare statism within the matrix of political power, a possibility about which he himself has come to be much less emphatic. See Offe 1996.

19. Offe notes that, whereas in the United States the erosion of the political support for welfare statism is prominently associated with 'tax revolts', in Western Europe cuts in welfare expenditure have primarily been presented as a necessary (that is, non-political) consequence of changes in both present and long-term 'economic indicators'. Thus, 'while the rise of a welfare state require(d) mass mobilisation and large political coalitions as a sufficient condition, its demise is mediated through economic imperatives as well as the silent and inconspicuous defection of voters, groups, and corporate actors whose heterogeneous structure, perceptions, and responses stand in the way of the formation of an effective defensive alliance. To put it somewhat simplistically, it takes politics to build a welfare state, but merely economic changes to destroy both major component parts of it and potential sources of resistance to such destruction' (Offe 1996: 175). As was noted above, this proposition may well underestimate the degree of resistance but the longer-term position remains unclear and Offe is clearly correct to emphasise the extent to which any future developments are politically contingent.

20. In considering the significance of this factor and its implications for Offe's general argument concerning the demise of welfare statism, it is important to bear in mind the comprehensive nature of his concept of the 'welfare state' as the site of crisis management in advanced capitalism. Thus, objectively, it is not only welfare expenditures narrowly understood which provide the source of chronic fiscal problems of welfare states but the tendency discussed in Chapter 3 for the socialisation of both important infrastructural production costs and of the costs of 'market failures', including those of speculation.

21. See, for example, the discussions in Chapter 3 and Chapter 6 in Offe 1984.

22. Once again, Offe's initial commitment to this position derived from his prior commitment to a systems-theoretic stance, leading to a judgement that certain political strategies were simply systemically precluded. In his

Introduction to Offe 1984, Keane notes and emphasises the importance of Offe's gradual abandonment of this theoretical perspective in favour of a much more action-theoretic position, which assesses the viability of political projects in terms of group conflicts within an overall matrix of social power; that is, there is a shift away from a system perspective on modes of welfare state capitalist domination to a concern with the possibilities of inter-group conflict.

23. There is arguably an insufficient emphasis in Offe's discussion on the degree to which corporatist arrangements exemplified a strategy of domination, the asymmetry of which became clear in the case of attempted 'corporatisations' such as that in the United Kingdom. The critical point in relation to domination and empowerment is the relationship between a range of corporatisms and the development of dualistic economies (see Goldthorpe 1984).

24. Beck argues that this leads directly to a demobilisation in relation to major forms of institutional politics and a consequent mobilisation at the level of sub-politics, particularly in the forms of a diversity of new social movements. Beck 1992, 1999.

25. But see below for a discussion of opposing views regarding the 'powerless state' such as Weiss 1998 and Mann 1997.

26. Anticipating objections that Wolin is writing in an American context, a context notably hostile to the implementation of the substance of a European social citizenship, it must be recognised that such 'citizenship' may be and has been viewed from a political perspective as involving incorporation and not empowerment.

27. Intended or not, the Foucauldian resonance of this proposition is quite clear.

28. The parallels with Habermas' discussion of these developments is clear. See the discussion in Chapter 5 below. Interestingly, in this perspective the much discussed 'control freakery' of the New Labour administration in the UK could be seen as not primarily the expression of personal authoritarianism (alone?) but as a structural phenomenon. Of course, as Weber noted a long time ago, dominant cultures have an elective affinity for certain personality types. Cometh the hour, cometh the men!

29. Wolin notes the power-enhancing role of marginalisation in the evolution of state-centred power into system-power: thus, 'the courts [in the US] have ruled ... that security guards in the employ of private companies are not subject to the same constitutional constraints that formally inhibit public law enforcement' (Wolin 1987: 492).

30. Wolin notes that the connection between the role of uncertainty and variability in the production of domination and the symbiotic relationship between polity and economy-civil society is demonstrated by the steady growth in the use of lie detectors and drug testing in both public and private sectors in the United States. The very fallibility of these procedures, he emphasises, actually enhances their efficacy as instruments of political regulation (Wolin 1987: 492).

31. Rose specifies 'governmentality' as being used in the sense that the term was used by Foucault: 'the deliberations, strategies, tactics and devices employed by authorities for making up and acting upon a population and its

constituents to ensure good and avert ill' (Rose 1996: 328; see also, Dean 1999: ch. 1). In what is in effect a theoretical and methodological position statement, Rose and his frequent collaborator, Peter Miller, offer three different meanings of the term 'government', one broad, one somewhat narrower and one quite conventional (Rose and Miller 1992). The broad version makes government co-terminous with all human interaction, the narrower version is wholly insensitive to and consequently negligent of the significance of differing institutional contexts, while the third focuses upon and implicitly recognises the importance of that very distinctiveness of politi-cal institutions, particularly states, which Rose and Miller wish to question and, following Foucault, dethrone (see Curtis 1995). See also Rose's discus-sion of 'governing "advanced" liberal democracies' (Barry et al. 1996). In the editorial Introduction to the latter volume, the suggestion is made that the 'retreat from the State' represented by policies and actions of the Thatcher government may involve 'a degovernmentalisation of the State' in favour of an autonomisation of 'entities of government' from the state. But surely, if we are concerned with the democratic character of government, that is, political freedom, then such a move from public to private represents a meaningful diminution of at least the principle of governmental account-ability, that is, a net transfer from power to domination.

32. The 'Declaration of Foucauldian Intent' underlining Rose's discussion of welfare statism and 'community' as differing political rationalities is to be found in the earlier paper, co-authored with Peter Miller, 'Governing Economic Life' (Miller and Rose 1990). Here, the elements of Foucault's perspective discussed in Chapter 2 above are identified, together with an appropriation of Latour's notion of 'action at a distance' (Latour 1987). In particular, Miller and Rose emphasised in typical Foucauldian fashion the importance of the 'how' as opposed to the 'what' of political processes; the role of language as an 'intellectual technology' serving to constitute the objects of politics; the dependency of 'governmentality' on the invention and evaluation of new technologies; the centrality of expertise to the exer-cise of 'modern power', particularly in terms of the creation of new, conso-nant subjectivities.

Highlighting the significance to 'modern forms of rule' of 'apparently humble and mundane mechanisms' such as technique of notation, computa-tion and calculation (only 'modern'? see, e.g. Mann 1986), Miller/Rose propose that 'the classical terminology of political philosophy and political sociology – State v. Civil Society, public v. private, community v. market and so forth – is of little use here.' Warming to their task, they continue:

> Such language needs to be investigated, to the extent that it functions in important ways within political rationalities and political programmes, providing them with an ethical basis and differentiating the legitimacy of varied types of governmental aspiration. But at the technical level, opera-tionalising government has entailed the putting into place, both inten-tionally and unintentionally, of a diversity of indirect relations of regulation and persuasion that do not differentiate according to such boundaries. In particular, the capacities that have been granted to expertise ... provide versatile mechanisms for shaping and normalising the 'private' enterprise, the 'private' firm, the 'private' decisions of businessmen and parents and

the self-regulating capacities of 'private' selves in ways that are simply not comprehended in these philosophies of politics. (1990: 8)

Even if one accepts the importance of identifying the power effects (or as I would wish to express it, the domination effects) of the capacities of expertise, why this should render the distinction between state and civil society redundant is by no means clear. That this is particularly so is underlined by the fact that most, if not all, of the examples discussed in the article are in fact concerned with government in the sense of the term that Miller/Rose wish to eschew, that is, with the exploration of the purposes and mechanisms involved in state/economy relations. Thus, discussing the issue of economic growth in the United Kingdom of the 1960s, they suggest, in an argument strongly reminiscent of Offe and Ronge's 'theses on the theory of the state' (1975), that government, while wishing to actively promote growth, could not intervene in the 'private' economy to do so. From this dilemma, they were rescued by the happy availability of the technique of Discounted Cash Flow Analysis. 'Social and private returns on investment could be reconciled, so it was held, by transforming ways of thinking about and calculating investments' (ibid.: 18). But would one seriously wish to argue that the failure of growth to occur was due to the lack of embeddedness of the 'technology of incessant calculation'?

Although Miller/Rose make much of the importance of recognising the nature of language as 'intellectual technology', they are, to say the least, equivocal about the substantive effects of such 'language games'. With more than a slight of air of having your cake and eating it, they adopt a stance of 'the world is a complex place and even government "at a distance" does not always work'. Moreover, their Foucauldian perspective on the inescapable heteronomy of social reality leads into what may be seen as a language game of their own. Anticipating Rose's discussion of 'the death of the social', Miller/Rose propose that 'the forms of political rationality that took shape in the first half of this century constituted *the citizen* as a social being whose powers and obligations were articulated in the language of social responsibilities and collective solidarities' (ibid.: 23, emphasis mine). Why 'citizen'? why not 'subject'? or does it not matter? Miller/Rose are obviously discussing in the UK context similar developments to those which Wolin is addressing in the US. Would not these developments be meaningfully illuminated by being considered in relation to processes of domination, processes rooted in a structuring of domination through welfare statism?

33. Rose cites Collini 1979, Clarke 1978, Donzelot 1979 and Procacci 1989 as illustrative texts dealing with England and France respectively.

34. These propositions are accurate but offer a very limited view of the complex reality. Certainly, in the United Kingdom, the level of intellectual and popular support for the welfare state remains remarkably high, given the unremitting onslaught against it. Any arguments concerning 'new political rationalities' have to be seen in that context and in addition, as Wolin suggests, in the context of the processes structuring the wider Economic Polity.

35. It is true that, at the very conclusion of his discussion of 'the death of the social', Rose does propose the possibility of identifying transformative possibilities in the social developments he explicates. However, the very brevity and generality of his comments contrasts sharply with the typically

Foucauldian documentation of the convoluted comprehensiveness of the new governmentality of 'community'. See Rose 1996.

36. Rose notes that, with regard to security, welfare statist universalism is being replaced by 'a variety of different ways of imagining security, each of which mobilises a particular sense of community'. One such image is Shearing's idea of 'a contractual' community, taking total responsibility for its own viability (Shearing 1995). The 'affluent ghettos' or laagers of West Coast America are a prime example (Davis 1990). A second image involves community 'as an antidote to the combined depredations of market forces, remote central government, insensitive local authorities in new programmes for the regeneration of delimited locales'. In either case, a highly centralised and technologically facile state further 'systematises' control in the name of decentralisation.

37. In the following discussion, no assumption is made regarding the overall world historical significance of 'globalisation'. (For useful general discussions, see Holton 1998 and Scott 1997.) Clearly, capitalism has been an indisputably central dynamic in any meaningful understanding of this development, creating a worldwide division of labour and market for capital and commodities. Holton usefully argues for the need for a 'top-down' perspective on globalisation emphasising the centrality of capitalism and the international system of states (as illustrated in Giddens 1991b) to be complemented by a perspective which recognises the significance of political and cultural developments in processes of global development. Holton sees Robertson 1992 as offering a positive example of the latter possibility, although one which understates the significance of economic developments. The present argument broadly understands the 'top-down' structuring of social relations as involving asymmetries of power equating to relations of domination while 'bottom-up' structuring refers to analytic, empirical and normative possibilities of collective action and possible empowerment.

Among this group of references Perraton and his co-authors, 1997, advance a distinctive argument concerning the existence of a hierarchy as opposed to a general collapse of national power relative to MNCs. Holton's discussion of the global economy, while fully recognising the asymmetries of power involved in its contemporary realisation, emphasises the growing importance of 'personalised networks of co-operation, exchange and trust in the successful constitution of global economic activity' (1998: 62). Importantly in the present context, Holton stresses the fact that governments and cultures enter into the constitution, reproduction and regulation of economic life (ibid.: 67). His argument here can be seen as paralleling the general thrust of Wolin's discussion analysed above. Whereas Wolin speaks of the emergence of the Economic Polity, Holton implicitly identifies a Political Economy.

38. Such a view would be supported by the cultural evidence offered by the recent genre of 'natural disaster' movies, the central common element of which relates to a world out of control and in the grip of irresistible elemental forces.

39. Within the terms of Mann's perspective discussed in Chapter 1 above, 'globalisation' has the capacity to play a role in both transcendental and

immanent ideological power networks. A critical difference from earlier ideological struggles may be that new technological media have qualitatively transformed both the spatial and temporal parameters of such networks.

40. As will be discussed below; however, this is quite an exception!

41. It has to be said that Castells also points to the evidence regarding the enormous importance of a facilitating 'home-base'. However, it seems simply anomalous for Castells to endeavour to conclude his argument by expressing agreement with those, such as Hirst and Thompson, who emphasise the continuing significance of state economic activity. His conceivable defence in terms of the necessity of contemporary states to negotiate with a variety of powerful collective actors, both territorially internal and external, would merely serve to undermine his general argument concerning the novelty of the prevailing situation since it is a central point in Weiss and Hobson's general argument about the continuing importance of states to economic development (see Hirst and Thompson 1996; Carnoy 1993; Weiss and Hobson 1995).

42. This is in a sense also the position adopted by Arrighi 1994 in terms of cycles of expansion. He, on the other hand, does raise the real possibility of the distinctiveness of the current situation.

43. Weiss does note that in recent decades, 'international capital flows have reached truly spectacular levels' (Weiss 1998: 178). While clearly correct to contest the 'unstoppability' thesis about the logic of capital in this phase of modernity and to emphasise the potential of and therefore for inter-state collaboration in relation to the regulation of money flows, her argument does not engage with the extent to which the current epoch demonstrates a profound transfer of economic resources within the world political economy.

44. Such devastation has obviously already been wrought by the successive crises in Mexico in 1983 and 1995. Further, at the time of writing, the East Asian miracle is looking decidedly less miraculous. In the Preface of her book, Weiss engages with this development and argues that, far from demonstrating the weakness of state power in relation to global markets, the current situation demonstrates the weakness of the relevant states with respect to what Weiss characterises as 'transformative capacity'. Weiss is right to dispute the unqualified 'logic of capital' case with its endemic fatalism; nevertheless, in the absence of existing organised power, either nationally or internationally, the continuing destructive capacity of financial markets seems clear (Weiss 1998).

45. For a strong statement of this position, see Mann 1997. Analysing the impact of four main factors – global capitalism, environmental danger, identity politics and post-nuclear geopolitics – he argues for the differential regional impact with a consequent dual outcome with respect to state-weakening and state-strengthening tendencies. Saskia Sassen proposes a similar assessment (public lecture, London School of Economics, 1 February 2000).

46. Significant examples of radical thinking with respect to the limitations of state power and possibilities for 'democracy beyond borders' are to be found in the work of Burnheim and Dryzek. Burnheim's normative theory of 'demarchy' is quite explicit about its intention to challenge 'the assumption that a centralised management of power ... is necessary to assure political order' (1986: 238). (This normative critique is reinforced by the contemporary

complexity of political and social determinations.) Dryzek argues in a similar vein for the necessity that the scope of immanent public spheres should in principle be derivative from the scope of the 'inter-est' identified by the participant members rather than being dictated by 'formal boundaries or jurisdictions, or obsolete notions of national sovereignty' (1995). Starting from a critique of neo-realist theory in the study of international relations, Linklater also explores possibilities for 'the transformation of political community' from a Habermasian perspective emphasising dialogue over domination in a post-Westphalian era (1998). For a systematic exposition and application of a civic republicanism argument to contemporary social realities – economic, political and cultural – see Sandel 1996.

Part II

5

Capitalism, States and Public Spheres I: Habermas' Political Journey

Part I of this study addressed three main issues: a critique of the chronic failure of modern political and social theory to recognise and/or sustain a necessary distinction between domination and power; the elaboration of a distinctive conception of power derived from the work of Arendt and Habermas; and the specification of capitalism and the modern states system as sites of domination in late modernity. The purpose of Part II is to explore the possibilities for political empowerment in late modernity against this conceptual and analytic background. This discussion is organised into four chapters: the present chapter and the next analyse the possibilities for empowerment which arise from the idea of the public sphere, an idea central to the political thinking of the leading contemporary advocate of modernity, Jürgen Habermas; Chapter 7 discusses the contribution that the discussion of citizenship may make to the analysis of empowerment, and Chapter 8 assesses the relationship between new social movements and such empowerment.

To an extent that seems strikingly obvious yet is at the same time surprisingly under-recognised, Habermas has been a consistently committed political theorist. This political dimension is most easily identified in the successive interventions Habermas has made in order to contest ideological challenges to the emancipatory rationalism he has consistently championed or in order to expose and engage with counter-democratic interventions into contemporary politics.[1] But Habermas' *oeuvre* is political at a more fundamental level: from the outset it has been centrally concerned with questions of power and politics, domination and emancipation, and these questions have provided a continuing motif in a wide range of works with apparently diverse concerns (such as the methodology of the social sciences and the nature and development of modernity). It therefore follows that any attempt to critically appropriate the concept of the public sphere as a focus for the analysis of contemporary possibilities of empowerment must first locate that concept within the trajectory of Habermas' evolving theorisation of power and politics in modern societies.

Given the scope of the important issues involved, the discussion is divided into two chapters. This chapter focuses upon Habermas' initial explication of the public sphere within the context of emergent modernity and then considers the subsequent development of his political thinking up to the definitive statement of the dual potential of modernity in *The Theory of Communicative Action*. The next chapter begins by completing the analysis of Habermas' political trajectory and then advances a critical appropriation of the concept of the public sphere and its implications for empowerment.

The Public Sphere

Against the background of his personal reaction to the genocidal domination of Nazism and his intellectual engagement with apparently terminal pessimism of the later Frankfurt School, the key question integrating Habermas' political concerns has been 'Is democracy possible?' in a rationalised world (McCarthy 1985).[2] To this question, Habermas has given a positive although, as will become clear, by no means consistent answer, whether in terms of content or scope. At the centre of this endeavour has been Habermas' discussion of the concept of the public sphere, a discussion which spans more than thirty years.

Habermas' initial statement of many of the political concerns which have been central to his work appeared with the publication of *Strukturwandel der Öffentlichkeit* (1962) (English translation, *The Structural Transformation of the Public Sphere* 1989; henceforth Habermas 1989a). Probably the most accessible of Habermas' major works, *The Structural Transformation* is at one level an historical account of the emergence and subsequent disintegration of the 'bourgeois public sphere' which Habermas locates in the context of a unique historical configuration, the civil society (*burgerliche Gesellschaft*) which originated in the European High Middle Ages. This civil society came into existence as the corollary of a depersonalised state authority. Activities and dependencies previously located within the framework of the household economy emerged to be reconstituted as the interface between private and public. Significantly, therefore, Habermas' initial specification of the public sphere was as a 'public of *private* individuals who join in debate of issues bearing on state authority' (Calhoun 1992: 7).[3]

Habermas identified a second crucial element in the formation of the public sphere: the press. The development of the press through its use by state authorities to promulgate instructions meant that those who were the addressees of state declarations genuinely became 'the public'. As a consequent part of such processes shaping the modern state, there arose a new stratum of 'bourgeois' – mainly jurists, doctors, pastors, officers and professors – replacing the genuine burghers, the old occupational orders of craftsmen and shopkeepers. At the core of the new stratum were the capitalists (that is, merchants, bankers, entrepreneurs and manufacturers). As Habermas remarks,

> In this stratum, which more than any other was affected *and* called upon by mercantilist policies, the state authorities evoked a resonance leading the *publicum*, the abstract counterpart of public authority, into an aware-ness of itself as the latter's opponent, that is, as the public of the now emerging *public sphere of civil society*. For these latter developed to the extent to which the public concern regarding the private sphere of civil society was no longer confined to the authorities but was considered by the subjects as one that was properly theirs. (1989a: 23)

Habermas identified the distinctive historical – and, as we shall see, normative – possibilities arising from these developments as twofold: first, the public use of reason as the proposed arbiter of power rela-tions understood as the generation of enabling and constraining rules; secondly, a transformation of the very nature of power claims themselves. The principle of control that the bourgeois public began to articulate against the claims of absolutism – and indeed against state claims in general – was, Habermas argues, intended to change domination as such. 'The claim to power presented in rational-critical public debate…, which *eo ipso* renounced the form of a claim to rule, would entail, if it were to prevail, more than just an exchange of the basis of legitimation while domination was maintained in principle' (ibid.: 28).

Thus, for Habermas, the critical element in the bourgeois idea of the law-based state, the binding of all state activity to a system of norms legitimised by public opinion, distinctively aimed at *abolishing the state as an instrument of domination*. 'Since the critical public debate of private people convincingly claimed to be in the nature of a noncoercive inquiry into what was at the same time correct and right, a legislation that had recourse to public opinion thus could not be explicitly considered as domination' (ibid.: 82). The intention lying behind the public opinion found in the critical debate of the public sphere was to abolish executive power as a source of social initiation, and thereby to abolish domination (*Herrschaft*) itself. 'The "domination" of the public, according to its own idea, was an order in which domination itself was dissolved: *veritas non auctoritas facit legum*' (ibid.). The key element in this transformation of *voluntas* (will) into *ratio* (reason) was the public competition of private arguments which produced a consensus about what was practically necessary in the interest of all.

Habermas showed no illusions about the gap which existed between the state of affairs formalised in such constitutional norms and the actual restrictive reality of bourgeois civil society. The autonomy of those private people whose interactions and critical debates constituted the public sphere was guaranteed by property; this autonomy was of equal importance with educational qualifications as a precondition of such a sphere. Even together petite and haute bourgeoisie only made up a minority of the relevant populations; the majority, the 'common people', were still governed by the rules, actors and institutions of precapitalist society.[4]

Nevertheless, Habermas maintained, the constitutions, written and unwritten, which provided the frameworks for the bourgeois public sphere, did contain *universal possibilities* in that they referred to citizens and human beings as such. Whatever the historical reality, 'the public sphere of civil society stood or fell with the principle of universal access. A public sphere from which specific groups would be *eo ipso* excluded was less than merely incomplete; it was not a public sphere at all' (ibid.: 85). Thus, while the empirical reality was that class interest was the basis of public opinion, Habermas nevertheless contends there was a congruence between such interest and a proposed general interest, to the extent that public opinion emerged from a critical public debate and could therefore be deemed to be rational. In other words, the criterion for political freedom is argued to be a question of institutional form and not substance, procedure and not content. From the outset Habermas' political position emphasised procedure over substance, formal justice over participatory actuality.

In setting out this account of the ascendant phase of the bourgeois public sphere, Habermas was quite clearly – and explicitly – contesting the limits of a purely ideological reduction of bourgeois political institutions.

as long as publicity existed as a sphere and functioned as a principle, what the public itself believed to be and to be doing was ideology and simultaneously more than ideology. On the basis of the continuing domination of one class over another, the dominant class nevertheless developed political institutions which credibly embodied as their objective meaning the idea of their own abolition: *Veritas non auctoritas facit legum*, the idea of that easy going constraint that prevailed on no other ground than the compelling insight of a public opinion. (ibid.: 88)

In the concluding chapters of *The Structural Transformation*, Habermas analysed the social developments which he identified as having led to the erosion of the limited reality and the emergent potential of the public sphere, thereby preventing the comprehensive institutionalisation of free speech and discursive will-formation. Central to these developments were the mutual interpenetration of greatly expanded economic organisations and equally expansive state administrations. Increased economic complexity and a consequent structure of economic conflicts and crises not soluble within the sphere of civil society led to a pattern of state interventionism ('neomercantilism'). However, emergent restrictions upon the autonomy of private actors did not *per se* undermine the private sphere as the essential precondition of the bourgeois public sphere. This erosion was only achieved when private corporate bodies appropriated dimensions of public authority in a process Habermas characterises as the 'refeudalisation' of society (ibid.: chs 5 and 6). This dialectic of a progressive 'socialisation' of the state simultaneously with an increasing 'stateification' of society is argued to have systematically eroded the separation of state and society, thereby destroying the basis of the bourgeois public sphere. The model of the bourgeois public sphere required the separation of the public and private realms in such a way that the public sphere, constituted by private people gathered together as a public and articulating the needs of society with the state, was itself considered part of the private realm. The intermeshing of state and society removed the social – and legal – basis of this public sphere. In its place, there developed an intermediate sphere involving state-absorbed social sectors and societally absorbed state sectors. This sphere was crucially distinguishable from the preceding bourgeois public sphere in that it lacked any element of rational-critical political debate on the part of private people.

The process of the politically relevant exercise and equilibration of power now takes place directly between the private bureaucracies, special-interest associations, parties, and public administration. *The public as such is included only sporadically in this circuit of power, and even then*

> *it is brought in only to contribute its acclamation.* (ibid.: 176, emphasis mine)

The effective subversion of the bourgeois public sphere was graphically represented in the transmutation of the concept – and content – of publicity. Originally, publicity referred to the *subject*-generated constitution (through rational-critical debate) of demands upon the state. With the erosion of the public sphere, publicity (and public opinion, public relations and so forth) came – and continues – to refer above all to an *object*-derived apparatus of manipulation and legitimation. Public opinion does not determine: it is determined and the resultant artefact has become a central element in the legitimation process. 'Critical publicity is supplanted by manipulative publicity' (ibid.: 178).

In Habermas' assessment, therefore, the interpenetration of state and society and the emergence of an intermediate sphere of semi-private, semipublic relationships created two tendential possibilities in those social (welfare) states that succeeded the liberal constitutional states in advanced capitalist democracies. On the one hand, the possibility of a political public sphere as the site of rational debate and general policy determination is both excluded and precluded by a process in which a range of dominant societal organisations (economic, cultural, religious) strive for political compromises with the state and with one another and do so as much as possible to the exclusion of the public.[5] An essential part of this process of 'incorporative exclusion' is the securing of plebiscitary agreement by means of manipulated publicity. On the other hand, Habermas sees this anti-democratic tendency as opposed by another in which the constitutional rights of all citizens are redefined by states committed to social rights in such a way as to facilitate genuine participation in the social and political order.[6] In these circumstances, the mandate of a critical publicity, under the bourgeois sphere required only in relation to the state, is potentially extended to all organisations acting in a state-related fashion.

> In the measure that this is realised, a no longer intact public of private people dealing with each other individually would be replaced by a public of organised private people. Only such a public could under today's conditions, participate effectively in a process of public communication via the channels of the public spheres internal to parties and special interest associations and on the basis of an affirmation of publicity as regards the negotiations of organisations with the state and one another. (ibid.: 232)

At this point, Habermas' position is that with the development of modernity, possibilities of power are increasingly dependent upon contexts of power over. Social-welfare states are the setting for a conflict between opposing modes of publicity: one is a rational-critical process of public communication; the other an anti-critical process of public manipulation. To the extent that the former prevails, Habermas proposes, we can speak of the democratisation of an industrial society constituted as a social-welfare state, in the form of 'the rationalisation of the exercise of social and political authority'.

The Public Sphere: A Model for Politics in Late Modernity?

We should be quite clear that the account advanced by Habermas is primarily not meant to be comprehensive but systematic.[7] It provides a framework within which Habermas sets out his *first* version of a political theory of late capitalism, a version organised around a distinctive conception of the institutional requirements of political freedom and grounded in an immanent critique of the norms embodying such freedom. The problem *Structural Transformation* seeks to address is the absence in late capitalist societies of meaningful political freedom. The solution it proposes is to renormatise and thereby democratise the state through the subjection of political and economic goals to rational and ethical reflection. 'According to Habermas, the clarification of what is practically necessary and objectively possible, of how to interpret norms and values, interest and needs in relation to technological possibilities, can be achieved only within institutionally secured public spaces that allow for the articulation of all needs, interests and values' (Cohen 1979).

The fundamental question Habermas seeks to address in *The Structural Transformation* is a critical one for democratic theory. Under what social conditions can a rational-critical debate about public issues be conducted by private persons willing to let arguments and not statuses determine outcomes? As Calhoun expresses it, *The Structural Transformation* 'aims to reach beyond the flawed realities of ... history to recover something of continuing normative importance ... an institutional location for practical reason in public affairs and for the accompanying valid ... claims of formal democracy' (Calhoun 1992: 1).

As Cohen argues, Habermas' concern with freedom as political democracy represented a major shift from his Frankfurt School predecessors (1979: 84). Their concern had been with freedom as happiness, a happiness conceived of primarily in terms of a reconciliation with nature and the re-establishment of communication between internal and external nature.[8] This perspective involved a completely negative assessment of objective institutions as invariably reified structures of domination. This proposition Habermas rejects in favour of a concern with the question as to what institutional arrangements facilitate intersubjectivity and interaction as the essential elements of discursive will-formation. Not for him the belief in or the search for a, indeed the, liberating revolutionary agent. In its place, Habermas focuses upon the necessity for a formal democracy based upon universalistic principles and legal guarantees.

The Structural Transformation therefore sets out an argument regarding the circumstances under which a normative concept of democracy had been developed, institutionalised and eroded and seeks to establish such a concept as a point of reference to critique contemporary political conditions. In advancing this argument, Habermas of course rejected key elements in the research tradition within which he was working. In particular, he rejected the Marxist view that political arrangements under capitalism were solely reducible to the clash of class interests.[9] The essential basis of this anti-reductionism lies in Habermas' location of the separation of state and civil society in the context of absolutism and not liberal capitalism. Thus, for him the duality of the state and civil society predates the distinction betwen state and economy. It is the former which provides the essential element in the necessary understanding of both the bourgeois public sphere and future alternatives. 'For it means that the presence of an independent private sphere does not hinge on an unregulated capitalist economy, *and a future repoliticisation of the economy need not entail the abolition of the private sphere and liberties guaranteed thereby*' (Cohen 1979: 76, emphasis mine).[10]

It is Habermas' contention that historically the dichotomy state/ civil society was not equivalent to the dichotomy state/liberal capitalist economy.[11] The term 'public' acquired its crucial meaning in relation to an emergent state administrative apparatus, distinguishable from monarchical power and a 'private sphere' comprised of those not holding power or office. Within this context, politics became not a matter of morality, not a normative terrain, but a matter of *technique*. Whatever its real limitations of class and gender, the normatively grounded, critical bourgeois sphere as it developed in the interstices of the public and new social spheres did – and for Habermas still can – provide a model of the form of democratic political possibilities.

The emancipating possibilities represented by the bourgeois public sphere were, however, dependent upon a particular institutional articulation. According to Habermas, a distinctive complex of institutional structures permitted the development of autonomy, privacy and individuality – within the context of the bourgeois family – and the transmission of these values, supplemented by reason and participation into the universal ideal of public freedom. *Contra* Marx and Hegel, Habermas argues that it was not the sphere of circulation *alone* which allowed the emergence of norms and conceptions of personhood and reciprocity, but also the communicative process of interaction of a politically functioning public of private persons. Only in connection with this politically functioning public – and an associated normative concept of public opinion – did universal principles attain a democratic dimension (Cohen 1979: 79).

Ideal or Idealisation?

The Structural Transformation is a clear example of what Habermas would later call 'a theoretically grounded history with practical intent'. The practical intent is clear: to set out the emancipatory case for a political democracy of informed and critical participation and will-formation. But with regard to that end, the argument suffers from two major defects. The first relates to Habermas' ambivalent conceptualisation of the bourgeois public sphere as derived, at least in part, from the bourgeois family. In order to advance this argument, Habermas must depict such a family as the site of intimacy and of discourse free from domination. Even making due allowance for the qualifications that Habermas makes to such a characterisation, the absence of any systematic incorporation of the hierarchical rootedness of the bourgeois family in relations of property and patriarchy was a major flaw in Habermas' argument.

Habermas' discussion of the bourgeois public sphere has been subjected to a powerful critique by Nancy Fraser (1992: 109–42). Drawing on the work of a number of scholars, Fraser noted that, despite the rhetoric of publicity and accessibility, the official public sphere was in fact constituted around a number of significant exclusions. In France, England and Germany, for example, the social construction of the public sphere was inextricably interwoven with processes of gender and class exclusion. There is, as Fraser notes, 'a remarkable irony here…. A discourse of publicity touting accessibility, rationality and the suppression of status hierarchies is itself deployed as a strategy of distinction' (ibid.: 115). Moreover, the idealised character of Habermas' account flows from his disregard of other non-liberal, non-bourgeois, competing public spheres.[12] Not only was there always a plurality of competing publics, but, equally importantly, the relations between bourgeois publics and other publics were always conflictual.

Fraser's critique introduces an element which has become a recurrent aspect in critical discussion of Habermas' work: this is the argument that the deficiencies of Habermas' account stem from the use he makes of a dichotomised understanding of public/private. As Calhoun also notes, 'when Habermas treats identities and interests as *settled* within the private world and brought fully formed into the public sphere, he impoverishes his theory' (1992: 35). We should be clear that Habermas' theoretical scheme requires him to locate the constitution of a general interest in advance of public life.[13] The limitation of his account involves not only the neglect of the unexamined exclusions of both private and public, but also a failure to thematise the reality and therefore the problem of difference, a problem which, as we shall see, was to become central to discussions of political empowerment in late modernity.[14]

The second defect of *The Structural Transformation* concerns the argument advanced regarding the dissolution of the public sphere. This argument can be summarised as follows: with the interpenetration of state and economy, the norms concerning the sovereignty of democratic will-formation embodied in the constitutions of the formal democracies become mere ideological formulas. This line of argument produces the 'central contradiction in Habermas' writings, one which is exacerbated rather than resolved in his later work' (Cohen 1979: 82). This contradiction arises from the juxtaposition of the proposition that the principles of the bourgeois public sphere still significantly inform politics under late capitalism with an argument concerning the erosion of the institutional loci upon which those principles were based. For Habermas, the radical discontinuity involved in late capitalism is manifest above all in the fact that democratic norms are increasingly irrelevant to the rationalised, reified mediatically determined institutions of the welfare state. This stance follows from Habermas' adoption of a systems and mediatic perspective towards societal integration and indicates the critical political consequences of his choice of functional adaptation as against social struggle for his central analytic focus. (See the discussion in Chapter 2 above.)

In spite of its emancipatory intent, *The Structural Transformation* offers neither an immanent utopia of political freedom nor a dynamic analysis of its possible development. Its implicit endorsement of the one-dimensionality thesis was reinforced by a series of arguments that Habermas subsequently deployed regarding the political impact of technocratic ideologies (Habermas 1971: chs 4–6). Such ideologies were argued to facilitate an anti-democratic, administered politics in two ways: first, technology offers a specialist or expert model of political decision-making which excludes a democratic model of the discursive discussion of ends; secondly, by rejecting alternative, politically derived legitimations and repressing ethics as a life category, such ideologies secure adaptive behaviour for administrative domination (ibid.: 81–122).

In such a situation, Habermas argued, it was important to distinguish between three possible models of political determination. Under the first, *the decisionistic model*, most fully explicated by Weber, politicians make use of technical knowledge, but decisions are basically made between competing value orders and convictions, inaccessible to rational discussion. In the post-Second World War period, however, the rationalisation of choice as such suggested an objective necessity constraining leadership decisions. These developments underpin the second, *technocratic*, model, in which politicians become in effect agents of a scientific intelligentsia. However, this technocratic model is vitiated by two major defects: first, it assumes the immanent necessity of technical progress, which illusion arises from the passively adaptive way in which social interests respond to technical possibilities. Secondly, the model presupposes a continuum of rationality in the treatment of *both* technical *and* practical problems.[15]

The defects of both these models – the rationality deficit of decisionism and the limited rationality of technocracy – could be overcome in Habermas' judgement, by a *pragmatistic* model, in which the strict separation between the function of the expert and the politician is replaced by a critical interaction. 'This interaction not only strips the ideologically supported exercise of power of an unreliable basis of legitimation but makes it accessible *as a whole* to scientifically informed discussion, thereby substantially changing it' (ibid.: 66–7).

How does each of these models correspond to the structure of modern mass democracy? The decisionist model relegates the public to an exclusively legitimising role.

> Decisions themselves … must remain basically beyond public discussion. The scientisation of politics then automatically accords with the theory developed by Weber, extended by Schumpeter, and now unquestioned by

modern political sociology, a theory that in the last analysis reduces the process of democratic decision-making to a regulated acclamation procedure for elites alternately appointed to exercise power. In this way power, untouched in its irrational substance, can be legitimated but not rationalised.

A similar diminution of democratic processes is implied by the technocratic model, in which 'a politically functioning public could at best legitimate the administrative personnel and judge the professional qualifications of salaried officials' (ibid.: 67–8).

By contrast, the pragmatistic model requires that the implementation of technical and strategic programmes depends upon mediation by the public as a political institution. Communication between experts and the agencies of political decision 'is based on a historically determined preunderstanding, governed by social norms, of what is practically necessary in a concrete situation. This preunderstanding is a consciousness that can only be enlightened hermeneutically, through articulation in the discourse of citizens in a community' (ibid.: 69).

The consequence of the turn toward hermeneutics involved in this discussion of the scientisation of politics and similar explorations was to produce two alternative exploratory strategies in relation to the politics of the public sphere (Crook 1991: 110). The first locates the public sphere within a topology of social spaces. The second builds upon the hermeneutic theme and identifies the politics of the public sphere with the communicative rationality of uncoerced discussion.

As Stephen Crook has pointed out, Habermas' paper on the scientisation of politics sits on the threshold of a shift of emphasis from the first of these possibilities to the second (ibid.: 111). In that paper, the fundamental problems of power over (domination) of modernity are identified not, as with Adorno and Horkheimer, as arising from the dialectic of enlightenment producing the pervasive domination of functionalised reason, but as the imbalance between such technical rationalisation and possibilities for communicative rationality expressed in discursive will-formation. An autonomous politics in late modernity is here assigned for the first time the role of critical mediator between technology (including social technology) and those 'social interests that arise spontaneously from the compulsion to reproduce social life'. In its absence, there is an inevitable degeneration of the public sphere. Habermas' subsequent concern with typologies of discourse greatly diminished the apparent concern with public sphere issues. But, as Crook also suggests, it is reasonable to see an underlying connection in that the resultant conception of critical theory as a 'reconstructive' *social science* enabled Habermas to move away from conceiving of issues of domination and emancipation as matters of self-reflection.[16]

The Structural Transformation revealed two problems as central to or definitive of Habermas' political theory: the absence in a modernised world of a structure of operative norms in relation to which there could be an immanent critique and the second absence of a dynamic in advanced capitalism leading to emancipatory developments. Habermas' elaboration of the implications of technocratic ideologies reinforced the first of these problems, leading to an attempt to ground at least the possibility of practical reason through the arguments that the politically corrosive effects of purposive rationalisation could be limited by limiting its scope and developing the communicative rationalisation which Habermas argued was the hidden face of modernity. The implications of this latter proposition were profoundly political in that they would involve the removal of restrictions on public discussion of both the efficacy and the ethical quality of action-orienting norms, whether such restrictions were advanced by technocrats, bureaucrats or whomsoever. The major limitation of this strategy was that Habermas' characterisation of late capitalism appeared to leave no possible breaks in relation to which the emancipatory potential of communicative rationalisation might meaningfully emerge.[17]

This deficiency Habermas sought to address in the text *Legitimation Crisis* (1976). In what might appear in the light of the subsequent trajectory of his work as somewhat ironic, the attempt involved (at the methodological level) a rejection of the functionalism of the Frankfurt School with its emphasis on rationalisation as an all-encompassing model. Rejecting what he considered an overschematic and pessimistic view on the functional connection between economy and culture/personality, Habermas introduced a more differentiated sociological model. The key distinction here was that between 'social' and 'system' integration, the former referring to the coordination of social action through the functional interconnection of action consequences, and the latter to the coordination of action through the harmonising of action orientations. In modern societies the analytic scope of system integration derives from institutional differentiation into polity, economy and family. In two domains particularly – the capitalist economy and state administration – the coordination of social action is functionalised. According to Habermas, both manifest a series of social actions which influence one another through unintended consequences. In addition, both implicate distinctive media of power: the capitalist economy, monetarised exchange in the market, the modern state, money and formal juridical power.

Such a system perspective must, Habermas argued, be complemented by that of social integration. In this instance, individuals orient their actions to one another because they cognitively understand the social rules of action. Unlike system integration, social integration cannot take place unless action consequences are compatible with the intentions of social actors and, consequently, can only be analysed from the internal perspective of those involved.

The distinction system/social integration was paralleled by a twofold conception of crisis. The first conception referred to the dysfunctionalities of the economy, world market and administrative processes when viewed as self-regulating systems. However, only those dysfunctionalities which derive from social integration and which generate crises of identity in individuals and collectives are crises in the second, significant conception. 'Systems are not presented as subjects; but ... *only* subjects can be involved in crises .... only when members of a society experience structural alterations as critical for continued existence and feel their social identity threatened can we speak of crises. Disturbances of system integration endanger continued existence only to the extent that *social integration* is at stake, that is, when the consensual foundations of normative structures are so much impaired that the society becomes anomic' (ibid.: 3).[18]

Habermas' elaboration of the nature of legitimation crises therefore had a double basis. First of all, it rested on a commitment to the position that private individual needs and desires are only meaningful if interpreted socioculturally. 'There is no individuation without sociation'. Secondly, Habermas is quite clear about the necessity of avoiding a one-sided emphasis on lived identity crises and of grasping the connection between system and social integration (Benhabib 1986: 232–3). On this basis, Habermas specified the sources and the potential consequences of a legitimation crisis as follows: given its ultimate fiscal dependency upon the economy, the capitalist state must intervene to facilitate and maintain the private appropriation of capital. However, the consequences of state-interventionist and regulatory policies may not result in the reproduction of mass loyalty to the capitalist system. In fact, state intervention may demystify the model of market exchange and self-regulation, producing demands for legitimation and political participation.

Habermas' argument in *Legitimation Crisis* hinged on three premises: first, that the dynamics of late capitalist societies can be analysed by means of a four-tiered crisis theory, which distinguishes economic, administrative, legitimation and motivation crises; secondly, the increased role of the state, necessitated by the dysfunctionalities of the economic system, can generate unintended consequences (Benhabib 1986: 233 seq.). Potentially ever new areas of social relations become politicised, requiring the identification of new areas of domination but thereby entering the political agenda as contestable claims generating new struggles of redistribution and/or recognition. This process leads in turn to a challenging of tradition. Both such consequences may result in a legitimation crisis, an increased demand for public justification of state action, leading to struggles between manipulative publicity – such as that of scientific expertise or national security – and the publicity of information and debate. Thirdly, therefore, Habermas argued that the rendering visible of the mode of production of meaning involved in both the occurrence and the resolution of a legitimation crisis destroys the possibility of the manipulative production of meaning.

> The public realm, set up for effective legitimation, has above all the function of directing attention to topical areas – that is, of pushing *other* themes, problems and arguments below the threshold of attention and, thereby, withholding them from opinion-formation. The political system takes over tasks of ideology planning (Luhmann). In doing so, manoeuvring room is…narrowly limited, for the cultural system is peculiarly resistant to administrative control. *There is no administrative production of meaning.* (1976: 70)

The possibility of a legitimation crisis rests therefore in the dynamics of state interventionism. In seeking to justify its actions, the state may demystify the power of capital. This possibility is increased to the extent that the state fails to generate values and meaning patterns. However, the culture of late capitalism does contain a barrier against legitimation crises in the form of various privatisms, civic, religious and familial; such privatisms block the development of participatory demands by compensating for dissatisfaction. In this way, Habermas seeks to make legitimation crises integrally dependent upon motivational crises.

The key assumptions which provide the background to *Legitimation Crisis* appear in the essay 'Technology and Science as "Ideology"' (1971: ch. 6). There the market alone provides the necessary legitimation for liberal capitalism. This argument is reinforced by an elaboration of the Weberian theory of rationalisation as the erosion of all legitimising tradition. In this process, traditional world views are reshaped into subjective belief systems. Capitalism solves the resultant problem by providing its own legitimations from the market system.

However, in *Legitimation Crisis* Habermas is quite explicit that the value form as an integrating mechanism is limited to the bourgeois. 'The loyalty and subordination of the new urban proletariat, recruited mainly from the ranks of the peasants, are certainly maintained more through a mixture of traditionalistic ties, fatalistic willingness to follow, lack of perspective, and naked repression than through the convincing force of bourgeois ideologies' (1976: 22; cf. Abercrombie et al. 1980).

From an analytic standpoint, the argument of *Legitimation Crisis* is important in two critical aspects. The first is its incompatibility with the position advanced in *The Structural Transformation*. There Habermas had proposed that the liberal state drew some of its legitimations from the institutions of the public sphere. While claims of justice might, formally at least, be advanced in terms of market ideology, claims regarding political freedom were based in the principles of the (bourgeois) public sphere (Cohen 1979: 87). The second, more significant point is that, by taking the Marxist model of liberal capitalism as his point of departure (a model which effectively collapses social integration into system integration), Habermas is unable to make effective use of his own conception of the private sphere and the much wider range of integrating and legitimising structures it implicates. As Cohen noted, 'the very thesis of the crisis potential of late capitalism rests on the assumption that traditions, world views and bourgeois ideologies have all been deactivated. The corresponding attempt to account for social identity in systemic terms prevents the important distinction between system integration and social integration from fully developing' (ibid.).

For Habermas, a political crisis necessarily had a dual dimension: a rationality deficit and a deficit of legitimation. The assumption of the normative underpinning of social action and of the grounding of administrative systems on normative structures is essential to the theory of legitimation crisis. *Habermas is quite explicit that the administrative generation of meaning is impossible.* The important consequence of any attempt to administratively manipulate cultural affairs is to focus public attention upon norms previously fixed by tradition. In an apparent paradox, the administrative use of strategic power (or in the present argument, domination) threatens the very genesis of power.

In the identification of the developmental trajectory of Habermas' political theory, *Legitimation Crisis* (*LC*) should be understood as an attempt to transcend the pessimistic statics of *The Structural Transformation*. *LC*'s central argument tied the occurrence of political crises to breakdowns in the ability of formally democratic institutions to sufficiently accomplish four requirements: to mobilise mass support in the absence of participation; to conceal the contradiction between administratively socialised production and private appropriation; to ensure the underlying motivations for civic and familial privatisms and to justify structural depoliticisation. The key factor in this theory was clearly that of state interventionism. The crucial distinction between the arguments of *The Structural Transformation* and those of *Legitimation Crisis* is the emphasis upon the centrality of such interventionism. State interventionism in Habermas' second political model involves a double threat: it erodes the separation of administration and citizen motivation (definitive of the liberal capitalist model) and it erodes those traditions and ideologies essential to the legitimation of depoliticisation through the system-driven elimination of those contexts which provide traditional supports.

The significance of interventionism rests upon the proposed impossibility of the administrative generation of meaning. The elements of universalism in the liberal capitalist state were provided by market ideology and a non-interventionist state. However, according to Habermas, there were in addition continuing memories of a generalised, universal morality. The conflict between such memories and the structures of late capitalism is viewed as resolvable in one of two ways: either there could be a movement from bourgeois formal law to a new political morality rooted in a communicative ethic or the socialisation process could be separated from the cultural system altogether. In the latter circumstance normative structures would no longer be internalised by individuals through socialisation. Social identity would become a systemic function, severed from norms and truth claims.[19]

Habermas did not rule out this possibility. But he did seek to provide an alternative in the form of an argument regarding the independent *evolutionary* logic of moral development. However, the inevitable abstractness of the resultant position vitiated any contribution Habermas wished to offer to practical emancipation. Moreover, this 'evolutionary escape' led Habermas too easily to disregard the vitality of tradition as a source of legitimation and equally, in the case of democratic tradition, of emancipation (Cohen 1979: 93). Such emancipation had provided the central focus of the rise and fall depiction of the public sphere in *The Structural Transformation*. The final stance of this account might be described as 'hope without possibilities', the latter being foreclosed by the one-dimensionality of rationalisation. *Legitimation Crisis* sought to rectify this position by developing a crisis theory of late capitalism. But, as Cohen noted, by asserting that rationalisation ... abolished those traditions that could provide legitimation and by assuming state interventionism has really undermined the emancipatory movements of the family, civil society and the public, Habermas ... blocked the analytical path to the very areas that might provide an answer to these questions, namely: the institutions of democratic traditions or national and political cultures of particular societies. The attempt to build a dynamic theory of late capitalism [is] bought at the price of a theory that might locate action-orienting, emancipatory norms in objective institutions. (ibid.: 94)

In other words, in a reversal of *The Structural Transformation*, *Legitimation Crisis* offers us 'possibilities without hope'. Possible scenarios, that is, for the emergence of crises in late capitalism but an absence of a contextualised analysis of emancipatory norms.

The Theory of Communicative Action: Pessimism or Potential?

Most of the critical reception of Habermas' massive two-volume work, *The Theory of Communicative Action*, viewed it as a contribution to the clarification of central theoretical issues in social theory (1984; 1989b – henceforth *TCA*). It is equally instructive, however, to see the work as being concerned with the clarification of analytical tools necessary to address a particular task: the understanding of the impact of the imperatives of material reproduction in everyday life in the era of modernity and the consequent political configuration characterising late modernity. Seen in this way, the thesis of *TCA* is as follows: the cognitive rationalisation of the lifeworld made societal rationalisation (the over-exclusive focus of Weberian concerns) possible. Paradoxically, the consequences of societal rationalisation undermine that rationality of the lifeworld which was the essential prerequisite of its emergence. There is an emancipatory potential in a rationalised lifeworld but this is constantly in danger of being eroded and overwhelmed by the dynamics of societal rationalisation in the form of capitalist development.

Within the extensive theoretical elaborations and excursi, much of the substantive argument of *TCA* is continuous with that of *Legitimation Crisis*. The thesis that late advanced capitalism requires an integration of economic and administrative systems is retained, as is the proposition regarding the repoliticisation of relations of production. A departure from the earlier work does occur, however, in that the significance attached to state interventionism in the generation of legitimation crises is now seen as resting primarily in its *form* rather than in its *content*. The significance of the elaboration of administrative mechanisms of the state is viewed in *TCA* as lying in its being a manifestation of system integration. Such system integration is stipulated as involving 'the non-normative regulation of individual decisions that extends beyond the actors' consciousness'. It requires 'mechanisms that stabilise the nonintended interconnections of actors by way of functionally intermeshing *action consequences*' (*TCA* 1989b: 117).

The integration of patterns of social action in such systemic terms is contrasted with a *social* integration of action 'produced ... by a normatively secured or communicatively achieved consensus' and involving 'mechanisms of action coordination which bring the action orientations of participants into accord with one another' (ibid.). As in *Legitimation Crisis*, social integration is conceived of in relation to the internal perspective of participant subjects. From such a perspective, society can be conceived of as the lifeworld of a social group. The distinctive quality of social relationships is that they are culturally and symbolically constituted; that is, they are *meaningful* relationships. In the terminology of *TCA*, the symbolic reproduction of the social is understood as the reproduction of the lifeworld. Advancing a composite, differentiated model of the lifeworld, Habermas argues that such a methodological device allows us to grasp the empirical fact of structural differentiation as the central characteristic of a rationalised lifeworld under the impact of modernity.

> In the relation of culture to society, structural differentiation is to be found in the gradual uncoupling of the institutional system from worldviews; in the relation of personality to society, it is evinced in the extension of the scope of contingency for establishing interpersonal relationships; and in the relation of culture to personality, it is manifested in the fact that the renewal of traditions depends more and more on individuals' readiness to criticise and their ability to innovate. (1989b: 146)

For Habermas, structural differentiation has created the conceptual space for and the potential reality of communicative action, where the latter is seen as a distinctive mode of sociation in which actors pursue a cooperative coordination of their actions through the mechanism of linguistic communication. The medium of communicative action is the correlate of the rationalised lifeworld.

The key question arising from such a perspective is the degree to which it is primarily intended as descriptive or prescriptive. To the extent that it is understood as the former, that is, a consideration of the pathologies that arise from the clash of two different principles of sociation, it fails to engage with major forms of domination in modern societies, such as patriarchy or racism, the dynamics of which cannot be understood in such terms. To the extent that it continues to be the case in late modernity that dominant forms of normativity reproduce rather than critique structures and processes of domination, Habermas' proposition regarding a rationalised lifeworld suffused by communicatively based argumentation must be seen as naive or downright misleading. In addition, if we understand Habermas to be using a 'weak' version of the lifeworld, analogous to a symbolic network in which validity claims are increasingly consciously accessible to actors, then the autonomy of such lifeworlds must be steadily eroded from within as social reproduction becomes increasingly rationally steered (White 1990: 101–3).[20]

The problem of reification as domination, central to the Marx–Weber conceptional amalgam of the Frankfurt School, is redefined therefore in *TCA* as the problem of system-generated pathologies of advanced modernity. The critical problem of power and politics in late modernity concerns the chronic disintegrative effects arising from the tendency for functional coordination in the form of money and (state) power to erode the boundary between system and lifeworld and overwhelm the integrity of lifeworlds whose immanent characteristic is substantial integration in terms of communicative rationalisation. In such an account, through the process of that societal rationalisation which so centrally preoccupied Max Weber, strategic action, liberated from traditional constraints, was institutionalised into systems of purposive-rational action, coordinated through the media of money and power. Empirically, such systems have been capitalist economies and state administrative systems. The objective and functional scale of such systems is such that they constantly threaten to overwhelm the boundaries between system and lifeworld and undermine the lifeworld as a site of meaning and freedom.

This is the general argument that provides the context for the discussion of political relations and possibilities advanced in *TCA*. As we have seen, Habermas' earlier discussions of such relations and possibilities in *Legitimation Crisis* had located the analytic significance of the legitimation system within the context of political interventionism in the economy, the erosion of traditionalism by capitalist development and the universalisation of normative-formal democracy. In such circumstances, the reproduction of capitalist democracies requires a barrier between a functionally necessary autonomous administration on the one hand and processes of legitimation on the other. (A substantive democracy of genuine political participation would highlight the contradictions betwen socialised production and private appropriation) (Habermas 1976: 36). The legitimation system therefore refers to processes which mobilise diffuse mass loyalty but avoid substantive direction. In this way, the public realm in capitalist societies is structurally depoliticised; that is, 'the citizenry, in the midst of an objectively political society, enjoy the status of passive citizens with only the right to withhold acclamation' (ibid.: 37). Legitimation is then reduced to two requirements: compensatory mechanisms for depoliticisation in the form of privatisms (notably, various modes of consumerism such as goods, media eroticised social relations) and social welfarism and ideological justification in one of two major forms, democratic elite theories or technocratic systems theories.

Clearly, empowerment in the form of structural *repoliticisation* would require projects and spaces of substantive or radical democracy in which active citizens would participate in processes of government, in particular self-government. The public sphere, or preferably, given the reality with which Habermas had failed to engage in *The Structural Transformation*, public spheres, would be at whatever spatial level – urban, regional, national, international and transnational – sites of struggle in relation to dominant normativity (cf. Linklater 1998).

The general diagnosis of the problem of politics in late modernity set out in *Legitimation Crisis* is substantially repeated in *TCA*. Once again, the central tasks of the state – in advanced capitalist societies – are the administrative monitoring of the requirements and consequences of the economic system. Thus, 'government intervention has the *indirect* form of manipulating the boundary conditions for the decisions of private enterprise, and the *reactive* form of strategies for avoiding its side effects or compensating for them' (1989b: 344). However, whereas the legal framework of capitalist relations – embodied in contractual relations – suffices to bind lifeworld and system, such is not the case, in Habermas' view, with political relations. Material exchanges do not and will not provide an adequate basis for political stability: 'only democratic procedures of political will-formation can in principle generate legitimacy under conditions of a rationalised lifeworld with highly individuated members, with norms that have become abstract, positive, and in need of justification, and with traditions that have, as regards their claim to authority, been reflectively refracted and set communicatively aflow' (ibid.).

On this account, to the extent that it depends upon processes of legitimation, political domination in late modernity is effectively unsustainable. For Habermas, the crucial problem of legitimation now has to be located within what he identifies as an 'indissoluble tension' between capitalism and democracy as distinctive principles of societal integration. 'The normative meaning of democracy can be rendered ... by the formula that the fulfillment of the functional necessities of *systemically* integrated domains of action shall find its limits in the integrity of the lifeworld, that is to say, in the requirements of domains of action dependent on *social* integration. On the other hand ... the internal systemic logic of capitalism can be rendered ... by the formula that the functional necessities of systemically integrated domains of action shall be met, if need be, even at the case of *technicising* the lifeworld' (ibid.: 345).

In posing the problem in this way, Habermas articulates in quite stark terms the contrast between a normative coordination of action rooted in processes of communicative rationalisation and a functional coordination of action rooted in systemic media which lies at the heart of his political analysis. The difficulty clearly emerges that, to the extent that functional rationalisation in the form of mediatic domination succeeds in suppressing/eroding the autonomy of lifeworlds, to that extent the basis for a substantively transformative democratic politics is eliminated. However, this is only the case to the extent that one finds the distinction between system and lifeworld a coherent conceptualisation of the modern world, being as it is, a conception which dichotomises the world into a sphere of mediatic domination and a sphere of normative coordination.[21] The alternative would be to place inclusionary struggles, whether of recognition (the excluded Other) or of redistribution, at the centre of political analysis, thereby accepting that normativity is as relevant to the analysis of domination as it is to the analysis of empowerment (Trey 1998: ch. 3). Moreover, to the further extent that the system/lifeworld distinction is found to be unsatisfactory, the scope for such struggles is greatly widened, becoming potentially coextensive with the modern world itself.

Notes

1. See Holub, *Jürgen Habermas, Critic in the Public Sphere* (1991) for an account of the major debates in which Habermas has engaged and for an argument regarding the strategy underlying these various debates.
2. On the formative influence of Habermas' reaction to the barbarism and irrationalities of Nazism, see Bernstein 1991.
3. The Calhoun volume is the definitive exploration of the theoretical and practical implications of *The Structural Transformation*.

4. Sensitive though he is to the class stratification of the public sphere, Habermas now notoriously failed to recognise its critical gendering, a failure which has been perceived as a major limitation by even otherwise sympathetic and radically democratic feminist critics. See, for example, Meehan 1995.

5. Here Habermas significantly anticipates later discussions of corporatism, literature which contains competing theorisations of the relationship(s) involved in this new configuration of state-civil society. See Crook et al. 1992; Jessop 1978; Lembruch 1977; Lembruch and Schmitter 1982; Schmitter 1974; Schmitter and Lembruch 1979.

6. Cf. T.H. Marshall, 'Citizenship and Social Rights' 1963: 67–127. Whereas Marshall's emphasis is on membership, Habermas adopts the stance that the development and extension of citizenship does represent real possibilities for participation in processes of will-formation. As he puts it, private autonomy is secured by political autonomy. Subsequently, he was to view state centred citizenship, particularly 'social citizenship', as much if not more as a medium of domination and control as of empowerment and emancipation but his positive assessment of the possibilities for a meaningfully participatory citizenship as against a citizenship of passive status has been a continuing source of criticism of his overall assessment of the political process in capitalist democracies. This has been particularly so for those writing from a postmodernist, Foucauldian perspective who find Habermas' engagement with the problem of state 'normalisation' in the form of citizens as clients wholly inadequate. See Ashenden and Owen 1999.

7. However, see Habermas in Calhoun 1997, where he proposes that his historical account has been substantially confirmed by later research.

8. See, for example, the discussion between Habermas and Herbert Marcuse in *Telos*, 38, Winter 1978–79, 124–53.

9. Subsequently, Habermas was to be equally emphatic in his criticism of what he saw as the anachronistic nature of Arendt's Aristotelian conception which seeks to see politics as the pure interaction of autonomous individuals severed from all social interests. At the same time, he endorsed the Arendtian identification of a distinctive generative – as against purely strategic – dimension of political action. See, for example, 'Hannah Arendt: On the Concept of Political Power' in *Philosophical-Political Profiles*, 1983: 171–88.

10. There are clearly conflicting interpretations of Habermas' account of the sources of the public sphere which substantially mirror tensions in that account. Thus, it is central to Cohen's appropriation of Habermas' argument that the public sphere finds its institutional location between state and civil society. Calhoun, on the other hand, predominantly emphasises an alternative point of view in which the determinate context is that of an emerging capitalism. See, for example, pp. 15–16 of his Introduction (1992). This position is, however, in its strong version, clearly at odds with that which sees both civil society and public sphere as made possible by the development of the modern state. See, for example, Calhoun's Introduction, p. 7 and p. 9 and his quotation from Habermas: 'Civil society came into existence as the corollary of a depersonalised state authority.' Additional support for the second position is provided by Calhoun's approving citation of Charles Taylor's argument that a key role was played in the development of

the modern self by 'the affirmation of ordinary life', a recognition of society in the relationships and organisations created for sustaining life.

11. The elision between these two distinctions continues to play a critical role in political and social theory.

12. See, for example, Mary P. Ryan, 'Gender and Public Access: Women's Politics in Nineteenth-Century America' 1997: 259–88.

13. See the further discussion of the limitations of Habermas' conception of the public sphere as a 'power-free' zone below, pp. 175–76.

14. Fraser's (it should be said, sympathetic) account of Habermas' analysis elaborates her earlier critique of the deficiencies of Habermas' argument in *The Theory of Communicative Action*, particularly with regard to gender politics, which she also sees as consequent upon a parallel dichotomy, system/lifeworld. See Fraser 1989a: ch. 6. See below for an analysis of the political implications of *TCA*.

15. A critique of this model and its unexamined assumptions in 'industrial society' lies at the heart of Beck's argument about 'risk society' as the expression of 'reflexive modernisation'. See Beck 1992 and 1994.

16. See, for example, Habermas 1973: 25–40, for a discussion of the impossibility of subsuming problems of social and political organisation into general processes of self-reflection.

17. For a discussion of the way in which this interpretation of late capitalism follows from Habermas' exclusion of any intersubjective possibilities from the world of work, see Chapter 2 above. For a serious attempt to explore the political possibilities of collective action in the modality of communicative rationalisation, see J. Forester 1985.

18. For a systemic interrogation of Habermas' specification of the system integration/social integration distinction in *TCA*, see Mouzelis 1992. Also, the same author's *Back to Sociological Theory* 1991: Appendix I. See also Giddens 1985a.

19. On the unsustainability of Habermas' separation of domination and normativity in late modernity, see the discussion of Trey 1998 below.

20. White argues that both these criticisms involve significant misreadings of Habermas' position. However, he acknowledges that Habermas' formulation offers little analytic assistance in addressing forms of domination which cannot be seen as arising from societal rationalisation. He further recognises that Habermas fails to offer us an adequate account of the interrelationship between normative judgements about justice and evaluative judgements about the good life (White 1990: 101–3). See also Benhabib 1992 and Stewart 2000: 55–72.

21. On the critique of the system/lifeworld distinction, see notes 18 and 20 above.

6

Capitalism, States and Public Spheres II: Empowerment in the Public Sphere

Re-enter the Public Sphere

As specified in Habermas' discussion in *TCA*, the tension between capitalism and democracy in late modernity is focused above all in the political public sphere. There two quite distinct and ultimately opposed understandings of public opinion contend with one another. From an action-theoretic perspective (that is, a perspective of power generation), the public opinion which emerges from votes, parties and associations is 'regarded as the *first link* in the chain of political will-formation and as the *basis* of legitimation'. From a systemic perspective, public opinion is a construct, 'the *result* of engineering legitimation ... regarded as the last link in the chain of production of mass loyalty, with which the political system outfits itself in order to make itself independent from lifeworld restrictions' (Habermas 1989b: 346). It is a mistake to oppose these understandings to one another, identifying one as 'normative' (will of the people), and the other as empirical. In fact, Habermas argues, the formation of political will – the structuring of 'interests' – which takes place via competition between parties is a result of both – the pull of communication processes and the push of organisational performances. Within the perspective of the political system, the general public is massified, functionalised into providing legitimation (mass loyalty) in return for social-welfare programmes but also through the exclusion of themes and contributions from public discussion. *Electoral arrangements amount in effect to a substantial neutralisation of the possibilities for political participation opened up by the role of citizen.*

It is in the systemic incorporation and subordination of consequentially circumscribed political actors that Habermas identifies 'the colonisation of the lifeworld' in contemporary late modern societies. Here the systemic media of power and money displace communicative sociation and erode the possibilities for the development of politically autonomous actors adopting a performative as opposed to an objectivising attitude toward other actors. White has argued convincingly that, in advancing this position, Habermas is not maintaining that some processes of lifeworld reproduction are substantively irreducible to processes of money and power. Habermas' theory is ultimately articulated around a particular conception of the human subject, in relation to which emancipatory arguments are developed. In this way, the theory specifies the centrality of communicative action to the reproduction of social and political life.[1] In other words, Habermas' concern is not primarily technical but practical (Brand 1990; Ingram 1987; McCarthy 1984).

Although Habermas makes it quite clear that he sees the colonisation of the lifeworld as being manifested in the systematically coordinated spheres of *both* economy and polity (via the roles of consumer and client respectively), it is no doubt significant that he chose to illustrate such colonisation by means of a political example, namely, the consequences of *juridification*. According to Habermas' hypothesis, a colonisation of the lifeworld can only come about under the following conditions:

(a) the structural differentiation of the lifeworld;
(b) when exchanges between the lifeworld and mediatised systems are around differentiated roles (employee, consumer, client and voter);
(c) the existence of compensatory mechanisms;
(d) the financing of such mechanisms according to welfare state capitalism and the channelling of the results into the roles of consumer and client.

The transition from societal integration to system integration is then argued to take a legal form. Reification in late modernity emerges as 'the symptomatic consequence of a *specific kind* of juridification, where juridification refers to a general increase in formal laws observable in modern society' (1989b: 349). This process of juridification has reached its zenith in the epoch of the welfare state, where the latter refers not only to the social provision of basic needs, but also, and perhaps more importantly, to the judicial containment of social conflicts and political struggles.[2] Habermas sees this epoch as the last (to date) of four such epochal juridification processes (ibid.: 359 seq.): (1) that of the *bourgeois state* which provided the political order within which early modern society was transformed into a capitalist market society. Central here was a legal order which formally guaranteed the liberty and property of private persons, the formal equality of all the subjects before the law and thereby, the calculability of all legally normative action. Subsequently, there emerged (2) the *bourgeois constitutional state*, in which the key development was the constitutional regulation of the state in which process the *modern* state acquired a legitimacy in its own right: legitimation on the basis of a modernised lifeworld. The third epoch was that of (3) the *democratic constitutional state*: during this phase, constitutionalised state power was democratised in that citizens were provided with rights of political participation. The central aspect of this configuration was the juridification of the legitimation process institutionalised through the extension of suffrage and the freedom to organise political associations and parties. Such developments represented a systematic extension of the bourgeois constitutional state in that a modern lifeworld continues to assert itself against the imperatives of a structure of domination abstracting from all concrete life-relations. In addition, Habermas argues, these developments finally complete those processes whereby modern power must necessarily be understood in relation to a comprehensively rationalised and differentiated lifeworld and not only in relation to the bourgeoisie.

The welfare state which provides the occasion and focus for Habermas' epochal typology is argued by Habermas to continue 'this line of freedom-guaranteeing juridification. The democratic welfare state represents the institutionalisation of power-balancing juridifications within an area of action already constituted by law.' At the same time, however, Habermas recognises that welfare statism cannot be seen simply as a mechanism of empowerment. It also contains the potential for further and more effective domination. Central to Habermas' theoretical and, above all, practical concerns is the concern that the policies of the welfare state involve the *'ambivalence of guaranteeing freedom and taking it away.'* The significant aspect of welfare state juridification is that its negative aspects are not a side-effect but result from the form of juridification itself. 'It is now the very means of guaranteeing freedom that endangers the freedom of the beneficiaries' (ibid.: 361–2). This danger arises from the fact that the bureaucratic implementation and monetary redemption of welfare entitlements take the form of *individual* legal entitlements which necessitate restructuring interventions in the lifeworlds of those who are so entitled (cf. Wolin 1987).[3]

The bureaucratic implementation of social welfare policies requires a process of 'violent abstraction' from the individual and social circumstances of the lifeworld, when social mechanisms intended to remove subjects from social constellations of commodification may easily become mechanisms of dependency and control. Even where the possibilities of this are recognised in the form of a perception of the limits of monetary compensation for societal damage, the elaboration of social services as mechanisms of therapeutic assistance merely reproduces the contradictions of welfare-state intervention at a higher level. 'The form of the administratively prescribed treatment by an expert is for the most part in contradiction with the aim of the therapy, namely, that of promoting the client's independence and self-reliance' (ibid.: 363).[4]

Habermas shows himself sensitive to the possibility that what he terms 'the dilemmatic structure of this type of juridification' may lead to the argument that *any* mechanism of participatory rights may involve restriction upon the freedom of the potential beneficiaries of such mechanisms (ibid.: 364). Habermas' answer here is a firm negative, consistent with his general evolutionary, anti-Foucauldian stance; accordingly, he argues that we cannot meaningfully speak of taking away freedom from the form of participatory rights but only from the *bureaucratic* ways and means of their implementation. Nevertheless, Habermas does recognise the sociological dilemma involved in the processes he is concerned to stipulate: the interplay of freedom and constraint, the necessity of a specification of rights within a necessary social context. Legal norms, he argues, must be classified according to whether they can be legitimised only through procedure or are amenable to *substantive* justification. He elaborates this possibility in relation to his general argument about the uncoupling of system and lifeworld. Law used as a steering medium within systemic integration is relieved of the problem of justification; by contrast, legal institutions belong to the societal components of the lifeworld and cannot be legitimised through a positivistic reference to procedure. What is clearly suggested by such a stance is a recognition of a reality that all legal norms are in principle fundamentally contestable. Consequently, their implementation and resistance to their implementation in modern societies cannot be politically understood in functional systemic terms but must always have the potential for struggles with respect to recognition. This is clearly illustrated in relation to the issue of civil disobedience which has become central to the politics of social movements in late modern societies.

Discussing its significance as a mode of political practice in late modern societies, Frankenberg argues that

Civil disobedience as symbolic practice and normatively limited and justified violation of rules casts doubt onto a system-theoretic understanding that conceives politics to be the production of binding decisions, as ordered transfer of power or as the production of mass loyalty. Those who practice civil disobedience cannot come to terms with the distinction between system and lifeworld. . . . *In action-theoretic terms, civil disobedience actualises the idea of democratically constituted political institutions and procedures as a plurality of public forums or 'transactional milieus' in which numerous agreements concerning collective goods such as peace, ecological balance, or biological security are 'constantly made, renewed, tested, revoked and revised.'* (Frankenberg 1992: 26, emphasis mine)[5]

In the terms of the present argument, civil disobedience is here characterised as representing the contestation of dominant norms as a key aspect of the functional coordination of late modern societies by social movements embodying the generation of power and the constitution of immanent political communities by means of deliberative democracy.

Thus, while Habermas recognises the tension within the process of juridification between domination and emancipation, his commitment to a systems theoretic perspective precludes his engaging with the consequent possibilities for political struggle. He notes that under the bourgeois state, civil law and bureaucratic domination exercised by legal means at least meant emancipation from pre-modern relations of power and dependence (Habermas 1989b: 366). The significance of the subsequent phases of juridification rested primarily in the fact that they involved the institutionalised restraint of the political and economic dynamics released by the legal institutionalisation of money and power. For Habermas, the democratic welfare state represents the zenith of this process of emancipatory restraint.

Habermas does recognise that the fact that welfare-state interventionism takes the form of law used as a regulative medium represents a major problem with respect to freedom in late modern societies. In the epoch of the democratic welfare state, the issue of political autonomy cannot be approached simply from the point of view of the lifeworld. Those aspects of juridification that are central to the democratic welfare state, such as social welfare law, do not, unlike the laws governing collective bargaining, involve intervention in areas already formally organised. Thus, the reification effect exhibited in the case of public welfare policy arises from the fact that the legal institutions guaranteeing social compensation become effective only through the use of social welfare law as a medium *for instituting new patterns of social relations* (ibid.: 367). The effectiveness of law in this context depends upon its capacity to reconstitute situations embedded in informal lifeworld contexts.

In this way, one of the major political concerns of *TCA* emerges as a focus upon the crisis of modernity represented in the conception of reification as juridification. The combination of juridification and a culture of expertise operates to produce a 'domain of dependency' (White 1990: 113). Central to this domain is the definition and normatisation of such lifeworld areas as family relations, education and mental health. Here, there is substantial overlap between Habermas' position and the social constructionism of postmodernist positions in general and of the Foucauldians in particular.[6]

The social consequences of the rise of expert cultures are also central to the other major dimension of Habermas' assessment of domination under the contemporary conditions of modernity. The context of this dimension is provided by Habermas' argument concerning the demise of ideology under the social conditions of an advanced modernity. A rationalised and differentiated lifeworld is argued to leave no space for ideological activity, whether in the form of control or critique. 'The imperatives of autonomous subsystems ... have to exert their influence on socially integrated domains of action from the outside, and *in a discernible fashion*' (Habermas 1989b: 354).

If a rationalised lifeworld has lost its structural possibilities for ideology formation, why has the competition between social and system integration not become more central to the political agenda? Because, says Habermas, late capitalist societies manifest a functional equivalent to ideology formation: the fragmentation of everyday consciousness (ibid.: 355). Such fragmentation involves the prevention of holistic interpretations of social process which could lead to movements of social change. In this process, a key role is played by the splitting off of expert cultures, leading to a general cultural impoverishment: 'the diffused perspectives of the local culture cannot be sufficiently co-ordinated to permit the play of the metropolis and the world market to be grasped from the periphery' (ibid.).

Although, as a number of commentators have noted, Habermas' discussion of 'fragmented consciousness' and expert cultures is frustratingly brief, it is possible and important to identify in his arguments here a distinct change of emphasis from the position set out in *Legitimation Crisis*. There Habermas identified as a major source of legitimation deficit and potential instability in late modern societies the disintegration of classical bourgeois ideology, combined with the fact that new ideology cannot be administratively generated.[7] The increasing visibility of the contrast between universal democratic values and patterns of institutionalised inequality was viewed consequently as a potent source of political and social change, although no arguments were advanced regarding forms of collective action. In contrast, the stance adopted in *TCA* is much more pessimistic: the emergence of that critical consciousness which had been viewed by Habermas as a key component of crises and change is now seen as being blocked by the diffusion of expert cultures, with the consequent fragmentation of everyday thought.

In the systems-based analysis of *Legitimation Crisis*, states in advanced capitalist societies were depicted as caught between the Scylla and Charybdis of economic imperatives on the one hand and the need to secure normative acceptance in terms of universalistic criteria on the other. In the argument of *TCA*, a combination of reification and fragmentation processes is argued to have greatly diminished the need for such normative agreement. This vacuum is now increasingly filled by 'instrumental attitudes, indifference and cynicism' (see 'Reply to my Critics' in Thompson and Held 1982). Again, of course, one has to say that analytically this stance derives in significant part from Habermas' commitment to a systems perspective and his subsidiary proposition that only tradition (decliningly) or communicative rationalisation offers a source of normativity. An alternative reality may be proposed: that dominant norms (in the sense of norms reproductive of existing forms of domination) play an essential role in late modern political and social orders.

Having in mind the institutional and normative limitations that I have argued characterise *Structural Transformation* and *Legitimation Crisis* respectively, one may reasonably ask whether any possibilities for change are identified in *TCA*. The answer must be yes and no: yes, in that in his brief discussion of potentials for protest, Habermas does argue that one may locate some such potential in *some* new social movements;[8] no, in that the discussion of protest potential seems to be located outside the major context of Habermas' argument.

For Habermas, new social movements correspond to new and distinctive types of conflict characteristic of late capitalist societies. Such conflicts are not concerned with questions of distribution but rather with 'questions having to do with the grammar of forms of life'. In the main, new social movements are therefore defensive; the only significant exception to this that Habermas identifies is the women's movement. Within the larger defensive category – composed of movements aimed at stemming formally organised domains of action for the sake of communicatively structured domains – Habermas proposes that we can distinguish between those which seek to defend tradition and social rank as against those which already operate on the basis of a rationalised lifeworld and are experimenting with new ways of cooperating and living together.

Judged by the standard of either *Structural Transformation* or *Legitimation Crisis*, the specification of oppositional politics in *TCA* is a circumscribed and pessimistic one. In Habermas' own words, '(the) new conflicts arise along the seams between system and lifeworld' (1989b: 395). The targets of protest are the institutionalised roles of consumer, citizen and state client. The solutions that the new social movements advance are characterised as involving at least a degree of de-institutionalisation and de-differentiation. However, such solutions are judged to be 'unrealistic' (ibid.: 396). But if de-differentiation is ruled out as even a partial solution, upon what strategy can an emancipatory politics focus? Greater institutional engagement and reformation? Projects of substantive democracy involving participation in argumentation, decision-making and social implementation, whether in the workplace, the locality, the region, the social movement? Apparently not. In the closing pages of the later text, *The Philosophical Discourse of Modernity*, Habermas argues for the necessity for an oppositional politics of the public sphere to remain disengaged from but also focused upon political institutions and the party system, clearly viewing the latter as a substantial mechanism of systemic integration (1990b: 364 seq.).

Seductive Systems?

How can we explain Habermas' pessimistic assessment of the possibilities for a critical politics under the conditions of late capitalism? It has been strongly suggested that the explanation may lie in the limitations of the dichotomy which provides the central analytic pivot of *TCA*, that of system/lifeworld (1989b: 125–7).[9] McCarthy in particular has argued that there is a continuity of concern with the implications of systems theory in Habermas' work and proposes that one should view *TCA* as an attempt to resolve the issues to which that concern gives rise (1985).[10]

In its earliest phase, Habermas' work, following the general perspective of the Frankfurt School, took a critical stance towards the implications of systems theory. Such theory was seen as the basis for dystopia in that the very idea of a cybernetically self-regulated organisation of society was identified as a 'negative utopia of technical control over history' (Habermas 1971: 81–122). This critical interrogation of systems theory initiated and characterised Habermas' long-standing debate with the doyen of German systems theorists, Niklas Luhmann. This began at least as early as *Legitimation Crisis*, continued through the extended public debate of *Theorie der Gesellschaft*, surfaced again in *TCA*, Vol. 2, and was continued in *The Philosophical Discourse of Modernity* (Habermas 1976, 1987, 1989b; Habermas and Luhmann 1971; Holub 1991). The main focus of this debate has been overwhelmingly political. Luhmann's central pre-occupation was to refute the idea that the basic reality of modern societies lies in their capacity to generate and sustain interaction systems. According to Luhmann's argument, demands for more *'personal participation in social processes are hopelessly out of touch with social reality'* (Luhmann 1982: 78). The nature and imperatives of societies as complex systems are defined by objective processes, *not subjective ones*, and can therefore only be grasped objectively.

Against the reification involved in such a systemic conception of society, Habermas has consistently urged the need to see society as the fundamental irreducibility of the lifeworld of a social group. The central problem to be addressed in social and political theory is identi-fied as the most effective way in which conceptions of society as both systematically and socially integrated may be combined. Recognising the difficulties involved in this endeavour, Habermas noted in both *Legitimation Crisis* and *Theorie der Gesellschaft* the problems raised for empirical analysis by the systems perspective, particularly with regard to questions of goal states, boundaries and functional struc-tures. These problems are rooted in the reality that social processes are inescapably – though not necessarily exclusively – symbolic in character. '(S)ocieties never reproduce "naked" life but always a cul-turally defined life.'

However, in spite of fully recognising the problems raised for social analysis by a systems perspective, Habermas nevertheless insists on its necessary place in any comprehensive specification of modern society. Such a proposition is recognised as having some plausibility with respect to market relations, which may be capable of being ade-quately conceptionalised as 'an ethically neutralised system of action in which individuals interrelate on the basis of egocentric calculations of utility in which subjectively uncoordinated individual decisions are integrated functionally' (McCarthy 1985: 85). The position is, how-ever, quite distinct with respect to *political* relations. As we have seen, Habermas' specification of politics in *TCA* is a broadly systemic one which substantially reiterates that set out in *Legitimation Crisis*. Political interaction is conceived of as being systematically integrated, formally organised and steered through the medium of power (over).

The conflicts of social actors around divergent values and interests do not enter this hermetically sealed world of objectivised, functionally integrated systems. *The predominantly pessimistic tone of TCA derives from this inability to recognise conflicts between institutionally located actors.*[11] Even if we were to accept the very reduced conception of politics in advanced capitalist societies which a systemic conception entails and consider only the administrative dimension of Habermas' argument, we might still question, as McCarthy proposes, the adequacy of characterising bureaucracies as systemically integrated. Following Parsons, Habermas proposes that the realisation of collective goals underpins power relations.[12] But to the extent that this is so and that there is a proposed shared interest by political actors in the realisation of such 'collective goals', why is not interaction within administrative bureaucracies socially rather than systemically integrated (ibid.: 39)? There is an obvious structural disparity between participants in a power relation. Under such conditions, compliance requires either the threat of sanctions (regarded by Habermas as an inadequate basis for stability) or a sense of obligation to follow orders. The need for an interactive as opposed to a functional perspective on political processes is supported by a range of studies confirming that procedural rules are often circumvented, selectively evoked and subject to both continual reinterpretation and negotiation.[13]

Consideration of the implications and limits of a systems-theoretic conception of politics and of the system/lifeworld distinction leads to an inevitable conclusion: *there is an irreconcilable tension between Habermas' normative position and his preference for conceptualising politics in systems-theoretic terms.* Recognising this, one can understand and assess the purpose of the subsequent *Between Facts and Norms* (1996) as the endeavour to resolve this tension by bridging the gap between the ideal and the real. Indeed it is in this text that one may argue that the consequences of the choice made previously by Habermas between an interactionist and a systemic conception of the social are worked through in their conservatising implications.[14] In what may possibly become the final formal if not definitive statement of Habermas' perspective on the drama of power and democratisation in late modernity, the major roles continue to be assigned to system differentiation and social integration respectively. As against the earlier statements of *Legitimation Crisis* and *Theorie der Gesellschaft*, Habermas now proposes system differentiation and its reproduction as the bedrock of social reality in late modernity. He is at pains to stress that there is no alternative. All political projects, including those of radical democracy, must accept and adapt to that reality and consequently practise an art of 'intelligent self-restraint'. Upon this premise, the further argument becomes that the only political game in town is concerned, not, as had been proposed by Habermas in earlier formulations, with the pursuit of justice in the struggle between democracy and capitalism (or, one might add, any other systematic structures of inequality such as, for example, those of gender or race) but rather with the problem of social integration in differentiated and pluralist societies.[15]

Habermas' answer to this problem of social integration is couched in terms of the efficacy of law as a means of achieving both optimal democratisation and social integration. In effect, Habermas' central argument in *Facts and Norms* is that law is realisable democracy in action, no less and no more. No less because without a consistent input of the authentic democratic publicity generated by reflexive communicative rationalisation the necessary degree of legitimation and therefore of social integration will not be achieved; no more because without a recognition of the inescapable necessity *that governments govern*, particularly in a world which both accepts and positively evaluates an irreversible system differentiation, there is a growing threat to system stability upon which social reproduction rests.

In *Facts and Norms* Habermas proposes literally – and presciently – 'a third way' between liberal and civic republican models of government. In the former, government regulates diversity in the interests of monitoring its efficient functioning; in the latter, generative power (to) constitutes the political community. In Habermas' proposed third way, the institutionalisation of deliberative democracy is specified through a combination of 'weak publics' (public opinions) and 'strong publics' (the legal procedures of the Reechstaat, the state of mights), which, according to Habermas, embody the integral connection between law and democracy.

When considered in relation to the distinction between and relation of domination and power in late modernity, a number of issues in the general argument presented in *Between Facts and Norms* are noteworthy. First, in terms of intellectual and/or political engagement, the problem of domination in the form of functional rationality ceases to be that of capitalist modernity – or indeed of any other general macro-structure of domination or empirical combinations of one or more of such forms.[16] The problem is now specified as the pathology of juridification leading to welfare state generated clientelism and passivity. Building upon the argument of *TCA*, Habermas characterises this problem in terms of a tension between the necessity of welfare state intervention formally intended to enhance power (to) and its potential to extend domination (power over). Reiterating the dilemma of welfare statism as comprising a 'dialectic of empowerment and tutelage', Habermas emphasises that 'built into the very status of citizenship in welfare state democracies is the tension between a formal extension of private and civic autonomy ... and a "normalisation", in Foucault's sense, that fosters the passive enjoyment of paternalistically dispensed rights' (1996: 79).

This reference to normalisation should not be taken as representing an accommodation with the fundamental argument of Foucauldian genealogy. Unlike Foucault and later Foucauldians, Habermas continues to propose in *Between Facts and Norms* that it is in principle possible to distinguish clearly between empowering and tutelary aspects of welfare democratisation according to the degree to which the relevant body of law can – or cannot – be demonstrated to be the product of democratic genesis as embodied in autonomous public spheres and the formal institutions of democratic legitimation.

> With the growth and qualitative transformation of governmental tasks, the need for legitimation changes: the more the law is enlisted as a means of political steering and social planning, the greater is the burden of legitimation that must be borne by the *democratic genesis* of law (1996: 427–8)

From a Foucauldian perspective, this suggestion represents at best a facile response to, at worst a denial of, the problem of that normalisation implicated in any governmentality.[17] It involves a basic failure to confront the central problem of power in modernity: *the dilution if not downright circumvention of juridical power (even if rooted in and therefore expressive of generative power) by disciplinary and governmental power.* Such a position encourages, if not requires, a narrowing of vision to institutional sites of political power, in particular that of the state. This modernist vision is more than inadequate; it is outmoded and should be replaced by a postmodern perspective that recognises the decentredness of power networks in *soi-disant* 'modern' societies.

It is certainly the case that the account of the relationship between the normative and the empirical offered in *Between Facts and Norms* is vulnerable to such criticism. This vulnerability arises from two main sources: to the chronic problems already identified as generated by Habermas' commitment to a system-theoretic perspective, there is added in *Facts and Norms* an intensive preoccupation with *the strict limits of radical democracy*. Habermas reiterates that the complexity of modern differentiated societies precludes the very possibility of new forms of concerted popular power. *Governments govern, managers manage, end of story*. In obviously Parsonian mode, Habermas thus identifies the problems of power and politics in late modernity as those focused not upon the pursuit of justice in the context of inequality and struggle but rather of destabilising and pathological forms across the borderline between system and lifeworld. If the Frankfurt School became pessimistic about overcoming the split between inner and outer nature, the possibility of realising the Good Life, Habermas was initially optimistic (if largely, uninformative) about the alternative possibility of establishing an emancipatory politics. Such an endeavour seems largely, if not wholly, abandoned in *Between Facts and Norms*, trapped as it appears in the 'realism' of a system-differentiated modernity on the one hand and the 'un-realism' of an allegedly communicatively rationalising lifeworld on the other.

On the premise advanced at the beginning of the previous chapter, that Habermas is above all a committed political thinker, the final effect of his journey from *Structural Transformation* to *Facts and Norms* is curious, not to say paradoxical. The attempt to grasp his formulation of an argument about domination and power in late modernity produces a Cheshire-Cat-like effect. The more one tries to identify the import of the argument, the more it disappears. In this account, domination (tutelary power over) is identified in the system coordination of functional rationality. Habermas' colonisation thesis envisages such systemic coordination as having an inherent dynamic of its own. The possibility of resistance to systemic domination is posited as lying within the lifeworld, the potential of which rests on its combination of irreducible tradition and expanding communicative rationalisation. A reasonable reconstruction of Habermas' intellectual trajectory would see it as focused upon the attempt to locate a structural and organisational basis for the implementation of such resistance. At the present terminus of *Facts and Norms* this basis is identified in democratically generated and therefore legitimate law. Critical to such legitimacy is the requirement that the reproduction of legitimate law through 'the forms of a constitutionally regulated circulation of power' should be 'nourished by the communications of an unsubverted public sphere rooted in the core private spheres of an undisturbed lifeworld via the networks of civil society' (1996: 408).

Democratic resistance to a totalising functional rationality thus continues to be significantly identified with the idea of an autonomous public sphere rooted in a diversity of private spheres. This identification serves to underline the fact that the very possibility of Habermas' claim to offer a critical social theory rests upon his use of the system/ lifeworld distinction *as both analytic and normative.* If the distinction is analytically deficient in its typification of the modes of coordination of economy and state – mediatic and functionally integrated – and lifeworld – intersubjectively coordinated – respectively, its normative use clearly rests upon 'a sociologised version of the public/private distinction [basic to liberalism]' which constitutes 'the "private" or "lifeworld" as a realm of freedom, autonomy and consensual action' (Ashenden and Owen 1999: 157). In this perspective, the 'lifeworld' is above all a power-free zone in any sense rather than the site of alternative generations of power, mobilisation and struggle. These alternative generations of power in terms of values, ideas and practices represent historically variable challenges to existing institutionalisations of domination and exclusion, as exemplified in but not restricted to that interpenetration of capitalism and state that Habermas documents in *Structural Transformation.*

The Limits of Habermas' Perspective

In sum, the possibilities for democratic empowerment directly offered by the explicit Habermasian political project are limited indeed, amounting to little more than a refurbished liberalism. The principal reasons for this are twofold: first, Habermas' commitment to a systems-theoretic perspective as an essential analytic tool for specifying the dominant characteristics of high modernity and, secondly, the related issue of the substantial retreat from history involved in the hypostatisation and elaboration of the system/lifeworld distinction. If the former substantially limits the possibilities for social transformation, on the grounds that the complexities of system differentiation set very definite limits to political agency, the latter misidentifies the nature of such political agency in late modernity as being directed towards pathologies of domination rather than towards political emancipation. As Trey suggests, Habermas' conceptualisation, by confining the normative integration of modernity to a communicatively rationalised lifeworld, obscures the extent to which the pursuit of normative integration in terms of justice, freedom and truth is characteristic of modern economic and political hierarchies (1998: 91). Rather than being the product and province of a power-free zone, the lifeworld, the dominant modern normativity 'which guides practices and serves implicitly as the justification for those practices, resides within the motivational structure of the capitalist mode of production...*the normative foundation of modernity is not freedom, truth and justice, in any universalistic sense; rather it is these ideals, conceived of in relation to production, profit and technical efficiency*' (ibid., emphasis mine).

Faced with the reality that history does not provide a collective agent as the instrument of total social transformation but wishing to retain the integrity and validity of critical Enlightenment ideals, Habermas' project evolved in the direction of identifying the telos of emancipation in the very structure of human communication itself. But the historical and political reality is that modern normativity is both more pervasive and more ambiguous than Habermas' account recognises. The dominant mode of normativity is just that: dominant. Yet political struggle focused on emancipatory norms is not confined to border-wars between system-imperatives and lifeworld but is a pervasive aspect of structural hierarchies, as specified in Chapter 2 above. Habermas' emphasis upon the need for self-restraint on the part of those participating in a range of public spheres, while clearly expressive of a practical and realistic concern about the dynamics of totalitarian movements in late modernity, is deficient in two respects: conceptually, it is indicative of the degree to which Habermas (in his defence of the project of modernity) remains fixed in the historical forms with which the emergence of that modernity was identified; in particular, state and civil society. And substantively, it fails to recognise the enormous asymmetries of power which characterise the political configurations of late modernity.

Thus, while *Structural Transformation* purports to chronicle the subversion of publicity from the key touchstone of a politically open society to the hallmark of a commercially manipulative consumerist society, Habermas' later formulations of the public sphere and its necessary boundaries presuppose an openness of communication in contemporary societies which is impossible to sustain. In his discussion of the 'politics of enlightenment', Trey, for example, analyses the way in which, in the context of the Gulf War of 1991, the anti-war movement in the United States found itself effectively constrained by 'a carefully constructed and controlled public sphere' and by its consequent inability 'to gain an adequate hearing, either within the existing sphere or through the construction of alternative spheres' (1998: 125). Underlying this are the enormous development and conglomeration of the media in the period between the Vietnam War (which Trey uses as a useful point of comparison) and the Gulf War, facilitated by the general process of governmental deregulation which, as we saw in Chapter 3, characterised the dynamics of capitalism from the 1970s onwards.

Equally, the realities of the *El Barzon* movement as analysed by Greider seem far removed from an explanatory model couched in terms of systematically distorted communication (1998: 259–84). Thus,

> a caravan of five hundred *campesinos* from Tepoztlan was en route to deliver a protest petition to the president when they encountered a blockade of three hundred state police. The police opened fire on the peasants, wounded thirty people and killed their aged leader. A similar clash had occurred the previous summer at Aguas Blancas in Guerrero, where seventeen peasants were massacred... (ibid.: 269)[18]

The realities of such struggles endlessly repeated over the globe by the dynamic of domination, dislocation and resistance, involving as they do the interpenetration of economic and political domination theorised by Habermas (and further complicated by processes of subordination and exclusion in terms of gender and ethnicity) cannot be addressed in terms of an appropriate relationship between system and lifeworld. Rather they require conceptualisation of the structuring of both domination and resistance and of the diverse struggles for empowerment arising therefrom. Of course, in so far as they are identified as implicating political projects of social transformation, a central aspect of those struggles concerns the reformulation of the agreed boundaries between public and private, of the contingent and fallible relationship between the justice of the general rules governing a political community and the plurality of understandings and corresponding practices of the good life contained within it.[19]

By limiting the possible parameters of a radicalised democracy to those of an appropriate relationship between civil society and the state via the cumulative impact of multiple 'weak' public spaces, Habermas in effect rules out the emergence of those 'democratic breakouts' identified by Ricardo Blaug (1999: ch. 7). As Blaug notes, discussions of the possibility of deepening democracy have been largely conducted in relation to the context of states and consequently must refer to 'a strategic game where one player is far more powerful than another' (ibid.: 132; see the discussion in Chapter 4 above). This state-centred focus has raised a variety of concerns – the problem of vanguardism, issues of feasibility and efficiency, volatility as characteristic of mass participation – which have resulted in the focus of democratic theory being upon those interactions that constitute the national state ('power over') and not upon the everyday interactions of ordinary people (the analysis of those processes of concerted action that constitute 'power to'). Thus, for example, as Blaug indicates, Habermas' own suggestion for 'peripheral' public spheres arises from a central concern with legitimacy in the political system as a whole (ibid.: 133).

Beyond the Limits of the Public Sphere: Democratic Breakouts

In Chapter 4 it was suggested that the alternative to a state-centred approach to power (over) and politics would be one which placed government at the centre of political analysis. In relation to the problem of deepening democracy, therefore, we must necessarily address the question of self-government. Here, we can usefully draw upon considerations reflective of the Arendtian conception of power. In his analysis of *Democracy, Real and Ideal*, Ricardo Blaug provides a powerful argument to the effect that any practical analysis of the nature of real democracy must proceed from the perspective of participants. From this perspective, Blaug argues following Wolin that real democracy above all concerns *the experience not the location of the political* (Wolin 1996). From such a point of view, real democracy is not an ideal but an empirically real phenomenon 'that occasionally *breaks out* among particular people in particular situations'. On such occasions, 'we find that we have risen above the power-saturated ways in which we normally interact and that something quite different is taking place between us' (Blaug 1999: 135).[20]

This participant perspective on experiential democracy as empowerment is found in a range of discussions including Arendt's specification of 'elementary republics', such as the innovations of the American and French revolutions and the examples of workers' councils in twentieth-century Europe.[21] Blaug explores the characteristics, problems and possible life cycles of democratic breakouts, noting their achievements, in particular the revelation of the realities and strategies of an otherwise taken-for-granted domination and the embodiment of both efficient and creative decisions. However, the general record is one of ultimate failure, for which he adduces a variety of causes, internal and external. (Unsurprisingly, most significant among the latter is the resistance of existing institutionalisations of power, using a variety of strategies from ridicule to direct and violent repression.) Nevertheless, their significance as exemplars of real empowerment should not be overlooked. Blaug argues that, on the contrary, they offer us the most useful context in which to systematically explore the possibilities of a real democratic politics as transient historical example and as current counterfactual ideal.

To that end, Blaug seeks to go beyond both the self-imposed and inherent limitations of Habermas' discussion of the public sphere by identifying and applying a series of normative tools which, while deriving from Habermas' theory, are applied to a new object domain: the functioning of deliberative fora (1999: ch. 8). (That is, Blaug attempts to advance our understanding of the operation of empowerment.) The central problem here concerns the conditions under which decision-making practices within a deliberative forum can be made legitimate, particularly given the reality that there must always be some trade-off between participation and effectiveness. Critical here is the need to recognise that the reproduction of empowerment – in Blaug's terms, the 'survival of the democratic moment' – depends upon the preservation of the deliberative capacities of the group. The key constituent in such capacities is judgement, the development and exercise of which relies upon a number of interdependent conditions: accessibility and provision of information, frequent and substantive practice, motivation, a realistic recognition that the development of the relevant skills is a learning process and a commitment to written procedures. (In the case of the last condition, there is a clear necessity to recognise the contingency and fallibilism of any set of political arrangements: that is, genuinely democratic constitutions cannot replace ongoing discursive capacity.)

Blaug's emphasis upon the acquisition and refinement of the skills necessary to sustain democratic breakouts finds further support in the argument advanced by Spinosa, Flores and Dreyfus (1997), which develops from a more directly critical appropriation of the Habermasian conception of the public sphere. This argument begins by noting that Habermas' account of the public sphere is clearly meant to present the paradigmatic form of democratic participation.[22] This form is articulated in terms of a number of key propositions:

1   The public sphere is a locus in which rational views are elaborated which are intended to guide government.
2   *Pace* Arendt, unlike the ancient polis or republic, the modern public sphere is self-consciously separate from power. 'It is supposed to be listened to by power, but is not itself an exercise of power'.
3   The public sphere does not play merely a limiting role upon the expansionist tendencies of the state but has the potential to be 'an intrinsic part of informed, collective decision-making'.
4   As such, the public sphere effectively 'constitutes large numbers of citizens as citizens' by promoting the understanding that democratic

participation involves the discursive specification of a consensus regarding the political issues of the day (1997: 85–6).

While accepting the importance of the public sphere as a bulwark of freedom – both negative and positive – nevertheless Spinosa et al. propose that forms of participation other than the rational argumentation stipulated by Habermas' model offer a superior paradigm of democratic citizenship. In particular, they claim, 'the most serious weakness of the public sphere is its contribution *to the loss of practical expertise*' (ibid.: 87, emphasis mine). In a passage which obviously parallels the argument advanced by Blaug with regard to the maintenance of democratic breakouts, Spinosa et al. state:

> Only by learning to distinguish a variety of situations and how to act appropriately in each can one acquire expertise. This learning requires interpreting the situation as being of a sort that requires a certain action, taking that action, and learning from one's success or failure. (ibid.: 87)

As against Habermas' emphasis on (communicative) rational argumentation, Spinosa and his colleagues argue that the highest kind of political discourse is that of *interpretive speaking*. Through an analysis of an exemplary political action group, MADD or Mothers Against Drunk Driving, they argue that such discourse 'allows some practice, thing or identity to appear as worthy of consideration by a mixed [that is, pluralist] community – …a community composed of a wider range of interests than those of a group of professionals or technicians' (ibid.: 99). Rather than the disinterestedness and detachment valorised in the Habermasian public sphere, the politics of interpretive speaking is rooted in the concrete experience of the lifeworld.[23] Indeed, its significance lies in the fact that it 'forces people to (1) remain true to the concrete experience of their subworlds, (2) acknowledge and respect the different experiences in other subworlds, and (3) seek opportunities for cross-appropriating practices from other subworlds' (ibid.).[24] If we locate this idea of interpretive speaking in the context of the argument concerning struggles for recognition developed in Chapter 2 above, we can identify interpretive speaking as the key mode of praxis (phronesis?) in a transformative politics of empowerment.

Spinosa et al. demonstrate the analytical and practical potential of their argument (regarding the transformative character of interpretive speaking as a mode of political action) in a discussion of the wide-ranging ecological movement developed in Brazil by Chico Mendes.[25]

Starting by organising a Rubber Tappers' Union as a defensive response
to the increasing encroachments of cattle ranchers, Mendes progressed
to the development of a wide range of alliances with other interested
parties. At the centre of this alliance network was that between rural
unionists and a number of international environmental groups, each
of which was forced to recognise the needs and aspirations of the
other. The dynamic of this process was critically determined by interpretive speaking as a mode of political action and a consequent cross-
appropriation of practices expressed in an immanent discourse of
recognition.

Of particular significance in this example are the international
dimensions of the Amazon movement mobilised through the processes
of interpretive speaking. Through these processes are created immanent communities of recognition and, Spinosa et al. suggest, citizenship. Thus, they argue:

> Normally, we would say that since there is no international state, there is
> no way to extend the rights and responsibilities of citizenship beyond the
> nation state. But with the development of social movements that cross
> borders, one becomes an ... international citizen by holding on to a
> disharmony and cross-appropriating various practices with as many local
> associations as possible, until the background practices of all relevant
> places are changed. (ibid.: 115)

So there are substantial grounds with respect to both the character
and the scope of contestatory struggles over the content of modernity
to reject the Habermasian terminus as being both unrealistic and
therefore pessimistic. One highly important example of this is illustrated in the preceding quotation with its emphasis on the potential
of international (and/or transnational?) social movements as sites of
struggle in late modernity. In something of a paradox (given his
emphasis upon the possibilities of a denationalised European citizenship), in his explication of the potential of the public sphere,
Habermas appears strangely wedded to the territorial boundedness
of the circuits of political power.[26] In spite of these important defects
in the Habermasian explication of the political possibilities identifiable in late modern societies, the model of deliberative democracy
does offer a significant focus for the analysis of domination and
power in the present epoch.

In the next two chapters, we will examine the possibilities for
empowerment arising from a critical analysis of citizenship and social
movements respectively.

Notes

1. Whether, as a matter of empirical projection, this centrality will continue is apparently viewed by Habermas as both an open question and a matter of political concern. See White 1990: 110; also, Abercrombie et al. (1980) for a statement of the position that such lifeworld mechanisms are not necessary for social domination and societal reproduction.

2. Cf. the discussion of Wolin's argument regarding welfare statism as the late modern form of Reason of State in Chapter 4 above.

3. Again, there is a clear parallel with Marshall's emphasis upon the unintended consequences of state interventionism in terms of the creation of new forms of social stratification – in Marshall's case – and new forms of social control in the case of Habermas.

4. In elaborating this argument, Habermas clearly follows Offe's initial analytic appropriation of the question of welfare statism discussed in Chapter 4 above. While, as we shall see, he does recognise the problem of 'normalisation' at the centre of the Foucauldian analysis of welfare statism, he does not engage with the type of perspective advanced by Wolin in his discussion of the Economic Polity. From Wolin's perspective, 'normalisation' is not simply an unintended pathology arising from problems of functional adaptation in late modern societies but a central aspect of process of domination in relation to such structures as those of class, gender and race in which process of political reproduction the containment and marginalisation of resistance plays a central role.

5. Frankenberg's argument engages primarily with the work of one of Habermas' major intellectual adversaries, the German systems theorist, Luhmann. However, as will be clear, *pari passu*, his comments would also apply to the doyen of systems theory, Parsons.

6. See the discussion in Chapter 4 above.

7. This proposition offers a key hypothesis about the structural determination of nationalist ideas as a typical basis for political mobilisation in late modern societies, together with populism as a variant of nationalism in an era of mass politics.

8. See Chapter 8 for a general discussion of the potential of social movements as sites for transformative politics.

9. See, for example, *New German Critique*, 35, Spring/Summer 1985, especially the articles by T. McCarthy and D. Misgeld. Also Rasmussen 1990: esp. ch. 3, and Ingram 1987: ch. 10. Stephen White, while recognising the limitations of Habermas' argument – especially its lack of institutional specification – nevertheless has a more positive assessment of the possibilities of Habermas' position and of the potential of the model of communicative sociation. See 1990: 125–7.

10. The following assessment of Habermas' appropriation of systems theory follows McCarthy's illuminating account closely.

11. See the discussion of Habermas' recognition of an alternative perspective of group struggle and his engagement with a systems perspective in Chapter 2 above.

12. See the discussion of Parsons' conceptualisation of power in Chapter 1.

13. See, for example, McCarthy's discussion of the studies by Buckley and Bittner, McCarthy 1985.

14. See Chapter 2 above.

15. On this general issue, see *Social Inclusion: Possibilities and Tensions* (Askonas and Stewart 2000).

16. For a clear statement of the necessity of identifying and analysing such empirical forms of domination as central elements of late modern societies, see Walby 1993.

17. See, for example, Ashenden and Owen 1999: 143–65.

18. As expressed by the defiant eponymous hero of the film *Cool Hand Luke*, moments before he is shot dead, 'We have a communication problem'.

19. On the inevitable contingency of political 'solutions' and the equally inevitable pressures for the decentralisation of political processes, whatever the institutional context, see Beck 1992: 191 seq. There he argues that in the new modernity of risk society 'both the formulation of [programmes] and the decision-making process, as well as the enforcing of those decisions, must be … understood as a process of collective action … and that means, even in the best case, collective learning and collective creation' (1992: 191). See also the same author's discussion of the societal determination of sub-politics in *The Reinvention of Politics* (1997).

20. The parallels with Benton's appropriation of the Gramscian analysis of empowerment explored in Chapter 2 above will be clear.

21. Blaug notes that we do in fact have a wide variety of characterisations of such democratic breakouts. Thus, for example, Pizzorno's 'mobilisation' type of political participation, Mansbridge's conception of 'unitary democracy', Phillip's 'internal democracy' and Moscovici's 'consensual' participation. See Pizzorno 1970; Mansbridge 1980; Phillips 1991 and Moscovici and Doise 1994. In addition to historical examples, Blaug cites a number of recent examples of democratic breakouts in the UK including those in the women's movement and among user groups challenging Community Care provisions.

22. Their account is based upon the argument presented in *Structural Transformation* and does not draw upon the subsequent developments in Habermas' work previously discussed in this chapter. However, were they to have done so, the consequence would have been to reinforce their depiction of Habermas' position.

23. Spinosa et al. (1997) speak of 'subworlds' but their understanding is broadly similar.

24. The emphasis here upon recognition of difference is critical for the development of a transformative politics in late modernity. See the discussion of citizenship in the following chapter.

25. Their source is Andrew Revkin's impressive study, *The Burning Season* (1990).

26. See the following chapter for a positive assessment of Habermas' discussion of European citizenship.

7

Citizenship: Constituting Political Community

Citizenship is fundamentally concerned with social relationships between people, and relationships between people and the institutional relationships of complex industrial societies. (Twine 1994: 9)

In the modern epoch, citizenship has been at the centre of the dialectical relationship between domination and empowerment. As the rallying cry of the French Revolution, the acclamation of 'liberty, equality and fraternity' literally and symbolically initiated the age of citizenship, stressing the root of empowerment as freedom, egalitarianism and solidarity. This initial perspective on citizenship was that of a participatory civic republicanism in which political agency was identified as the source of political community, the necessary and irreducible context for socially derived rights and obligations. Subsequently, this central emphasis upon concerted action came to coexist with and arguably to be displaced by an emphasis upon citizenship as a status, a status deriving from membership in a political community not the creation of purposive interaction but rather a function of recognised coercion within a specified territory and, as such, definitive of status.

The discussion of citizenship has become an increasingly important aspect of the analysis of power relations in late modernity (Andrews 1991; Bader 1997; Beiner 1995; Bottomore 1992; Brubaker 1989, 1992; Janowski 1998; Lister 1997; Roche 1992; Turner 1986, 1990; van Gunsteren 1998; van Steenbergen 1994; Vogel and Moran 1991). At a theoretical level, it has been proposed that this development represents a 'natural evolution in political discourse because the concept of citizenship seems to integrate the demands of justice and community membership' (Kymlicka and Norman 1994: 352).[1] The reasons for this development are doubtless multiple and complex but the following are clearly of particular importance: the collapse of the

Leninist project of state-centred social change in the East; a renewed focus upon the nature and conditions of political membership as a source of social integration in the context of changing state–market relations in the West; the remobilisation of old – in some cases, ancient – ethnic and sectarian disputes and the emergence of new ones; the enforced addressing of the nature of political membership against a background of ever-accelerating mass migrations and the rise of new supra-political forms such as the European Union; the ubiquitous clash between modernism and postmodernism, with a consequent interrogation of the feasibility of a universalist citizenship from a standpoint valorising particularism and difference.

Given the diversity of such causes, it is unsurprising that within the renewed discussion of citizenship there are an equal diversity of positions. Michael Mann has proposed that citizenship is most fruitfully viewed as offering a range of possibilities within a repertoire of ruling class strategies, while Bryan Turner, although positively assessing Mann's argument as a general advance upon the work of T.H. Marshall, nevertheless criticises that argument as economically reductionist and analytically restricted. Seeking to negotiate these shortcomings, Turner outlines a theory of citizenship organised around a twofold matrix, public/private, active/passive (Mann 1987; Turner 1990). Alternatively, Roche has implicitly critiqued both such positions as excessively state-centred and has argued for the necessity of disconnecting the discussion of circuits of citizenship from one particular political form (Roche 1992).

Even this small selection from the range of variations on the theme of citizenship becomes less problematic if one adopts the position advocated by both van Gunsteren and Leca, that citizenship is a contestable concept, lacking a fixed meaning and requiring specification in terms of its use by 'historical participants' in varying historical contexts (Leca 1992; van Gunsteren 1978). Such a stance is strongly supported by Derek Heater's extensive survey of the historically variable usages of the concept of citizenship, leading to the conclusion that 'from very early in its history the term already contained a cluster of meanings related to a defined legal or social status, a means of political identity, a focus of loyalty, a requirement of duties, an expectation of rights and a yardstick of good behaviour' (Heater 1990: 163). This argument leads to the further conclusion that we may reasonably question 'the modern assumption that the status (of citizenship) *necessarily adheres to the sovereign nation-state*. [It] can be associated with any geographical unit from a small town to the whole globe itself' (ibid., emphasis mine). This question as to the necessary linkage between citizenship and any particular site of political agency and struggle is, as we shall see, central to any assessment of citizenship as a focus of empowerment in late modernity.

In order to clarify the issues at stake in citizenship analysis, it is necessary to recognise that there is a tension at the centre of the contemporary discussion which on occasion amounts to a contradiction. This tension arises from the juxtaposition of two different conceptions of citizenship, one state-centred and immanent, the other democratic, non-state-centred and imminent. The former conception involves the identification of citizenship with the elaboration of a distinctive, formal legal status, which elaboration is co-terminous with the emergence of national-states and their diverse lineages.[2] We may identify this as *state citizenship*. The second conception involves the elaboration of citizenship around shared membership of a political community and requires the *non-identification* of such political communities and states. In this conception, citizens as political actors constitute political communities as public spaces. We may identify this as *democratic citizenship*.

The first conception, state-centred modern national citizenship, was, as Brubaker notes,

> an invention of the French Revolution. The formal delimitation of the citizenry; the establishment of civil equality, entailing shared rights and shared obligations; the institutionalisation of political rights; the legal rationalisation and ideological accentuation of the distinction between citizens and foreigners; the articulation of the doctrine of national sovereignty and of the link between citizenship and nationhood; the substitution of immediate, direct relations between the citizen and the state for the mediated, indirect relations characteristic of the ancien regime – the Revolution brought all these developments together on a national level for the first time. (Brubaker 1992: 35)

Central to this conception is the idea of citizenship as a general membership status. The definition of citizenship is *abstract and formal, not concrete and substantive* (ibid.: 40). The context of this definition is the diverse struggles whereby centralising, rationalising territorial monarchies gradually subordinated the liberties, immunities and privileges of feudal lords and corporate bodies (Bendix 1964; Poggi 1978). This status of citizen is thus from the outset the correlate of emerging modern state power, that is, of a distinct form of political administration and control and the legitimation thereof. As Brubaker argues further, *pace* the classical Weberian definition of the state, states are not only territorial but also membership organisations, in which the capacity to determine membership and to enforce the resultant decision has been fundamental to state power.

This is clearly the conception of citizenship which Mann utilises in his discussion of ruling class strategies. Here citizenship is merely one of a number of such regime strategies identified in the course of comparative analysis. In this overwhelmingly class-reductionist account, the possibilities for and the institutionalisation of different dimensions of citizenship are essayed purely as the function of ruling class power (over); citizenship emerges as an element in variable strategies of domination. In such an argument, *any* connection between citizenship and power relations is severed and citizenship becomes merely a function of relations of hierarchical domination. This leads to the treatment of the dubious concept of 'social *citizenship*' as if it were separable from any conception of civil and political freedom and thereby to the treatment of Nazi Germany and the Soviet Union as the exemplars of ruling class strategies in which such social citizenship was maximised. Such an unproblematic treatment of welfare as social citizenship may explain in part Mann's unfortunate proposition in the 1980s that authoritarian socialism 'appears no less stable than other enduring types of regime' (Mann 1987: 350). T.H. Marshall was more accurate when he tellingly observed that the provision of welfare without civil and political citizenship stunted the growth of liberty (1981: 170). Of course, the converse is also true, as Fraser and Gordon argue: namely, that in the absence of meaningful social citizenship, the effective exercise of civil and political citizenship will be impossible to realise (Fraser and Gordon 1994).

In contrast, Brubaker argues that much of the significance of citizenship in the modern world flows, not from its functional, but from its *formal* properties as a specification of membership (and non-membership) in a world which is universally divided into a system of states, bounded both territorially and also in membership terms (see also Baubock 1994: Part I; Ruggie 1993). He further proposes that, within this context, the politics of citizenship has been shaped around a number of 'distinctive traditions of nationhood – by deeply rooted understandings of what constitutes a nation' (Brubaker 1989: 7). Thus, in France the politics of citizenship has historically reflected the fact that the nation has been conceived of mainly in relation to the institutional and territorial framework of the state. Political unity, and not shared culture, has been the basis of nationhood and the universalist, inclusive theory and practice of citizenship have depended on confidence in the assimilatory workings of the major institutions. By contrast, because national feeling developed in Germany *before* the nation-state, 'the German idea of the nation was not a political one, nor was it linked with the abstract idea of citizenship'. Over time, this produced a politics of formal citizenship which focused upon exclusion rather than inclusion.[3]

Both these specific variants of national citizenship can be further contrasted with the case of Britain. The absence of a clear conception of British nationhood has been paralleled until recently by the absence of a clear conception of citizenship.

> The concept of citizenship as membership of a legal and political community was foreign to British thinking. Legal and political status were conceived instead in terms of allegiance – in terms of the vertical ties between individual subjects and the king. The ties of allegiance knit together the British empire, not the British nation. (Brubaker 1989: 10)

With the end of empire, Britain had to redefine itself as a nation-state and seek to create a national citizenship. The absence of both of these has 'contributed to the confused and bitter politics of immigration and citizenship during the last quarter century.... While other countries were debating the citizenship status of immigrants, Britain was debating the immigration status of citizens' (ibid.: 11).

Within the state-centred perspective, therefore, the institution of citizenship is inextricably bound up with the formation of the modern state and the modern state system. But as Brubaker rightly points out, the converse is also true. The formation of the modern state and state system cannot be understood apart from the emergence and institutionalisation of citizenship. As well as territorial organisation, states are membership associations constituting themselves and delimiting the field of their jurisdiction by *constituting* their citizenry. The literature on citizenship has repeatedly emphasised universality and inclusiveness but Brubaker is right to emphasise the inherent duality of modern nation-state citizenship, 'a status at once universal and particularistic, internally inclusive and externally exclusive.... [Such] citizenship is inherently bounded. Exclusion is essential both to the ideology of national citizenship ... and to the legal institution' (Brubaker 1992: 72; see also Bader 1995, 1997; Lister 1997; Roche and van Berkel 1997).

As in the past, in the contemporary world this defining process of inclusion/exclusion is not an undifferentiated one. It is not the case that all those subject to the authority of a given state can be meaningfully thought of as occupying the same status, as being 'included' to the same extent. A simple distinction between *Ausländer* and *Inländer* will not do. A more accurate and useful distinction is between foreign nationals, denizens and citizens: foreign nationals are those who are citizens of another state, who have not been granted full residential rights in the state in which they are domiciled and who therefore should be thought of as having a temporary status; denizens, in contrast, are those who, although they are not citizens of the country in which they have their domicile, nevertheless do have a legal and a permanent resident status (Hammar 1990: 12 seq.). Following the large-scale migration patterns consequent upon the recruitment of foreign labour, there were by the late 1980s some 12 million foreign citizens resident in the Western industrialised states, 50 per cent of whom have been estimated to be denizens (ibid.: 19 and 23). From a state-centred perspective, therefore, citizenship should be seen historically and increasingly not in terms of a simple dichotomy but rather as the pinnacle of a hierarchy of legally defined statuses which together comprehend internal state-membership (Brubaker 1989). Such citizenship status confers full rights, privileges and obligations upon some members, several rights upon denizens and virtually no rights upon short-term visitors. Within this perspective, citizenship questions concern the basic rules for decisions and judgements about who are citizens and who are not. Questions as to precisely what rights flow from being a citizen are on the whole not addressed and neither are questions regarding the relationship *between* such rights. The main qualification to this generalisation concerns the matter of political rights which have usually been thought of as central to the idea of full citizenship. Hence, as Hammar proposes, two types of questions are generated within this perspective: those concerning the extent to which political rights should be given to those who are not formal citizens and those regarding the extent to which and the conditions upon which formal citizenship should be given to foreign residents with a long period of residence (Hammar 1990: 3). To these we may reasonably, and I would propose necessarily, add a third type of question: with the emergence of both supra-national and sub-national forms of political organisation of actual or potential great significance, this type of question concerns the relationship between citizenship as full formal membership of a nation-state and membership of other forms of political organisation at whatever level.

The Welfare-rights Version of Citizenship

A seminal contribution to the discussion of citizenship was made by T.H. Marshall. In his initial exploration of the topic, which has become a sociological classic, Marshall defines citizenship as follows:

Citizenship is a status bestowed on those who are full members of the community. All who possess the status are equal with respect to the rights and duties with which the status is endowed. There is no universal principle that determines what those rights and duties shall be, but societies in which citizenship is a developing institution create an image of an ideal citizenship against which achievement can be measured and towards which aspiration can be directed. (1963: 87)

Marshall further proposes that citizenship requires a particular kind of social bond involving 'a direct sense of community membership based on loyalty to a civilisation which is a common possession. It is a loyalty of free men endowed with rights and protected by a common law. Its growth is stimulated both by the struggle to win those rights' and by their enjoyment when won' (ibid.: 96).

As is well known, Marshall argues that the analysis of citizenship in the modern world would be greatly facilitated if we were to differentiate citizenship rights into three types. These are civil, political and social rights, each type being associated with a particular institutional sphere. Marshall uses this typology of rights to advance an account of the development of citizenship in Britain, focusing upon the impact of the institutionalisation of citizenship upon class inequality.[4]

Having been absorbed into a conventional sociological wisdom concerning the institutionalisation of class conflict, Marshall's discussion was substantially neglected for some time but more recently has received an increasing amount of attention and critical analysis (Bulmer and Rees 1996; Dahrendorf 1988; Giddens 1982a, 1985b; Lockwood 1992; Turner 1986, 1990; van Steenbergen 1994). Part of such analysis concerns Marshall's treatment of the role of the state in the development of modern citizenship. Thus, Giddens spoke of Marshall's depiction of the evolutionary development of citizenship being helped along by the 'beneficent hand of the state' (Giddens 1982a: 171). Turner also saw Marshall as taking the British nation-state for granted, thereby neglecting the important question of the link between 'the notion of national citizenship' and 'the constitution of the nation-state' (Turner 1986: 46).

Such criticisms, however, have failed to identify the central deficiency in this area of Marshall's discussion. As far as a state-centred discussion of citizenship is concerned, Marshall's elaboration of his argument in relation to Britain was singularly inappropriate.[5] As Brubaker makes clear in his instructive comparative analysis, the striking characteristic of the British case is the absence of a state-derived conception of citizenship (see also Hammar 1990: 23).[6] Within this perspective, Marshall's analysis in *Citizenship and Social Class* is most usefully thought of as contributing to our understanding of the changing relations between legally defined status and other dimensions of social structure, most notably class inequality.[7] Such changing relations must be seen in the British case, however, as taking place alongside a high degree of fundamental continuity in the constitution of political actors as *subjects of political sovereignty*. Initially, this sovereignty was first exclusively monarchical; subsequently it took the form of parliamentary sovereignty. Clearly, such subjects are defined and constrained by their location within a structure of domination and not by their contribution to a configuration of power (to).

In spite of this limitation, Marshall does have a real contribution to make to our understanding of differing conceptions of citizenship. In explicating this contribution, we have to take note of his account of the transition to market society in England, an account which presents us with a fruitful paradox (Marshall 1963). On the one hand, central to that account is the proposition that there is a fundamental incompatibility between citizenship as a universal status within a community of rights and a market society. On the other hand, citizenship (specified by the indices Marshall uses) and market society had coexisted until the time of Marshall's account. Marshall's explanation of this apparent paradox is that 'the core of citizenship at this stage (that of market society) was composed of civil rights'. Such civil rights were an indispensable part of a competitive market economy, allowing each *man* to engage in economic struggle and denying him social protection on the grounds that he was able to protect himself.[8]

The real content of legal citizenship in market society was extremely constrained, as Marshall fully recognised. In practice the right to justice, to true equality before the law, did not exist, due to the existence of obstacles between formal rights and possible remedies. Such obstacles were principally of two types: one subjective, that is, class prejudice, which Marshall considered to have been substantially eroded by cultural change and social mobility; the other objective, in the sense of material obstacles to legal equality. The latter Marshall considered to have been somewhat ameliorated by such measures as the Legal Aid provisions advanced by the Labour government in Britain after the Second World War. In a contrast which highlights the paradox to which I have referred, Marshall identified these objective changes as stemming directly from a commitment to 'equal social worth' as against 'equal natural rights'. Such a commitment is crucial to an emancipatory conception of democratic citizenship. This conception is distinct from, in tension with and frequently in contradiction with a state-centred conception of citizenship.[9]

Implicit in Marshall's argument, therefore, are distinctive conceptions of citizenship. The first, elaborated around the concept of equal *natural* rights, is formal and individualistic and wholly compatible with the premises of market society. Such a conception, however, as Durkheim argued, is incapable of supplying an adequate basis for social integration.[10] Marshall implicitly recognises this limitation when he invokes a second emancipatory conception of citizenship articulated around the concept of equal *social worth* as being necessary for social integration in an otherwise fissiparous market society.[11]

Given Marshall's concern with the impact of state intervention upon social inequality, the particular focus of his analysis was upon 'social citizenship', which, although viewed as distinctive, is nevertheless treated as both continuous with and complementary to civil and political citizenship.[12] However, the relationship between the provision through centralised state mechanisms of those welfare rights seen as definitive of social citizenship and a proposed consequent enhancement of individual and group autonomy was viewed as unproblematic. Marshall did not consider the possibility that there may be at the very least a tension between a welfare-rights version of (social) citizenship and a conception of citizenship focusing on emancipation and autonomy.[13] As Roche argues, Marshall 'implies that the *citizen "world" or community* is a sphere in which rights-claiming citizens have their claims serviced by the state-based institutions of the law, parliamentary democracy and the welfare state' (Roche 1992: 21). The consequence of this was the institutionalisation of a passive status, the social citizen, as mainly and effectively a culturally and institutionally subordinate dependant rather than a worthy claimant of those rights necessary to sustain a position of equal worth within the political community.

As was pointed out in the previous chapter, this erosion of the distinction between citizen and client is central to both the Habermasian and the Foucauldian perspectives on state power and normalisation, although they reach contrasting judgements on possible outcomes.[14] Such erosion carries with it a dual danger: demoralisation and depoliticisation (ibid.: 31–2; 34–7). In the case of the former, the moral character of social participation (for example, in the welfare state) involving notions of interactional reciprocity and a logical and practical connection *between rights and duties*, is lost, with a consequent loss of freedom and moral autonomy for dependent clients.[15]

These considerations have an obvious relevance to a second danger, that of depoliticisation. As Roche notes:

> The status of citizen is essentially a legal and political status of membership in a civil and political community which both makes and also abides

by its own laws. It thus implies political rights and duties. In the light of this the idea of social citizenship ... is not at all clear and well grounded, whether in practice or in principle. (1992: 35)[16]

Viewed in this way, a state-based operationalisation of particular social rights requires a prior institutionalisation of democratic political status to enable the effective maintenance of citizenship. 'De-moralised individuals are unlikely to be able to see themselves as being credible bearers of the civil and political powers, the identity and status, of full citizenship' (ibid.).[17]

Citizenship as (Universal) Status

Both the formal membership and the welfare-rights versions of citizenship are therefore state-centred. As such, they inextricably locate citizenship within a framework of domination and exclusion. While institutionalising rights in the form of passive claims, both the membership and the welfare-rights versions tend to institutionalise hierarchy and dependency. These limitations significantly derive from the particular conception of citizenship which lies at the heart of both the foregoing versions: the conception of citizenship as status. As Oldfield argues, the emphasis on status in what is fundamentally an individualistic conception of citizenship 'gives rise to a language of "needs" and "entitlements" which are required both for human dignity and for the possibility of individuals being effective agents in the world' (Oldfield 1990a: 178). The status 'citizen' involves such entitlements as 'rights' defined by collective definition, i.e. the state, and supplied by collective provision.[18] Parallel duties are strictly circumscribed by the payment of taxes and the possibility of military service in defence of the state. Within this conception, social relations are narrowly *contractual*. Consequently, activity in the public realm is a matter of choice for, in principle, autonomous *individuals*. Such a conception 'generates no social bond ... [and] neither creates nor sustains any social solidarity or cohesion, or any sense of common purpose' (ibid.: 180).

Marshall and many others have charted the historical struggles which led to the establishment of such citizenship rights (Barbalet 1988; Bulmer and Rees 1996). A number of such accounts, including Marshall's own, have been criticised for casting their narrative in an evolutionary framework, thereby giving a strong sense of irreversibility to the institutionalisation of rights, which developments in the United Kingdom and elsewhere in the closing decades of the twentieth century have clearly demonstrated to be false. Perhaps more fundamentally, there has been a continuous discussion as to the meaningfulness of particular combinations of citizenship rights in relation to the empowerment of equally autonomous individuals. The central thrust of much of the study of social stratification, for example, has been to demonstrate the manner in which patterns of systematic social inequality in the form of class, gender, sex and race serve to render many formal rights just that.

From a very different standpoint, the reaffirmation by the New Right of the necessity of re-establishing the unregulated market as the central institution of capitalist societies led to a direct challenge to Marshallian arguments regarding citizenship in general and social citizenship in its welfare-rights version in particular. Typically, Peter Saunders argued that 'only ... a liberal social order of market capitalism can generate the conditions for full citizenship [and] that [the] pursuit of egalitarianism and the construction of socialist political institutions tend necessarily to undermine it' (Saunders 1993: 57). In short, it is proposed that the market alone can empower and facilitate social membership and participation; political interventions to rectify market-generated inequalities which effectively nullify formal equalities of citizenship status or which represent the decommodification of social relationships cannot do so and will, moreover, merely lead to the generation of new forms of inequality.

The pivotal notion of negative freedom at the centre of this critique is of course open to challenge. In a series of interventions, Raymond Plant has questioned the coherence of the argument that seeks to separate the formal freedom to pursue given ends from the ability to do so (Plant 1988, 1990, 1992). Social rights in the form of collective provision are argued to be an essential precondition for even the possibility of meaningful membership status within an association of citizens. Two critical questions then arise in considering the implications of such an argument for relations of power: the first concerns the extent to which such 'facilitating' rights are usefully thought of as a separable social citizenship, rather than an integral element in a wider network of citizenship relations; the second question concerns the political significance of different modes of securing the necessary collective provision (in terms of the relationship between power to and power over and the social constitution of political communities of participation and commitment as against hierarchical structures of depoliticisation and demoralisation). It should be clear that it is not only neo-liberals who have questioned the welfare state's relationship to the social construction of citizenship as democratic membership, but also both Habermas and various Foucauldians.

A Differentiated Citizenship?

The degree to which a conception of citizenship as universal status, whether in terms of analytic perspectives or possible practices, can provide a coherent focus for either integration and/or empowerment has been subject to critical scrutiny not only within terms of a direct interrogation of the historical accuracy, analytic utility and internal coherence of the Marshallian perspective, but also from completely different perspectives which question both the theoretical and political defensibility of any universalist perspective on citizenship. In particular, a large body of feminist theory has developed a substantial critique of both liberal citizenship theory and its major alternatives (principally variants of civic republicanism) with regard to their hidden reliance upon gendered assumptions, both conceptually and practically. Equally, the proposition advanced by Marshall and others that both justice and social cohesion could be achieved via integration into the shared identity of a common citizenship status has been challenged on the grounds that such a position always was – and increasingly continues to be – at odds with that pluralism which characterises societies in late modernity, the denial of which on the basis of an unconsidered and therefore formalistic universalism can only serve to legitimise various forms of social exclusion. For this reason, it is argued that justice and a citizenship of equal worth require *a politics of recognition and difference*.

The central propositions of the feminist critique of both liberal theory focused on citizenship as status (defined by passive rights) and its main alternative, citizenship as active membership (in a community of rights and obligations, civic republicanism: Oldfield 1990b), are that, with respect to both historical constitution and conceptual implication, the exemplary citizen has been and continues to be (white) male and that such constitution and implication are critically dependent upon a conceptual and practical division of the world into compartmentalised public and private spheres.[19] Women's secondary status in terms of citizenship must be seen as more than a matter of simple exclusion from a formally universal status – although historically speaking women's achievement of formal rights has been, and continues to be, the focus of protracted struggles. As Carole Pateman pointed out, the complexity of women's political status has in fact *derived from their difference*; that is, from their having been excluded and included on the basis of the same distinctive political attributes (Pateman 1992). On the one hand, women have been excluded from citizenship on the grounds that their natural (sexual) differences from men indicate their inability to participate in an arena of public affairs stipulated in male terms. On the other hand, these differences, notably their capacity for motherhood, became the basis upon which women were assigned a distinctive political duty, one that legitimised their exclusion as citizens while assigning them the critical task of producing citizens. Within the existing patriarchal conception of citizenship, there consequently exists what Pateman usefully terms 'Wollstonecraft's dilemma'.

> On the one hand, to demand 'equality' is to strive for equality with men (to call for the rights of men and citizens' to be extended to women), which means that women must become (like) men. On the other hand, to insist ... that women's distinctive attributes, capacities and activities be revalued and treated as a contribution to citizenship is to demand the impossible; such 'difference' is precisely what patriarchal citizenship excludes. (ibid.: 20)

In the citizenship struggles and successes definitive of modernity, the empowerment of men as citizens has depended upon the subordination of women. This domination was formulated and enacted in terms of women's difference.[20] Reviewing a range of historical examples of this process, Pateman indicated that all illustrate the way in which, even after the substantial achievement of formally equal citizenship rights by women, there continues to be a real opposition between the apparent 'equality' of such citizenship and 'difference' and that, via the difference of 'difference', women continue to occupy a subordinate position within the political order (ibid.: 28). From this she concludes that 'whereas "equality" in some of its possible meanings can encompass "difference", no sense of "equality" compatible with a genuine democratic citizenship can accommodate subordination....for citizenship to be of equal worth, the substance of equality must differ according to the diverse circumstances and capacities of citizens, men and women' (ibid.: 29). Within the terms of the present discussion, therefore, location in an overall structure of domination must preclude the possibility of access to political processes of power to.

These feminist arguments identify and interrogate the limits of the conception of citizenship as a universal status and its implication in meanings and practices constitutive of systematic asymmetries of power (over). They have been complemented by a further range of arguments concerning the need for a positive political engagement with the realities of group difference and multiculturalism as characteristics of late modernity. From very different standpoints, Iris Young and Will Kymlicka have set out the most important versions of these respective positions (Young 1989, 1990; Kymlicka 1989, 1995). Both positions can be recognised as seminal expressions of the dialectical relationship between structures of power (over) and mobilisations of power (to) in the circumstances of late modernity.

Noting that modern political thought has generally equated universality of citizenship in the sense of citizenship for all with universality of citizenship in the sense that citizenship status transcends particularity and difference, Young proposes that the ideal of universal citizenship in fact carries two meanings beyond citizenship for all: first, universality as generality: what citizens have in common as opposed to how they differ; and, secondly, universality as equal treatment: the implication of citizenship in laws and rules blind to both individual and group difference (Young 1989: 263–4). Young argues that these two meanings are in effect in tension with any project of an inclusionary, participatory citizenship and that this provides an important explanation for the situation of liberal capitalist societies in late modernity in which a wide range of social groups are treated as second class citizens.[21]

The idea of universality as generality must lead and has led inevitably in Young's argument to the effective creation of groups of second class citizens whose 'otherness' is perceived as being incapable of assimilation into any general political community. On this ground, Young proposes that a coherent and defensible citizenship of inclusion and participation in public discussion and decision-making requires mechanisms for group representation. Equally, the idea of universality as equal treatment when applied to those characterised by differences with respect to 'capacities, values and behavioral styles', is argued to lead both logically and practically to disadvantage and oppression.

Central to Young's elaboration of the case for a 'differentiated citizenship' is a critique of the idea of impartiality and its consequences in terms of political subordination (1990: ch. 4). It is from just such a standpoint of liberal neutrality that Kymlicka develops a substantially similar case for group representation in the form of multicultural citizenship (Kymlicka 1989, 1995. See also Phillips 1993, 1999). In an argument which echoes Plant's emphasis upon the importance of ability in relation to the assessment of a meaningful equality of rights and possibilities for participation, Kymlicka proposes that it is 'cultural structures' which provide the necessary context within which there develops the capacity to judge as the essential precondition for the effective exercise of individual choice. Communities which are marginalised or even threatened with disintegration are clearly constrained in the extent to which they can provide such contexts of assessment and, consequently, need special recognition and support.

In exploring the possibilities for and limits to a politics of difference and recognition, Kymlicka locates his argument in the context of multiculturalism as an accelerating characteristic of late modern societies. Within the diverse meanings attached to such multiculturalism, he distinguishes in particular between 'multinational' states (those in which cultural diversity arises from the incorporation of previously self-governing, territorially concentrated cultures into a larger state) and 'polyethnic' states (where cultural diversity arises from individual and familial migration). This distinction gives rise to the further distinction between 'national minorities' (in multinational states) and 'ethnic groups' (in polyethnic states: 1995: ch. 2). Obviously, these are very 'different' groups and their political mobilisation is associated with the pressing of different demands with very different implications for the conception and practice of citizenship. Thus, Kymlicka distinguishes between self-government rights (the delegation of powers to national minorities, often through some form of federalism), polyethnic rights (financial support and protection for certain practices associated with particular ethnic or religious groups) and special representation rights (guaranteed seats for ethnic or national groups within the central institutions of a larger state: ibid.).

Relationships of power are implicated in these arguments about group representation in two ways. First of all, the critical terms of a political agenda specified in relation to both structured inequality and political and social integration are identified in terms of relations of domination. Young is emphatic in arguing for the necessity of seeing politically relevant groups as *the products of social relations*, relations of solidarity through reciprocal identification and of shared oppression (1989: 272).[22] Such groups, central to the dynamic of politics of recognition, must, Young argues, be distinguished from the classification of persons into aggregates on the basis of a potentially infinite number of attributes and collectivities in the form of associations such as corporations, political parties, unions or interest groups. What distinguishes social groups in this account (whether privileged or oppressed) from aggregates and associations is their specific implication in a wider structure of power relations. In Young's argument, the distinguishing characteristic of oppressed groups is the existence of one or more of the following conditions in all or a large proportion of its members: exploitation, marginalisation, powerlessness, cultural imperialism and vulnerability to violence and harassment (1989: 261; also 1990: ch. 2).

Young's discussion illustrates the possibility of linking citizenship analysis to a wider analysis of asymmetries of power. Similarly, her proposals for group representation are clearly intended to facilitate processes of empowerment:

> a democratic public, however it is constituted, should provide mechanisms for the effective representation and recognition of the distinct voices and perspectives of its constituent groups that are oppressed or disadvantaged within it. Such group representation implies institutional mechanisms and public resources supporting three activities: (1) self-organisation of group members so that they gain a sense of collective empowerment and a reflective understanding of their collective experience and interests ...; (2) voicing a group's analysis of how social policy proposals affect them and generating policy proposals themselves, in institutionalised contexts where decision makers are obliged to show that they have taken these perspectives into consideration; (3) having veto power regarding proposals that affect a group directly, for example, reproductive rights for women or the use of reservation lands for Native Americans. (ibid.: 274–5)

Together the various arguments for a differentiated citizenship represent a radical development in citizenship theory. The Marshallian perspective had focused on the idea of citizenship specified in terms of an equality of individual rights. In contrast, the model of differentiated citizenship relates empowerment and integration into a political community to a process of incorporation, involving not only individuals but also the members of certain groups whose consequent rights would depend upon their membership of these groups. Justice and democracy are viewed as demanding a politics of recognition and difference and, as such, requiring differential restructuring of institutional resources.

The new pluralism of a differentiated citizenship offers a powerful critique of the conception of citizenship as a state-centred universal status.[23] Going beyond Marshall's viewing of the idea of citizenship as a counterweight to the oppressions and exclusions of the systemically generated inequalities of capitalism via a formal equality of legal statuses, the model of differentiated citizenship proposes that the equal treatment of the unequal merely perpetuates old and/or creates new forms of domination.[24]

This argument concerning the oppressive consequences of the political intervention represented by the pursuit of an impartial citizenship has provoked, in turn, substantial criticism from the standpoint of impartiality. It is objected that a differentiated citizenship offends against the principle of equality, since granting particular rights to specified oppressed groups on the basis of group membership must inevitably serve to create a hierarchy within citizenship, albeit a fluctuating one; further, that a radical pluralism depends upon an incoherent and therefore arbitrary state partiality, precluding even the possibility of just procedures and therefore doomed to lead to fragmenting and divisive recognition struggles; and that consequently, in the absence of any clear principles of state intervention, differentiating citizenship will both appear and be arbitrary (Hindess 1993; Kymlicka 1989, 1991; Meyer 1998; Phillips 1992; Taylor 1991, 1992; van Dyke 1985).

The central thrust of these criticisms is that, whatever the merits of radical pluralism's critique of the idea of citizenship as universality of treatment, its proposed solution is a recipe for accelerating conflict and fragmentation. Kymlicka himself recognises the dangers involved, noting:

> On the one hand, many of these groups are insisting that society officially affirm their difference, and provide various kinds of institutional support and recognition for their difference, e.g. public funding for group-based organisations.... On the other hand, if society accepts and encourages more and more diversity, in order to promote cultural inclusion, it seems that citizens will have less and less in common. If affirming difference is required to integrate marginalised groups into a common culture, there may cease to be a common culture. (quoted in Beiner 1995: 6)

Must such a politics of recognition and group empowerment lead to a politics of fragmentation?[25] Not necessarily, as Kymlicka argues, if we distinguish between different kinds of group rights: special representation rights (for disadvantaged groups), multicultural rights (for immigrant and religious groups) and self-government rights (for national minorities) (Kymlicka and Norman 1994: 372–3). Viewed realistically, claims for both representation rights and multicultural rights are claims for inclusion in a reconstituted but thereby valued and potentially cohesive political community. Calls for the recognition of difference are articulated in pursuit of a more just and therefore a more, rather than a less, viable ethical community, a project of particularity within generality.

Self-government rights are, however, Kymlicka argues, a different matter. Unlike representation and multicultural rights which take the wider political community for granted – else why press for recognition? – self-government rights question the 'very nature, authority and permanence' of that wider community (ibid.: 375). This being the case, Kymlicka proposes, we must accept that 'self-government rights ... are the most complete case of differentiated citizenship, since they divide the people into separate "peoples", each with its own historic rights, territories, and powers of self-government, and each, therefore, with its own political community' (ibid.). In such circumstances, he concludes, 'it seems unlikely that differentiated citizenship can serve an integrative function'.

For all the difficulties involved, this is to overstate the case: the general argument here would appear to presuppose an idea of *exclusive citizenship* located within the context of a single political community.[26] This seems unrealistic in a world increasingly characterised by multiple political identities which do, as a matter of fact coexist, sometimes relatively harmoniously, at other times less so.[27] Kymlicka's argument locates the problem 'of differentiated citizenship too firmly *in* and too closely *to* the context of national states and therefore too firmly in the context of what he terms a 'societal culture' (1995: 76).

It is precisely this location which is contested by Habermas in an argument for the historically contingent nature of the linkage between nation and citizens, between national independence and participatory republicanism which seeks to optimise self-government. 'The nation of citizens', he proposes,

> does not derive its identity from common cultural and ethnic properties but rather from the praxis of citizens who actively exercise their civil rights....the republican strand of 'citizenship' parts company completely from the idea of belonging to a pre-political community integrated on the basis of descent, a shared tradition and a common language. (1994: 23)

In support of this position, Habermas notes the important distinction between two fundamentally different, indeed contradictory, conceptions of citizenship. In the first perspective, citizenship is conceived on an analogy with a model of *received* membership in an organisation which secures a legal status. In this interpretation, 'individuals remain external to the state, contributing only in a certain manner to its reproduction in return for the benefits of organisational membership'. In the second interpretation, citizenship is conceived in an analogy to a model of *achieved* membership in a self-determining ethical community. Here, 'the citizens are integrated into the political community like parts into a whole' (ibid.: 25). (This distinction is a clear exemplification of the distinction between 'power over' and 'power to'.)

Habermas fully recognises that the second understanding of citizenship stands in sharp contrast with the many sectional and strategic aspects of modern bureaucratic politics. In this latter organisational model, ultimately isolated individuals are subject to surveillance within a contractual relationship which regulates an exchange of benefits for functionally specified contributions. The holist (or what I characterise below as an imminent) model emphasises in contrast that political autonomy – as an irreducibly relational phenomenon – 'is a purpose in itself, to be realised not by single persons in the private pursuit of their particular interests but rather only by all together in an intersubjectively shared praxis. [In such a reading] citizen status is constituted by a web of egalitarian relations of mutual recognition' (ibid.: 26).[28]

Considering the example of the emergent European Union, Habermas poses the question: does the idea of an active community-building citizenship have any meaning or analytic value in relation to such a supra-national entity? Here, he notes that the proliferation of multiple sites of membership – in the sense of both access to and participation in – is characteristic of functionally ever more differentiated social systems in late modernity. However, such proliferation of memberships tells one nothing about increases or losses in autonomy; 'it says nothing of the actual use made of active citizenship by means of which the individual can him- or herself bring influence to bear on democratic changes' (ibid.: 31).

In the context of a globalised and corporatised economy and a bureaucratic and technocratic administrative apparatus, citizens are potentially reduced to the status of clients. In response to these possibilities, Habermas reiterates the need to reassert an active citizenship through struggles to realise democratic will formation through a mobilised public sphere. As we saw in the previous discussion of the public sphere, however, Habermas' concern with the possible erosion of liberal procedures in the face of irrationalist movements of traditionalist nostalgia leads him to an overly conservative position as far as the democratisation of (existing) democracy is concerned. While he refers to the potential significance of new social movements as vehicles for resistance and communication in relation to the institutionalisation of functional rationality, he fails to recognise their potential as sites of empowerment through the constitution of alternative communities of citizenship (see Chapter 7 below). *An active model of citizenship must be tied to contexts not only of communication but also of decision making.*

Whatever the limitations of Habermas' conception of democratisation in late modernity, it clearly points to a model of active citizenship which endeavours to transcend the problem of national particularism and the restriction of the idea of citizenship within it. To that extent, one can identify in such a conception of citizenship a clear resonance with the Arendtian conception of power as collective action in an inescapably plural world. As we have seen, whatever its limitations in regard to the substance of political struggles in modernity, it is the singular contribution of Arendt's argument to reassert the need for theory to be expressly *political*, 'because she directs us toward the public aspect of human life and toward the human activity that determines all other human relations and arrangements in demonstrable ways' (Dietz 1991: 246). As Dietz argues, the Arendtian conception of plurality as politics resonates with Iris Young's notion of a 'politics of difference' and thereby emphasises the heterogeneity of citizens. Difference as plurality is proposed as the ground of politics, not as its insurmountable obstacle (ibid.: 247).[29] Here we have the groundwork for a political theory of both action and difference and a conception of civic 'publics' of constitutive citizenship, spaces where plurality can manifest itself.[30]

These considerations about the relations between plurality, collective action and citizenship can be advanced by a sympathetic critique of the most commonly proposed modality of a publicly based politics in late modernity, that of deliberative democracy (Bohman and Rehg 1997; Dryzek 1990). In the present context, this critique can most usefully be located between two contrasting possibilities: on the one hand, formulations of a postmodernist politics of difference that effectively discount the possibility of any reasonably coherent and politically feasible articulations of the political around constitutive engagements between generalisable conceptions of justice and pluralistic versions of the good life; and, on the other hand, recognisably modernist formulations of such constitutive engagements which place various conceptions of deliberative democracy at their centre. In developing such a critique, Iris Young agrees with the deliberative critics of the dominant alternative perspective – that of an interest-based democracy – that it is preferable to have a conception of democracy that understands politics as the meeting of people to decide public ends and policies in a rational way (1996: 121). As she quite reasonably remarks, 'Such deliberative democracy appears most often in our current experience in the decision-making structures of voluntary associations outside the state' (ibid.).

The central conception here is that the process of political discussion consists in reasoned argument. Clearly, such a process is dependent upon a broadly specifiable set of conditions which Young sets out in a largely Habermasian manner. In deliberative democracy, assent is dependent upon the force of the better argument, the freedom and equality of the participants, the absence of domination, and an acceptance of the goal of a general consensus, which goal predominates even in situations of majoritarian voting.

Against such a conception of deliberative democracy, Young presses the following criticisms: first, that the specified processes are exclusionary in that they privilege certain cultural modes of social process over others; second, that the conception involves variations around

[margin note: critique of deliberative democracy]

an either explicit or implicit idea of unity, whether deriving from a community's prior shared understandings, as in the case of Michael Walzer, or, involving the re-establishment of a disrupted consensus, as in the occasional case of Habermas. In the case of this second criticism, Young rightly argues that the pluralistic nature of modern societies makes the notion of shared understandings substantially unviable;[31] and that the assumption of a prior unity effectively negates the genuine autonomy of a generative politics productive of new articulations of the relationship between justice and alternative versions of the good life. Notions of unity are potentially, if not inherently, exclusionary and, as such, inhibit genuine dialogue.

Young's proposed solution speaks directly to the possibilities for a citizenship of empowerment in late modernity: this solution identi- *communicative democracy* fies difference *not as a problem but as a resource.* Recommending a perspective of communicative democracy rather than deliberative democracy, she argues that such communicative democracy depends upon three conditions: significant interdependence, formally equal respect and agreed-upon procedures. These conditions, while 'thinner' than those most frequently proposed for deliberative democracy, are, Young argues, consequently more viable. They permit more realistic encounters, of communications between different perspectives with at least the possibility of their transcending one another. 'Communication among perspectives that transcend one another preserves the plurality that ... Arendt understood as a condition of publicity' (that is, as the ground of the political) (1996: 127). In such a model of communicative democracy, understanding does not require identification but rather a realistic recognition of the possibility of arriving at limited public objectives through appeals to justice as opposed to tradition or self-interest.

Young's formulation of communicative as opposed to deliberative democracy is explicitly intended as an engagement with the problems of collective action in the plural world of late modernity. As such, it seems particularly useful as a model for a non-state-centred conception of citizenship directed towards the constitution of imminent political communities. The importance, both conceptually and practically, of detaching the conceptualisation of citizenship from any integral association with the national-state – or indeed, for that matter, from any territorial specification – is powerfully suggested, not only by a widespread perception, both academic and popular, of the declining significance of this particular context but further and more importantly by the emergence of a wide range of multiple and overlapping alternative contexts (Hall and Held 1989: 183). Elizabeth Meehan has persuasively argued that 'a new kind of citizenship is emerging that is neither national nor cosmopolitan but that is *multiple* in the sense that the identities, rights and obligations associated ... with citizenship ... are expressed through an increasingly complex configuration of common [European] Community institutions, states, national and transnational voluntary associations, regions and alliances of regions' (1993: 1, emphasis mine).

Democratic Citizenship and Community

The emergence of multiple sites of governance and political struggle characteristic of late modernity indicates the necessity of relating the possibilities for and the limitations upon differing conceptions of citizenship to the context(s) which give them meaning. This necessity is illustrated in an early contribution to the contemporary discussion of citizenship in Britain. Writing of the reconstitution of status that had accompanied the rise of citizenship, Halsey noted how important it has been that the possibilities for citizenship have been defined in the context of the nation state (1986: 62). In pursuing the goal of creating a national political community, the British Labour party found itself in a paradoxical situation. In its emergence as a serious political force, the Labour party was significantly dependent upon the solidarity of local class communities. To a very real extent, community was the critical resource base for the development of particular forms of citizenship. However, the welfare rights conception of citizenship, which was central to Labour party thinking and institutionalisation for at least four decades after the Second World War, crucially depended upon continuing economic growth and change. However, apart from the depoliticising effects of the statist model noted above, economic change also produced changes in the occupational structure which steadily diminished the size of the traditional working class and eroded working class communities.[32] Recalling Brubaker's argument, it seems reasonable to conclude that with respect to both citizenship as formal membership and citizenship as a source of social solidarity through the delivery of formal and substantive rights, the task of constructing a national political community in Britain remains to be achieved. And there may be good reasons to believe that the historical possibilities of realising such a task have been exhausted. Constitutional reforms by way of a pre-emptive devolutionism are obviously intended by the United Kingdom's New Labour government to ward off the centrifugal dangers of nationalist independence movements, but there are powerful indicators that the dynamic of at the very least a federal system may well be unstoppable (Nairn 2000).

An Alternative Conception

What emerges clearly from the foregoing discussion of state-centred conceptions of citizenship in both the formal membership and welfare-rights versions is the degree to which conceptions are implicated in a discursive field of meanings and practices involving passivity and conditionality, at the centre of which are hierarchies of control and exclusion. This is to say that within this discourse any possibilities of power to are critically dependent upon structures of power (over). Possibilities for the collective creation of political community (or communities) remain unrealised. Behind formal legalisms and political rhetoric, the sociological realities are those of subjects, clients and consumers, not those of citizens of equal social worth and decision-making capacity. The construction of political communities clearly requires an alternative conception of citizenship. Such a conception involves political actors, rights and duties and a conception of political forms as *subordinate and adaptive* to a variety of citizenries, rooted in the divisions and diverse purposes of civil society.[33] Such democratic citizenships are created and reproduced through the constitution of substantive communities of reciprocity and balanced rights and duties, involving conceptions of 'equal social worth'.

In contradistinction, therefore, to conceptions and specifications of citizenship centred upon nation-states, the political communities which provide the contexts of democratic citizenship are, as Michael Walzer has argued, 'phenomenological and imminent' (1983: 26). For this reason, such political communities are able to encompass group as well as individual citizenship and their social sites are potentially widespread, both sub-national and transnational, the city and the region as well as the Community and the Federation. Such political communities need not, indeed should not, as Habermas rightly argues, be thought of as embodying some anterior organic identity of territory or blood. Exploring the possibility for the emergence of a European political community, Tassin argues that just

> as the institutionalised community cannot fall under the statist logic of the monopoly of legitimate violence, so its constituent parts cannot establish themselves against each other in a relationship of domination. What is required rather is a principle of 'participation in government' ... which can only be guaranteed by a *public space*....[Therefore, instead] of being

the precondition for a public space, the European community is actually its result: it is a community resting not upon an amalgamation of interests, feelings and wills, but on the contrary upon a politically constituted public space in which the plurality of political initiatives stand face to face. (1992: 188)

Tassin's further explication of this conception of a non-state-centred citizenship demonstrates its implications for our earlier discussion of a formal membership approach to citizenship. Arguing the case for the development of a European fellow-citizenship, he notes that the nation-state principle of citizenship is based on a deliberate conflation of the concepts of general will and national will or on that amalgamation of nationality and citizenship which Habermas precisely contests. The construction of a European political community, however, requires citizenship to be broken away from nationality.

> The right of foreign residents ... to vote in local elections ... is an essential and obligatory step in the formation of this new community citizenship. It indicates that participation in the life of public institutions takes precedence over nationality; that, whatever the citizen's cultural or national identity, his or her insertion in public political space is elective and not 'native'; that it derives from a political choice and not from birth (*natio*) or an identity passed on by history. (Tassin 1992: 189)

Within the imminent conception of democratic citizenship, therefore, political communities are above all the *product of citizenship practice*. The distinctive characteristics of such a conception *vis-à-vis* the state-centred conception of citizenship may be further clarified by recognising the divergent relationships between political interests and political contexts implied by each. Within the state-centred conception of citizenship, it is assumed that preferences, interests and identities are given *exogenously in advance of public discourse and deliberation*, whether by explicit state specification or implicit state prioritisation among the many competing possibilities contained within civil society. The conception of democratic citizenship does not make or require such an assumption. It 'appreciates, rather, that preferences, interests, and identities *are as much outcomes as antecedents of public deliberation*; indeed, they are discursively constituted in and through it' (Fraser 1992: 130, emphasis mine).[34]

The crucial contextual referent of democratic citizenship is thus common membership of a shared and imminent community. In that specific sense, such democratic citizenship requires us to acknowledge the other members as being of equal social worth. Within this context, 'citizenship is an explicitly *political* activity, in which people who are equals address collective and general concerns' (Phillips 1991: 82, emphasis mine). The case for the 'absolute primacy of politics' in the elaboration of a conception of democratic citizenship has been forcefully argued by Phillips (ibid.: 82–7). Drawing upon the contributions of two US feminists, she elaborates the case that a democratic citizenship is *necessarily* implicated with the political, public sphere. Thus, such citizenship requires – if you will – a movement, certainly symbolic and phenomenological, frequently literal, from the private world of family and work to an involvement in more general, public concerns. Equally, however, democratic citizenship does not require a false dissociation from the reality of group identities. Rather, political organisation in a democratic citizenry occurs around such group identities but is only fully realised through interaction with others, in which interaction we are necessarily reminded of others' claims. Thus diversity and contingency are *inbuilt conditions* of genuinely democratic citizenship: 'there is no way to know in advance whether the outcome of a deliberative process will be the discovery of a common good in which conflicts of interest evaporate as merely apparent or the discovery that conflicts of interest are real and the common good is chimerical' (Fraser 1992: 130).

The combination of the structural and organisational dimensions of globalisation and the political uncertainties and possibilities characteristic of an emerging post-national era has accelerated theoretical debate and practical conflict around the meaning and implementation of citizenship. As Linklater notes, 'as the present [now the last] century draws to a close, the subnational revolt, the internationalisation of decision-making and emergent transnational loyalties in Western Europe and its environs reveal that the processes which created and sustained sovereign states in this region are being reversed' (1998: 113).[35] In this situation, he urges, it has become essential to question whether citizenship has no meaning apart from the sovereign nation-state. In a vein wholly consistent with the present argument, he notes that a major obstacle to the effectiveness of such questioning arises from the fact that 'the main strands of modern social and political theory ... have assumed that there is a stark and immutable contrast between domestic and international politics [and are consequently] woefully ill-prepared for the task of imagining new forms of community which promote the development of a transnational citizenry' (ibid.: 117).

The overwhelming characteristic of modern states, whatever their variable characteristics, has been monopoly: monopoly control of violence, monopoly right of taxation, monopolistic intentionality towards political identity and political obligation, monopolistic arbitration of legal dispute and monopolistic claim to membership of international society (ibid.: 118). However, with the erosion of these state monopoly powers the possibility has been increased 'that alternative sites of power and competitors for human loyalty will emerge'. As we saw in Chapter 3, both the internationalisation of relations of production and the unregulated dynamic of global financial markets have limited state capacity to autonomously determine national economic policy. The consequence is a global if differential immersion in Beck's 'risk society', but equally the emergence of a clear distinction between those for whom the response to 'risk' is an intensification of their identification with their 'nation-state' and those for whom the diminution of individual state powers represents a welcome opportunity to create and participate in the citizenship of multiple political communities.

Notes

1. For a discussion of the major models specifying the relationship between the universal and the particular, praxes of justice and praxes of the good life, in late modernity, see Stewart 2000.
2. The term national-states is to be greatly preferred over the more conventional, but analytically unhelpful, nation-states. While it may be true to argue that all modern states are national states, sharing characteristics of centralisation, coordination and differentiation within the context of circumscribed territory, they are by no means all nation-states if what is being conveyed by that term is ethnic or linguistic homogeneity. The complexities of citizenship analysis concern issues of participation and integration which arise precisely in the context of the relationship between national-states and diverse modes of membership both self- and other-designated of which ethnonationalism is only one. Clearly a major driving force behind changes in this relationship is global capitalism. See Jessop 1999; Mann 1993, 1997; Tilly 1975.
3. Cf. the discussion by Jessop of *Volksnation*, *Staatsnation* and *Kulturnation*. This represents a more refined discussion of the bases of nation-states but the essential point regarding state-centred *membership* remains. Jessop 1999.
4. For an illuminating and important consideration of the status of Marshall's typology – historical hypothesis or ideal type – see the concluding discussion by Bulmer and Rees 1996. As they suggest, viewing the typology as an example of an ideal type permits a fruitful comparison and extension in terms of Hirschman's triad of exit, voice and loyalty. Upon this basis, they argue, we can see the integral links between civil rights and capitalism, the exercise of political rights and 'active involvement in the affairs of the community and ... dialogic relationships both within and between bounded political units' and social rights and issues of social cohesion. Bulmer and Rees 1996: 270–1.

5. For an exemplary and systematic engagement with the 'Englishness' of Marshall's account, see Rees 1996.

6. Turner potentially recognised this particularity in his 1990 article but failed to draw the appropriate conclusions:

> A more important point is that the constitutional settlement of 1688 created the British citizen as the British *subject*, that is a legal personality whose indelible social rights are constituted by a monarch sitting in parliament. *The notion of citizen-as-subject indicates clearly the relative extensive notion of social rights but also the passive character of British civil institutions.* (1990: 207, emphasis mine)

7. See Turner 1988.

8. As Fraser and Gordon note in their exemplary explication of the real limitations of historically constituted civil citizenship: 'Civil citizenship made property rights the model for all other rights, thereby encouraging people to translate all sorts of claims into property claims. It is not surprising ... that those who were excluded from civil citizenship were usually those who did not own property, either because they were unable to get their resources defined as property (for example, women, tenants) or because they *were* property (slaves)'. Living in a different time, Marshall clearly failed to recognise the gendered nature of that civil citizenship which is such a necessary component of a capitalist economic order; that is, he fails to recognise the central importance of the core cultural and therefore political meanings of civil citizenship, which Fraser and Gordon so clearly explicate (1994: 98).

9. In effect, Marshall endorses that political intervention on behalf of a disadvantaged group (here a working class systematically disadvantaged by the nature of the capital–wage labour relationship) which was to become a central element in the radical pluralism of the late twentieth century. He makes no mention of other forms of systemic inequality such as those implicated in the gendering of domination or institutionalised racism and therefore does not engage directly with the issue of difference. However, his argument does anticipate later concerns with the problem of unintended consequences in the form of the substitution or parallelism of one hierarchy for or with another.

10. See Lockwood 1992.

11. Marshall further compounds the confusions and complexities surrounding these conflicting conceptions of citizenship by invoking national consciousness as an additional source of social integration, placing at the centre of the integrative processes of citizenship 'a direct sense of community membership based on loyalty to a civilisation which is a common possession' (Marshall 1963). For an argument regarding the context of these differing conceptions of citizenship, see the discussion of models of social order focused on social contract and social compact respectively in Stewart 2000.

12. For a critical interrogation of the possibility that Marshall's identification of the idea of social citizenship lends itself to a downgrading of the central importance of political citizenship, see the discussion by Himmelfarb, in Rees 1996.

13. For an interesting attempt to consider the normative justification for treating welfare provision and citizenship as intrinsically linked, see

King and Waldron 1988. The authors do not consider, however, the degree to which different dimensions of citizenship may be in tension with one another.

14. See also Chapter 5 above. For an exemplary analysis of the power-saturated (including gendered) nature of the cultural and political meaning and realisation of 'dependency' in the United States, see Fraser and Gordon 1994.

15. In addition to Roche's illuminating discussion and the references therein, see also Habermas 1989b.

16. See also MacIntyre 1985.

17. For a parallel discussion of the depoliticising effects of the welfare state institutionalisation of economic rights, see Sheldon Wolin 1992: 245–6. Thus, 'Economic rights, or ... "entitlements" do empower people. There is a gain in dignity, autonomy and well-being, and no democrat should believe otherwise. *But this must not blind one to the anti-political consequences resulting from the preoccupation with economic rights*' (emphasis mine).

18. Of course, the immediately human benefits of such a conception are clear and important. As Macedo proposes, albeit somewhat exaggeratedly, it places 'certain human goods (security, prosperity, and freedom) within the grasp of nearly all, and that is nothing less than a fantastic human achievement' (quoted in Kymlicka and Norman 1994: 355). However, the central point here is that the conventional organisational delivery of this achievement is necessarily dependent upon an arrangement of power over. See the discussion of state power in Chapter 4 above.

19. Ruth Lister proposes that these elements may be expressed in the form of a set of dichotomies permeating the fabric of citizenship. Here, the public male citizen characterised in terms of abstraction, rationality, impartiality, independence and a humanising political agency is contrasted with the private, female, non-citizen characterised by particularity, irrationality, partiality, dependency and imbrication in the natural: Lister 1997: 69–70; see also James 1992. The degree to which the general perspectives of Arendt and Habermas express this dichotomy will be obvious. But, as we shall see, to recognise this is to identify a critical reality of late modernity but does not remove either the problem or the possibility of imminent politics not necessarily constrained by a gendered agenda. On the gendered characteristics of liberal political theory, see Landes 1988; Nicholson 1986; Okin 1989; Pateman 1988.

20. Yeatman proposes that such exclusionary symbolisations of and practices in relation to 'the other' are a general characteristic of processes of domination and marginalisation: Yeatman 1994.

21. It is important to emphasise that Young is quite explicit about this factor providing only part of the explanation for domination in the circumstances of late modernity. Another 'part of the answer is straightforwardly Marxist: those social activities that most determine the status of individuals and groups are anarchic and oligarchic; economic life is not sufficiently under the control of citizens to affect the unequal status and treatment of groups.' Taken together, it seems reasonable to view Young's position as one which formally identifies structures of domination in terms of capitalism and state, although her examples make it clear that empirically she regards

gender and race as equally important in the explication of processes of subordination. Kymlicka also recognises that inequalities of power are a function of economic inequalities as much as differences of social and cultural identity. See, for example, Kymlicka and Norman 1994: 370. Thus, the arguments for a differentiated citizenship have to be located within both a politics of redistribution and a politics of recognition.

22. 'In the women's movement, gay rights' movement, or elders' movements, differential social status based on age, sexuality, physical capacity, or the division of labour has been taken up as a positive group identity for political mobilisation' (Young 1989: 272). As Charles Taylor notes, what is critically at stake here is not only the reality of cultural diversity but the diversity of political and social positions that the members of cultural groups occupy within any political system. See the discussion in Gianni 1998.

23. For an illuminating comparison between this new pluralism with its celebration of heterogeneity, diversity and difference and the older Anglo-American pluralism of the 1950s with its celebration of political stability through the medium of competitive interest groups, see Phillips 1993: ch. 8. Not the least merit of Phillips' discussion is its acknowledgement of the evolution of the thought of Robert Dahl towards a systematic critique of the original pluralist theory of democracy.

24. Seen in this way, the argument for a differentiated citizenship represents a classic statement of the central political issue in late modernity, the relationship between justice (generality) and the good life (particularity) or, in Habermas' formulation, between autonomy and solidarity. See, for example, Askonas and Stewart 2000, *passim* and, in particular, Stewart 2000: 55–72. It has to be said that the general form of the differentiated citizenship argument – the unintended consequences of the granting and implementation of equal rights – is quite consistent with a similar concern in Marshall's account.

25. The work of Anne Phillips throughout the 1990s represents a systematic, nuanced but troubled engagement with the issues raised by a politics of difference, most particularly but not exclusively from a feminist perspective. This work identifies, celebrates and advances the feminist critique of the 'universalist pretensions' of mainstream political theory and its systematic imbrication of gendered, racist and hegemonic assumptions. Phillips is quite clear that the consequence of this critique is to enable a more accurate analysis of diverse sites and processes of domination. Nevertheless, her work manifests a continuing concern that a valuable politics of difference has the potential to develop into a politics of enclaves in which a vested interest in the amplification of grievance will lead to a new institutionalisation of the old pluralism and preclude a politics of dialogue (albeit between diverse groups) and imminent community. See Phillips 1992, 1993, 1995.

26. See the discussion of Linklater below for an engagement with this issue.

27. See the discussion of Meehan, Tassin et al. below.

28. In support of this position, Habermas quotes Taylor's argument regarding a participatory conception of citizenship: 'Full participation in self-rule is seen as being able, at least part of the time, to have some part in

the forming of a ruling consensus, with which one can identify along with others. To rule and to be ruled in turn means that at least some of the time the governors can be "us" and not always "them"'. However, Habermas subsequently takes issue with the communitatarian basis of Taylor's argument: Habermas 1994: 26 seq.

29. For the best contemporary statement of this position, clearly influenced by Arendt's thinking, see Bernard Crick's classic, *In Defence of Politics* (1992).

30. Dietz also importantly notes the great limitation of those critics of Arendt who dismiss her arguments as 'too rational'. (Unquestionably this criticism has gained momentum from Habermas' appropriation and development of her 'communications theory of power', which is more vulnerable to the charge of being overly rationalistic, although, as Holub and McCarthy remark, for very understandable reasons.) As Dietz notes, 'Representative thinking, the mentality that distinguishes action in the public realm, is a good example of a form of reason that defies characterisation in terms that would have us drive a wedge between reason and passion. It encompasses and incorporates both' (ibid.: 249).

31. Substantially seems appropriate here. It is both fashionable and inaccurate to exaggerate the fluidity of shared understandings at whatever level of social process.

32. Cf. the discussion of Offe's general analysis of this development in Chapter 3 above.

33. Adrian Oldfield has elaborated an alternative conception of citizenship to that embodied in the liberal-individualist conception of citizenship as status: the civic-republican conception. Thoughtful and stimulating though his discussion is, he does not address the contextual dimension which is central to the present argument. For a consideration of the limitations of a communitarian approach to political practice, which I believe the present argument avoids, see the discussion by Michael Walzer. Oldfield 1990b and Walzer 1992: 89–107.

34. My argument here is an adaptation of Nancy Fraser's argument which is directly concerned with developing a contrast between competing views of the public arena. See Fraser 1992.

35. See also Linklater's highly important, *The Transformation of Political Community* (1998), which develops a Habermasian perspective on international relations.

8

New Social Movements: Politics of Identity and Politics of Distribution

From the 1950s onwards, a new phenomenon entered the power discourse of capitalist democratic societies. Both conceptually and substantively, new social movements became an additional, distinctive site for projects of empowerment. Following the Civil Rights Movement in the United States, the women's movement of Second Wave Feminism, the Campaign for Nuclear Disarmament in the United Kingdom and parallel anti-nuclear movements in Europe and the United States and the anti-Vietnam War movement(s) across the international arena, there was a proliferation of new social movements throughout the globe. While the 1970s began with an explosion of industrial conflict across Europe, as that decade progressed the post-Second World War settlement in Europe, embodied in the variants of welfare state corporatism, was increasingly characterised by stasis and disintegration, while the United States became enmeshed in a succession of constitutional crises.[1] With the New Right regimes of Reaganism and Thatcherism, political settlements that focused on a variety of compromises between capital and labour were abandoned and the domination of capital both nationally and internationally was enhanced. Classes as sources or sites of collective action were argued to have been both defeated and/or eroded.

In this context, new social movements were identified as both novel and significant forms and forces of a new politics (Dalton and Kuechler 1990; Kriesi et al. 1995; Markoff 1996; Touraine 1981).[2] In relation to our thematic concern with the interrelationship of domination and power in late modernity, this discussion of new social movements raises two questions in particular. First, to what extent can the proliferation of such movements be identified as corresponding to major changes in forms of domination emerging in late modernity? And, secondly, to what extent are the characteristics of *some* new movements expressive of new constructions of the political, new projects intended to realise communicative democracy both with respect to goals (generally speaking, challenging expert or dominant-interest formulations of culturally problematic models of social order) and processes (participation and an emphasis on non-hierarchical models of political agency)?[3]

Such a discussion can usefully begin from Eder's location of new social movements within the social production of modernity. Eder's argument begins from a reading of the history of modernity in terms of certain social groups 'characterised by an evolutionary new form of communication [which] have had a profound effect in triggering modernisation processes' (Eder 1993: 21). Such groups, Eder proposes 'try to organise their mode of association and communication according to ... principles of *equal* and *discursive* handling of disputes. This type of discourse is based ideally on the free and equal exchange of arguments, that is, on *Aufklärung* (enlightenment)' (ibid.: 21–2).

This proposed new type of discourse is not an abstracted ideological development: it can and must be related to associations as the contexts which make possible its various historical manifestations. Eder identifies three such contexts: first, those groups in the eighteenth century which identified themselves as bearers of enlightenment (Cohen and Arato 1992: 200–10; Koselleck 1987);[4] secondly, the working class movement, which modified the content but not the form of the earlier associations (Thompson 1978; Tilly 1978);[5] and, finally, the associations of the new middle class seeking to defend a lifeworld against the encroachments and disruptions of a subversive and dominating functional rationality.

What is centrally important in these examples, according to Eder, is not the content but the logic of discourse involved. Within the terms of this logic, a reflexive use of communication (a communication about communication) is practised which is in effect the starting point for the social production of a specifically modern society. 'Those who participate in modern associations know that they are taking part in a collective learning process' (Eder 1993: 23). Accordingly, Eder contends, what specifies the social in modernity is precisely its realisation in such collective learning processes. Following Habermas, Eder proposes that 'the mechanism constituting modern associations since the eighteenth century can ... be defined as *discursive communication*' (ibid.).[6]

Such communication can be defined by two principles: equality and the discursive handling of conflicts. 'Modern learning processes are based on the principles of ceaselessly testing the universalizability of the normative order of civil society. Their mechanism is the resolution of contradictions by argumentation or "critique"' (ibid.).[7] Collective learning processes have therefore become the foundation for the model of modern society; the greater the extent to which social relations can be organised and integrated through the medium of such processes, the greater the possibility of the democratic organisation of the well-being of society (ibid.: 24).

Lest his argument appear an overly optimistic or utopian reading of modernity, Eder is emphatic about the obstacles to the realisation of the potential of collective learning processes. As he puts it: 'Associations [as the product and vehicle of collective learning processes] do not exist in the thin air of discussion.' They are inevitably implicated in the wider social order of domination and struggle and, consequently, 'the symbolic universe produced by discursive communication is used for legitimating purposes' (ibid.).[8] In particular, symbolic practices become implicated in and a critical aspect of those power struggles which Eder recognises as endemic to capitalist modernity. In effect, Eder proposes that domination (power over) and struggle are focused upon the contestation of legitimising practices and the wider social orders they produce and reproduce. This is the appropriate context within which to locate social movements conceived in terms of collective action leading to the emergence of (diverse) collective actors.

From the perspective of empowerment, Eder's argument can be seen as a valuable elaboration of analytic possibilities around a conception of power as concerted action. As such, it offers immediate and obvious parallels with the discussion of political mobilisation set out in Chapter 6 above. In particular, Eder emphasises the active and critical role of collective action in the constitution of collective actors, whether through the process of acting together, the defining of the boundaries of collective action (that is, through the constitution of political communities) or the reproduction of collective identity through cognitive practices.[9] Similarly, Eder's argument concerning the necessity of analysing the production and reproduction of collective action with respect to three different levels – micro, meso and macro – is informed by a thematic concern with empowerment through the process of acting together in the course of struggles within the context of institutional frameworks (ibid.: 49–60).[10]

At the micro-level, concerted action most immediately produces the 'group' as a 'social construction produced by actors drawing boundaries between the collective action they contribute to and its environment' (ibid.: 53).[11] What translates collective action into a collective actor is the emergent variable of group identity, which identity derives from the self-production and self-reproduction of groups through cognitive practices, in the ideal case through collective learning processes (ibid.: cf. Touraine 1977).[12]

This discussion adds considerable depth to a conception of power as concerted action. The elucidation of the way in which collective actors are constituted represents a clear and analytically useful elaboration of the Arendtian/Habermasian conception of power set out in Chapter 2 above. This conception emphasises both a critical *relational* argument concerning power and equally the manner in which power as relation implicates the necessary *social* generation of power *and irreducible plurality* as the vital context of human empowerment. Like Arendt, Eder proposes that collective action cannot be derived either from an individual strategic, instrumental model of social relationships nor from one which stresses the holistic power of groups over individual actors (that is, power over cannot produce a generalisable and therefore just power to). It must be recognised that engaging in collective action

> triggers reflective cognitive processes. As collective action produces the reasons for joining a collective action, it becomes itself a mechanism of collective learning .... market models and discourse models are related to each other in the way that mechanism and logic are related to each other. (ibid.: 54)

This perspective makes it possible to draw upon the findings of rational choice models to elaborate the structural parameters within which communicative discourse is likely to be maximised. We can recognise that group heterogeneity (always perceived as the major stumbling block to meaningful concerted action), group size and the relative number of activists facilitate 'outbreaks' of communicative democracy in the following manner: heterogeneity (the Arendtian plurality) produces argumentative conflicts, feeding the dynamic of communication; group size accounts for a diversity of discourses and activists stimulate public debate and discursive struggles (ibid.).[13]

If Eder's explication of the micro-level analysis of collective action involves a significant elaboration of the conception of power as concerted action, his discussion of the meso-level highlights the degree to which the effective pursuit of objectives arising from social movements on the basis of such power raises possibilities of hierarchy and domination.[14] The intensity and degree of psychic and other resources, both relational and material, required to sustain 'outbreaks' of communicative democracy create a strong probability of their transience and fragmentation. The 'solution' has typically been the creation of social movement organisations (SMOs) situated at the meso-level of institutional relations. Analysis of this level gives rise to questions concerning appropriate organisational forms, relations with diverse branches of the state apparatus specifying the space of political opportunity structure within which SMOs must operate and the consequences of the different logics of collective action available to different collective actors in terms of a differential ability to mobilise different kinds of resources (ibid.: 55–6).[15] In general terms, all these questions concern the inevitable tensions surrounding the relation between communicative democracy and efficiency discussed in Chapter 6 above.

Finally, at the macro-level, Eder proposes that collective action 'manifests itself as social movements transcending the limits of an institutional system and relating to historical alternatives of societal development' (ibid.: 50). Thus, in the terms of the general argument presented here, those social movements identifiable as protest or emancipatory movements are examples of empowerment, collective action directly challenging existing structures of domination and inequality on the basis of contradictory readings of the potential of modernity.[16] Historically speaking, major examples of such transformative movements have been: those pursuing political emancipation to the extent that they have pursued a chronic agenda of radical democratisation; those pursuing economic emancipation, most notably socialist movements; feminist movements to the extent that they have involved transformative as against integrative political projects and the ecological movement subject to a similar qualification concerning social transformation as against social regulation and amelioration.

The concept of class has been the putative bridge at the macro-level between a conception of capitalism as a system of asymmetrical power (equated here with domination) and the generation of both historically and socially variable collective actors.[17] However, the changes in the structuring of capitalism analysed under the headings of 'disorganised capitalism' (Lash and Urry 1987) or 'postfordism' (Crook et al. 1992) are seen as having eroded the potential for the production of subordinate classes *as collective actors*. In addition, a wide range of social movements are proposed to be not susceptible to adequate analysis on the basis of class relations. For this reason, Eder advocates the retention of class as a component in the analysis of social movements but proposes that the term should be seen as detachable from its implication in the historical experience of industrial capitalism. Classes (understood in terms of a commonality of experience given by a specific location in society) should be seen as functioning 'like a *social opportunity structure* for collective action that underlies movement politics' (ibid.: 61).[18] Within this framework of an effective cultural reproduction of social inequalities, 'the macro-level analysis of collective action involves identifying the context of public communication within which collective action reproduces its conditions of existence. This implies leaving the context of organisation behind and locating social movements in the public sphere, [since] the public sphere is the macro-condition *par excellence* of the constitution of collective action' (ibid.: 60; cf. the discussion of Chico Mendes in Chapter 6).

As we have seen in Chapter 3, capitalism continues as a dominant form of late modernity within which there has been a significant shift of power in favour of capital. Against that background, the capacity of class-specific collective actors has become systematically restricted with the result that a key problem becomes that of the nature of collective political action in modern societies. Major (European) theorisations of new social movements have advanced power-saturated interpretations of both these phenomena and the crises of social reproduction to which they 'correspond'.[19] Capitalism may require new forms of regulation but there is no reason in principle to propose that these will not be forthcoming. As discussed in Chapter 5, Habermas attempted to sustain the crisis perspective by shifting the focus from accumulation to legitimation but, as also noted, his account is significantly characterised by probabilism ('there is a potential but not a necessity for this to happen') and a growing absence of structurally related collective actors. Following the linguistic turn in Habermas' work, there is a marked retreat from the attempt to ground the analysis of social change in terms of possibilities for struggles leading to the implementation of the results of normative critique in structural conflict or systemic crisis. Transformative possibilities become attached to the expansion of communicative rationalisation as an integral dimension of modernity. By the time of *Between Facts and Norms*, however, any political projects in these terms are emphatically subordinated to procedural constraints and elite agency. The complexity of modern social systems is assumed to require that the political is a matter of discussion and legitimation and politics therefore a matter of strategic negotiation. Possibilities for communicative rationalisation appear subordinate to the necessity of instrumental rationality; power to is subordinated, conceptually and historically, to power over.

This compromise appears to concede that the dominant normativity of late modernity is that of the functional rationality of capitalism (Trey 1998: ch. 3). As Eder notes, if we recognise the diversity of modernities, we have 'to consider modernity as a social construction .... the results of social constructions are to be located within social relations of power and competition ... again embedded in social structures' (1993: 189). History will not guarantee the success of communicative action. Communicative democracy has a chronic agenda involving fallibilistic projects of justice and the good life (Stewart 2000).

Seeking to refurbish the notions of contradiction and class conflict as contexts for the analysis of social movements, Eder argues for the utility of recognising the critically *political* nature of contradictions. What is needed is 'a theoretical "middle ground", *a theory pointing out the role of antagonistic definitions of the social world, that creates and reproduces a reality outside individual motivations and beyond their social-structural determinants*' (Eder 1993: 191, emphasis mine).[20]

In a manner consonant with the possibilities discussed in Chapter 2, Eder relates the occurrence of social conflicts to such antagonistic definitions but contextualises such conflicts within a proposed class politics where the latter refers to 'processes that separate and coordinate social actors quasi-objectively into classes of actors'. Politicising the notion of contradiction leads to the proposition that modern society is subject to an endemic crisis arising from blocked class politics. Since class relationships are based on interpreted contradictions, crisis discourses are a way to give meaning to contradictions. 'Crisis therefore has a double meaning: it is a process of social self-blockading *and* a critique of this process. [Such] critique, however, is inevitably bound to conflictual relationships' (ibid.: 192). Echoing Honneth's critique of Habermas' decision to adopt a systemic rather than a conflictual group perspective on the trajectory of modernity,[21] Eder proposes that 'the object of class politics [in K.E.'s refurbished sense] no longer concerns either the systemic logic of modern societies or its regulation. *The proposition is that constitutive of class politics is the situation in which alternate ways of perceiving and reacting to adaptive problems collide*' (ibid.: 193, emphasis mine).

As we saw in Chapter 6, Habermas' commitment to a systemic perspective leads him to characterise the 'new social movements' of recent decades substantially in terms of identity politics, to the relative exclusion of a concern with issues of redistribution, whether national or international. In common with a number of social movement theorists, Habermas proposes that contemporary social movements are distinct from earlier movements to the extent that they address symbolic rather than instrumental needs.[22] Consequently, in *TCA* the new social movements are argued to be mobilisations around 'the grammar of forms of life' such as equal rights, individual self-realisation or participation as against the previous concern of earlier forms of collective action with distributive issues such as social justice and systemic inequalities (Habermas 1989b: 392). 'The bond that unites these heterogeneous groups is the critique of growth' (ibid.: 393). Noting the diversity of new social movements, Habermas argues for the differentiation of emancipatory potentials from those of resistance and withdrawal (ibid.).[23] Broadly speaking, this distinction seems to correspond to that between projects of (at least potential) universalisability and projects intended to realise and/or defend particular versions of the good life.[24]

Whether offensive or defensive, as is well known, Habermas' discussion in *TCA* identified the conflicts involving social movements as occurring 'along the seams between system and lifeworld'. Thus:

> alternative practice is directed against the profit-dependent instrumentali-
> sation of work in one's vocation, the market-dependent mobilisation of
> labour power, against the extension of pressures of competition and per-
> formance all the way down into elementary schools. It ... takes aim at the
> momentarisation of monetary services, relationships and time, at the con-
> sumerist redefinition of private spheres of life and personal lifestyles ....
> the relation of clients to public service agencies is to be opened up and
> reorganised in a participatory mode, along the lines of self-help organisa-
> tions. (1989b: 395)

In addition to the limitations of Habermas' formulation of the distinction between system and social integration, the very formulation itself tends to encourage an integrative rather than a transformative perspective on power relations; that is, it is a perspective on patholo-gies rather than conflicts. Moreover, with *Between Facts and Norms* at a practical level Habermas has become primarily preoccupied with the problem of social integration defined in relation to an irreducible system complexity: he sees the critical political issue as 'how may we stabilise existing structures of social integration' and argues that communication must play a necessary but constrained role in such stabilisation. This is not a perspective from which one can approach empowerment as self-government via concerted action.

Nevertheless, Habermas' proposal that offensive movements are those which represent the potential for that advanced cognitive-moral learning, both associated with and necessitated by post-conventional morality, is a useful way of considering the orientations of collective actors. We can, as Ray suggests, then consider the degree to which any movement repoliticises the public sphere by 'salvaging practical questions from ... privatism ... or de-politicised administration (technocracy)' (Ray 1993: 62). What is lacking, however, in Habermas' very general discussion is any detailed analysis of the relationship between oppositional movements and processes of colonisation (Berger 1991). In keeping with his systems orientation, Habermas uses the framework of anomie to 'explain' movement 'reactions'. However, as was argued in Chapter 2, and as Eder and Melucci among others point out in relation to social movements, collective action is never simply reactive. It is always constructed and, moreover, constructed at multiple levels: cognitive, affective and organisational (Bagguley and Hearn 1999; Eder 1993; Eyerman and Jamison 1991; Melucci 1989, 1996a). Further, Habermas' unvarying commitment to the idea of the lifeworld as a 'space without power' leads him to overlook the degree to which there can be a dialectical relationship between the growth of economic and/or political domination which leads to an oppositional appropriation of 'systemic' resources.

What is required therefore is an analytic strategy which will enhance our understanding of the factors conducive to the successful construction of offensive/oppositional movements specified in Habermasian terms. Ray offers an illuminating suggestion in this context, drawing upon the arguments of the leading American school of social movement analysis: resource mobilisation theory (RMT) (McCarthy 1987; Zald and McCarthy 1987). The central insight of RMT identified by Ray is that the success or failure of a social movement in influencing public agendas derives not only from organisational abilities or strategies but also from the structural conduciveness of the social networks these movements attempt to deploy (1993: 64). Ray argues that, whatever other limitations are involved, this RMT notion of networks is central to the Habermasian notion of the lifeworld and therefore can be of real assistance in addressing the critical question: what factors promote political opportunity structures conducive to offensive or defensive social movements?

Before turning to a consideration of those recent structural developments against which we can assess this question, it may be salutary to note that the relationship between power (as concerted action) and domination (as power over) make even tentative answers to such a question both complex and problematic. As Ray, for example, notes:

> One should be wary about celebrating the autonomy of social movements which 'by-pass the state', since this might underestimate the recuperative power of regulatory systems to neutralise protest by marginalising it into alternative lifestyles. (1993: 66)

In this regard, for example, the movements of life-politics (or self-actualisation) that Giddens proposes as a complementary parallel to an emancipatory politics of the public sphere can be seen as implying an essential privatisation of potentially public issues, a displacement from public to private tendencies (Giddens 1991a). Such a consideration reinforces the arguments concerning the limitations of structuration theory as a basis upon which to approach the relationship between power over and power to, since in this instance the diffusion of individualistic appropriations of the dominant practices of the market consumerist ethos of the Economic Polity inevitably leads to the privatisation of public issues. In the same way, the celebration by Melucci of the centrality of lifestyle politics to the new social movements conduces to the marginalisation and particularisation of critical issues from the public sphere (Luke 1990; Melucci 1996a; Ray 1993).

These considerations suggest the very real constraints operating upon social movements as effective sites of political empowerment in late modernity. Equally, they indicate the necessity of combining structural and agentic dimensions in any analysis of empowerment in relation to social movements. In late modernity, outbreaks of communicative democracy may well be emblematic and fragile, correspond to episodes of crisis and be empirically intertwined with narcissistic and expressive motivations. On the other hand, a critical dimension of emancipatory movements involves their communication – both internal and external – of alternative value orders for the organisation of public affairs. The development and viability of emancipatory/transformative movements is proposed to depend upon structural change (which clearly represents constraints as well as possibilities) but also on a committed engagement with the dilemmas of communicative democracy in a pluralistic world.

Structural Considerations

Central to any discussion of sites of domination and political struggle in late modernity are processes associated with the restructuring of a globalised capitalism, emergent systemic crises and corresponding projects of regulation and opposition. The relatively high stabilisation of domination and incorporation associated with the institutionalisation of welfare state capitalism had been organised around the prioritisation of a historic class compromise, with an accompanying exclusion and depoliticisation of any and virtually all other dimensions of social cleavage in relation to dominant institutional political agenda (Jessop 1990). The substance of power struggles was overwhelmingly concerned with matters of redistribution, their form was intensely bureaucratic and hierarchical and the critical context was one which rendered invisible, indeed naturalised, those operative assumptions of the particular division between public and private discussed above (see Chapters 5 and 6). In this situation,

> Class politics evolved into orderly and routinised processes cemented by formal rules and less formalised corporatist deals. Within this framework, the class/interest conflict transformed into a support of the sociopolitical status quo. Opposed interests were articulated in the form of bureaucratically framed and negotiable policy demands which were aggregated within corporate blocs and systematically resolved through bargaining, arbitration and conciliation. The dominant role in these processes was played by bureaucratised elites, *and the level of grass-roots involvement was low. Class milieux were the reference points rather than participants in political processes.* (Crook et al. 1992: 142, emphasis mine)

Social movements coexisted with this institutionalised order of an Economic Polity as a largely excluded other of emancipatory critique, drawing, out of structural and institutional necessity, on social networks excluded from the dominant order but also of necessity constructing new political identities; that is, generating new forms of power as concerted action. The dynamics of power struggles focused on liberal issues of incorporation such as the Civil Rights Movement in the United States and the liberal vanguard of Second Wave Feminism acted both internally and externally as media whereby what were initially perceived as particularistic struggles could be perceived as integral parts of systemically generated but distinctive inequalities.

The systemic crisis of accumulation and regulation associated with the oil crisis of the early 1970s but actually having much deeper roots was manifested in an explosion of class conflict and a major destabilisation and delegitimation of corporatist forms of intermediation. The subsequent restructuring of capitalism associated with such terms as 'disorganised capitalism' and 'postfordism' clearly had a critical impact on both sites and forms of struggle, an impact associated with the erosion and demobilisation of classes as sites of political struggle, the increasing hegemony of market-based models of social order and process and a crisis of social theory and political praxis in relation to models of social transformation.[25] At the macro-level of movement analysis, the necessity has been recognised of focusing on the global system as the most general context of social determination. As Melucci notes, 'The analysis of contemporary movements must today take a systemic, global point of view ... it cannot be applied in a mechanistic way to a national or state level .... societies are today inextricably inserted in a global system, participating in a shared world dominated by a set of central cultural models' (1996a: 191). Similarly, Dieter Rucht proposes: 'Analogous to the shift from local to national social movement that began centuries ago ... today we are witnessing a gradual shift from national to transnational movement activity' (della Porta et al. 1999: 206).[26]

The dynamic interrelationship of new forms of domination and new forms of concerted action is explored in an exemplary analysis by Donna Dickenson (1997). Dickenson notes that, contrary to arguments concerning the liberating, 'empowering' effects of economic globalisation and the modernising of Third World economics by the marketising projects of neo-liberalism, the direct impact was generally to intensify their subordination and exploitation. While the diffusion of globalised capitalism through structural adjustment programmes has, as discussed in Chapter 3 above, had a fundamental impact on a transnational basis, Dickenson argues that its effects have been substantially gendered. Thus, she notes that, among other consequences,

- women did not benefit proportionately from the 1970s development loans which caused the international debt crisis and consequent structural adjustment crisis, because their reproductive labour was undervalued and because they rarely owned land;
- women suffered disproportionately from SAPs (Structural Adjustment Programmes), which created a triple burden of low-paid work in export processing zones, traditional subsistence labour and housework;
- women have been the direct objects of subordination and depoliticisation in a range of fundamentalist political projects seeking to defend 'traditional' ways of life (centrally articulated around the practical – economic, social and sexual – and symbolic subordination of women) (1997: 100–6).

Considering women's political response to these and related restructurings of empirically intertwined forms of domination, Dickenson argues that this response is most accurately viewed as a form of reinventing democratic politics, 'entailing a new notion of democratic political community' (ibid.: 106). The various constraints upon female political participation discussed in our previous consideration of citizenship are identified as determinants of women's pursuit of alternative forms of political engagement, an engagement which has occurred both below as well as across and above national state boundaries.

Dickenson offers an analysis of the Beijing Women's Conference in 1996 as an example of the possibilities and problems associated with a transnational political movement. In particular, she argues that Beijing marks the emergence of a fully globalised women's movement.[27] Previous meetings of the Women's Conference had significantly foundered in relation to the problem of cultural diversity, to which Third World feminists had seen their First World counterparts as having a knee-jerk and condescending reaction. In an obvious parallel with the critique of the male-saturated universalism advanced in feminist discussions of citizenship, Mohanty argued: 'Universal sisterhood, defined as the transcendence of the "male" world, ... effectively erases material and ideological power differences within and among groups of women, especially between First and Third World women (and, paradoxically, removes us all as actors from history and politics)' (Mohanty 1991). In contrast, the Beijing Platform for Action deliberately eschews relativistic clauses which would 'count women out'. Whereas the earlier 1994 Cairo Conference on Population and Development declaration included the limiting – not to say fudging – phrase 'respecting cultural values and religious beliefs' in delineating rights of women and girls, the Beijing text did not.

Dickenson's discussion of the transnational women's movement indicates how the emergence of communication and transport networks has transformed spatial and temporal obstacles to the development of supra-territorial movements (see also Castells 1997).[28] In a very real sense, the possibility of the historical emergence of imminent political communities of communicative democracy has been fundamentally altered by the development of communicative networks transcending territorial limitations (McAdam and Rucht 1993). As Buechler notes, 'global social structures are now providing ... incentives for the mobilisation of transnational social movements. [Moreover], such movements are particularly likely to coalesce around issues that *inherently transcend national boundaries and borders*.... the human rights movement appears to be the largest, whereas the environmental movement is the most rapidly growing transnational social movement' (2000: 77, emphasis mine; see also J. Smith 1994, 1997a, 1997b; Castells 1997: ch. 3).[29]

As well as providing the essential context within which to analyse the generation of a variety of *transnational* movements, a globalising world also provides the appropriate macro-context of determination and explication for a variety of *national* developmental movements. In this regard, Ray proposed both the possibility and the necessity of extending a Habermasian analysis of offensive and defensive movements into the context of developing societies in late modernity (Ray 1993). In an argument consonant with that advanced by Eder, Ray argues that social movements can be seen as carriers of alternative forms of modernity within the context of struggles over the meaning and organisation of modernity. In this instance, however, rather than communicative developments in the form of transnational movements transcending territorial boundaries, it is the variable insertion of particular peripheral states into the diverse structures of globalisation which is proposed to provide the macro-context for the generation of competing forms of modernity.

If the dynamics and insections of a multi-dimensional globalisation provide the necessary macro-context of social movement analysis, social movements continue to be significantly realised and politically constructed at a national level. Within this context, there is an unsurprisingly complex relationship between social movements and the dynamics of power relationships. Following Buechler, we can initially distinguish between at least two senses of the political (2000: 165 seq.). Thus, state politics can refer to collective action directed towards influencing state policy, including those circumstances in which it seems possible to consider such 'influence' as amounting to projects for the transformation of state power through a significant power generation and an envisioning of alternative projects of modernity. These may be helpfully differentiated into offensive and defensive movements along Habermasian lines.[30] Here, power over is centralised and hierarchical, that is, referential to integrated institutions of domination. In contrast, social politics is proposed as a referent for power struggles around diverse social institutions and cultural practices, including those compartmentalised into a depoliticised, unproblematic 'private' sphere. 'In this conception, power is diffuse and decentralised, and challenges to this form of power take a wider variety of tactical, strategic, and expressive forms' (ibid.: 165).

As Buechler rightly notes, the overwhelming institutional focus of political analysis in the dominant modes of political and social theory – whether theoretical or empirical – has left little room for an integral analysis of social movements as oppositional and transformative forces.[31] The possibilities seem stark but unreal: a world of diversity without difference; a world of manipulated uniformity without historical or social movement; or an 'economised' world which ignored pluralism and therefore politics, and consequently had nothing coherent to say about an illusory world of economic transformation. Pluralist theory saw power struggles as public and open; elitist theories document the history and social manifestation of singular group power and class theory proposed that, whatever the complexities of the relationship between capitalism as a mode of production and individual social formations, the collective action of social classes was the analytic key and practical formula for social transformation and the inauguration of realisable social justice.

Against the background of such theoretical closure, only in recent decades have the dynamics of a diversity of oppositional movements, whose various projects brought them into direct confrontation with the state, forced a recognition of the interactions of states and social movements.[32] The important reality that states can most usefully be seen as providing not one but multiple contexts of determination and struggle has been helpfully identified in Buechler's advocacy of a multi-level structural approach to the analysis of states and movements (2000: *passim* but especially ch. 7). At the global level, all states are variously inserted into a global capitalist system and an international system of states, shaping and being shaped by a growing number of transnational social movements. At the national level, states remain as highly significant territorial nodes of regulation and coordination. At the regional level, which Buechler appropriately specifies in analytic and not spatial terms, the state continues to be the guarantor of structures of domination rooted in the dynamics of class, race and gender. And, finally, at the local level of direct and unmediated interactions, states continue to structure and engage in surveillance in the pursuit of projects of both system and social integration.

In general terms, the relationship between social movements and structures of domination in late modernity is unsurprisingly complex. Following Habermas' distinction between offensive and defensive movements and Giddens' distinction between emancipatory movements and those mobilised around life-politics projects with their clear commitments to narcissistic self-actualisation and trajectories of privatism, it is clearly necessary to recognise that by no means all movements exemplify struggles for empowerment in the conception of power to in pursuit of generalisable interests adopted here. The growing emphasis in Habermas' work upon the centrality of procedural forms as critical bulwarks for both the interactive forms of communicative and instrumental rationality he deems necessary for a modern social order – whether local, regional, national, international or transnational – clearly stems from a concern about the particularistic, non-generalisable basis of many movements rooted in exclusivist versions of the good life. Such versions are articulated around such rigid versions of the Manichaean relationship between collective self and other as to leave no scope for argumentative democracy. From such a perspective, it is entirely reasonable to view the potential relationship between social movements and structures of domination as one of positive correlation, if not causation, as the history of the last century indisputably demonstrates.

Such a consideration is reinforced if one considers the relationship between movements and predominant forms of domination from the other end of the telescope, so to speak. Contemporary social movements are inescapably, in some ways irreducibly, although not exclusively constructed. What makes the link between modernity and movements an integral one is the fact that such construction has always been and continues to be mediatic. Movements as symbol artefacts are in important senses constructed in and by the media, within whatever given historical parameters those media are. Movement struggles are in significant part struggles around the construction of public spaces with respect to both their integrity and their content. This reality is what underpins the growing efforts of hegemonic states to systematically orchestrate media coverage of the militarisation of political processes, as the discussion of Trey's analysis of the Gulf War in Chapter 5 illustrates.[33] Of course, such considerations have equal analytic application to significant dimensions of movement reproduction. In a number of important ways framing is a matter of the creation and reinforcement of identity through the manipulation of images. (Leni Riefenstahl knew that – as did Picasso.)

Although valid, these inevitably schematic considerations about the generally ambiguous relationship between social movements in general and their relationship to the reproduction of domination substantially underestimate the significance of social movements as sites of struggle and empowerment. This significance can be approached in relation to both questions of substance and questions of form, although, as we shall see, it has been perhaps the major contribution of both the theory and the practice of emancipatory movements to interrogate the content of this distinction as it has been institutionalised, indeed naturalised, in dominant forms of modernity.

In terms of substance, it is beyond dispute that social movements have fundamentally transformed the public sphere with respect to the creation of new arenas of public policy making. As della Porta et al. note: 'These new loci of decision making vary in terms of their openness, duration and extent of power' (1999: 239). What they share in common and contribute to the contestation of existing forms of technocratic domination are forms of legitimation rooted in new generations of power and heightened degrees of visibility.[34] While the public commissions of enquiry that della Porta and her colleagues cite as the principal example of such innovations have to be carefully assessed in terms of their specific outcomes, their contribution to the creation and reproduction of open public spaces based on forms of generative power and concerted action should not be underestimated (cf. Forester 1985). Beyond these individual instances of social movement contestation, new social movements have involved a plurality of diverse challenges to the scope and direction of state policy. Thus, state ministries and local government agencies have found it necessary to establish an enormous diversity of consultative institutions on an equally large range of issues. Inevitably such initiatives may represent strategic actions in multi-faceted struggles of domination and exclusion in which institutionalisation and cooptation are as frequent outcomes as transformation. Nevertheless, such struggles have served to greatly widen the scope of multiple public spheres, not least with respect to the de-territorialisation of political communities, which is clearly the central potential of empowerment in late modernity.

Social movements as the primary forms of extra-institutional power mobilisation have acted as major countervailing forces against agendas institutionalised around the mobilisation of bias. Social movement mobilisation, for example, is the single largest explanatory factor for the politicisation of issues such as divorce, abortion and environmental degradation. Of course, the fact of such issues becoming politicised merely serves to denaturalise existing forms of social organisation, identify potential areas of social struggle and thereby create potential agendas of communicative democracy, agendas which, in the absence of teleological perspectives of a formulaic historicity, must be literally communicative and therefore tentative and potentially transient. Any and all dominant orders are mobilised around particular articulations of regionalised domination – the bases of which are extensive but historically have focused on class, gender, race and religion – the reproduction of which is dependent upon the defence of certain logically formulable but sociologically problematic limits (Melucci 1996a). Particular regimes of domination have become increasingly sensitive to and proactive in relation to these limits. The marketisation of institutional political processes has led to a focus-group strategy of political determination in which it is not individual products but *the validity of the overall system of need-determination and allocation* that is crucially being legitimised and practically reproduced. Where such general marketisation ('business as usual') clearly fails, there is more and more resort to a scientisation of politics. This in turn, however, serves to delegitimise existing channels of need-determination and problem resolution with a consequent potential for the repoliticisation and re-ethicalisation of the dilemmas raised by a technological innovation fuelled by capital competiveness – as in the case of genetic engineering whether with respect to food technology or human biological constructivism.

Within the concerns of the present discussion, social movements are most usefully thought of within the processual problematics of the political: processual because, as will hopefully have been clear from the foregoing, discussions of social movements once again highlight the complex relationships between deep structural antagonisms and the complexities of collective action, whether in terms of super- or subordination. Here, structure specifies social opportunity ranges and problematises the possibilities for various kinds of collective action. But also, problematics of the political because of the necessity of recognising that the political refers to fundamentally generative forms of concerted action, whereas politics refers to ongoing strategic interactions, asymmetrically defined in terms of differential access to resources whether material or symbolic (Wolin 1996). Thus, singular or sustained engagements between institutional orders and oppositional movements inevitably create dual possibilities: either for instrumental cooptation and domination or for novel redefinitions of legitimate and sustainable relationships between current understandings of universal justice and agendised versions of the good life.[35]

Such considerations, important although they are to a nuanced and analytically sensitive assessment of social movements as sites of empowerment, should not obscure the central contribution of social movements in general and emancipatory movements in particular to a praxis of empowerment: the creation of a new conception of democracy. As one analyst of the anti-roads movement in the United Kingdom notes: the 'impact of [new social movements] in the advanced democracies has been immense in that it both signified and contributed to the wider societal development of new "participatory" ideologies, non-institutionalised modes of political action and the politicising of cultural, environment and moral issues that were hitherto generally considered apolitical' (McNeish 1999: 72). As the number, salience and success of social movements proliferated through the closing decades of the twentieth century, it was widely recognised that cumulatively they represented a 'challenge to the political order', central to which was not merely a contestation but an outright rejection of bureaucratic parties and state administrations (Dalton and Kuechler 1990; Offe 1985). The critique of the scientisation of electoral politics and of the substitution of technocratic rationality for participatory will formation was a central and common element in the value structure of emancipatory movements.

As Kitschelt argues:

> The stakes and the struggles of the left and libertarian social movements ... invoke an ancient element of democratic theory that calls for an organisation of collective decision making referred to in varying ways as classical, populist, communitarian, strong, grass-roots or direct democracy against a democratic practice in contemporary democracies labelled as realist, liberal, elite, republican or representative democracy. (1993: 15)

In this perspective, social movements must be positively assessed as sites of political empowerment, as diverse projects of concerted action, the complex dynamics of which must be analysed not merely with respect to the empirical tension between efficacy and participation but equally within the framework of strategies and resources of domination, including media manipulation and Mann's emphasised organisational outflanking.[36] Late modernity is increasingly characterised by a replacement of bureaucratic party systems with a mediatic populism based upon a seamless fusion of money and technology. Thus, in an accurate comparison, Rohrschneider (1993) argues that, if mass political parties were the contagion from the left and a demobilised democracy via mass media the contagion from the right, it is necessary to contextualise social movements as a contagion from below.

If therefore a genuinely reflexive modernity is dependent not merely upon a wide range of public spaces, where the pluralism inherent in modern societies may be optimally represented through communication and conflict, but also upon the exercise of agency and decision-making capacity, then it seems indisputable that social movements can significantly contribute – at a range of levels from the local to the transnational – to the generation and reproduction of empowerment.

Notes

1. For a perceptive and illuminating analysis relating these constitutional crises to the development of what he terms the Economic Polity and its blurring of the boundaries between public and private spheres, see Wolin 1989. See also Chapter 3 above.

2. Both the theoretical and the empirical analysis of social movements, largely inspired by the emergence of American, European and East European 'new' movements in the decades after the Second World War, have become a virtually autonomous area of academic enquiry, raising many issues with which the present chapter is not intended to engage. For comprehensive and illuminating surveys, see della Porta and Diani 1999; Giugni et al. 1998.

3. The emphasis upon 'some' new movements here is an important one. As will become clear, it would certainly be inaccurate and impossible to regard all new social movements as having even the potential for social transformation in that they might arguably be said to be projects embodying generalisable interests. Traditional and fundamentalist movements therefore must be viewed as authoritarian projects of closure articulated around various categories of 'otherness'. This is not meant to imply that there exists a coherent model of the relationship between justice and the good life but rather to underline the necessity of recognising the need in a pluralist world of viewing any and all projects as both discursively constituted and potentially open to interrogation.

4. Cf. Habermas 1989a.

5. Eder's argument is historically inaccurate and consequently conceptually deficient here to the extent that it fails to engage with the significance of the particularism of an objectively subordinate working class movement.

6. Unfortunately, Eder does not consider the extent to which this process of reflexive constitution is an exclusive indicator of modern normativity or one process to be compared with the constitution of the societal through the specification of national-state boundaries or the constitution of asymmetrical structural antagonisms in terms of the differential location of capital and wage labour.

7. Here, Eder appears to fall into the trap that Trey (1998) identifies in the work of Habermas: the confinement of normativity to the sphere of communicative intersubjectivity.

8. Cf. the similar argument produced by George Trey concerning the possibility that discursive normativity merely acts as a cloak for the systemic norms that really certify modern activities. Trey 1998: 91.

9. See, in particular, Eyerman and Jamison 1991.

10. As Eder notes, research at the second meso-level is characteristic of a predominantly American approach to the analysis of social movements, that of resource mobilisation theory. See, for example, the work of Zald and McCarthy 1979, 1987.

11. It is interesting to contrast this conceptualisation of the formation of groups with that proposed by Iris Young, discussed in Chapter 6 above. Whereas Young stresses a distinction between groups on the one hand and aggregates and associations on the other and specifically relates the emergence of groups to a shared experience of oppression (that is, arguably

relates group and difference), Eder valorises the constitution of groups through collective or concerted action. Clearly, in general terms both aspects are important; equally clearly, whereas Young wishes to address directly the normative aspect of power relations (how group difference may be recognised and procedurally incorporated so as to maximise empowerment), Eder focuses upon the analysis of social movement mobilisation and locates the self-constitution of groups within that framework.

12. Eder notes the empirical intermingling of strategic and communicative elements in such collective learning processes. However, like Habermas, he offers an overly rationalistic account of these developmental possibilities, excluding any consideration of the integral affectual dimension of social interaction and of both the creative and destructive role of unconscious processes in the constitution of the social. Eder's emphasis on the critical role of interpretation in processes of collective action has become central to the conceptualisation and theorisation of social movements in the form of discussions of framing. See, for example, della Porta and Diani 1999: ch. 3; Donati 1992.

13. This suggests an important qualification to the position set out by Iris Young regarding group mobilisation in relation to structures and processes of exclusion. Obviously, this may occur but Eder's argument points to a second possibility: may it not be that in some instances an awareness of various forms of power over only arises as a result of projects of power to; that is, only by engaging in collective action (as in the case of MADD, for example – Spinosa et al. 1997) do the participants develop an awareness of macro-structures of inequality and consequently enter into the second and third phases specified by Eder for the emergence of a collective actor from collective action?

14. Michels' so-called 'iron law of oligarchy' remains the classic statement of these possibilities. See Michels 1959.

15. For the classic statement of the different logics of collective action, see Offe and Wiesenthal 1980.

16. For a distinction between emancipatory and life-politics movements, see Giddens 1991a.

17. However, the specification of this relationship between structural location and propositions regarding the dynamics of class action has always been problematic. See, for example, Lockwood 1981.

18. Another leading analyst of social movements in the context of contemporary social change, Alberto Melucci, having begun from a similar position, has now concluded that the conceptual baggage of the concept of class is too great to allow for an effective reconstruction. Melucci does, however, still wish to retain an important structural component in his own theoretical framework for the analysis of social movements. See Melucci 1996a.

19. In addition to Habermas' discussion in *TCA*, see the work of Touraine (in particular 1992) who has consistently articulated an actionist/movement perspective on social processes over several decades.

20. These theoretical possibilities concerning mobilisation struggles are explored in Chapter 2 above. See also the discussion of the importance of 'framing' below.

21. See Chapter 2 above.

22. Both the accuracy and consequently the utility of what virtually amounts to a categorical distinction in Habermas' discussion of social movements have been questioned. Thus, many of the so-called 'new' social movements can be argued to have a much longer history than such labelling would imply, while the possibility of meaningfully separating expressive and instrumental goals is also called into question. See, for example, Ray 1993: ch. 4.

23. Habermas (1989a) also speaks of 'offensive' as opposed to 'defensive' movements. In *TCA*, he distinguishes the anti-nuclear and environmental movement, single-issue and local movements, the alternative commune movement, the minorities movement, the psychoscene, religious fundamentalism, the tax-protest movement and the women's movement among others. Clearly both between and within these movements, there is enormous variation in the degree to which the relevant movement and movement organisations involve a commitment to power as concerted action in relation to both practices and critique.

24. Empirically, the Green movement, for example, encompasses both of these analytic possibilities.

25. Analytically, this was not only associated with the critique of valorising class cleavages in terms of social division and conflict but also with an increasingly generalised critique of growth and its implicated social priorities which rendered a dominant 'productivist' reading of Marxism more problematic. See, for example, Cohen 1982 and Gorz 1982.

26. On the local to national shift, see the outstanding body of research by Charles Tilly 1979, 1984, 1995. On the emergence of transnational movements, see Smith et al. 1994. See also, for example, Castells 1997: chs 2 and 3.

27. Dickenson emphasises the extent to which the social realisation of the Beijing Conference was critically dependent upon prior and subsequent communication via 'Women's Net', a global community of women activists and organisations using computer networks for information sharing, broadcast and collaboration with the aim of increasing women's rights. 1997: 109. IT has been central to the rise of transnational social movements.

28. One should not exaggerate the importance of such developments, however. While it is certainly a major purpose of the present work to support the proposition that communicative democracy is a coherent and transformative process of empowerment, it is equally emphasised that the contestation of structures of domination, upon whatever basis and at whatever level, necessarily involves a process of struggle.

29. Once again, Buechler notes the way in which these developments are characterised by the tensions between universalism and particularism identified herein as central to late modernity. Thus, '[on] the opportunity side, transnational … movements may appeal to multiple governments as well as nongovernmental organisations to exert pressure on a particular nation or group of nations. On the constraint side, cultural differences and political fragmentation can pose severe obstacles to cross-national coordination of social movement efforts' (2000: 77).

30. The 1989 revolutions in Eastern Europe are the most resonant contemporary examples of such a possibility. Once again, however, we must bear in mind the need to contextualise these processes in relation to one or

more systemic crises, struggles over competing projects of modernity – in particular, marketisation versus self-government.

31. By integral, I wish to convey here an analysis which considered 'movements' in terms of their rational political and/or cultural relationship to the dominant institutional order rather than in terms of deviant status within a proposed unproblematic order.

32. For the early pioneering work in the resource mobilisation tradition linking movements and states see Tilly 1978 and McAdam 1982. This work has been subsequently elaborated in terms of states as political opportunity structures generating typologies of both types and levels of state structures leading to different kinds of social movement and also to a significant body of illuminating and suggestive comparative research. On political opportunity structures, see McAdam et al. 1996 and Tarrow 1996. For comparative studies, see Kriesi et al. 1995 and Rucht 1996.

33. Similar processes have been identified in relation to the NATO intervention in Kosovo and the Russian assault upon Chechnya.

34. The continuing saga represented by the processes involving and following the racist murder of the young black British teenager, Stephen Lawrence, including the consequent politicisation of endemic institutional racism, is a prominent but not isolated example.

35. For a classic discussion of the dilemmas and probabilities of cooptation, albeit within a framework of contestation and not transformation, see Piven and Cloward 1977. On the limitations of public enquiries and processes of symbolic manipulation through a translation of political issues from political choice to administrative decisionism, see Forester 1985.

36. For a systematic analysis of both the internal dynamics and the strategies of containment and repression in the case of one social movement committed to a non-hierarchical politics of concerted action, the Greenham Common Women's Peace Camp, see Roseneil 1995.

Conclusion

The present work had two main purposes. The first of these was to propose the necessity for conceptually, analytically and politically distinguishing between structures and processes of domination on the one hand and structures and processes of power on the other. Dominant usage within political and social theory effectively treats the two terms as synonyms to be interchangeably used within a privileged understanding of power relations as relations of strategic interaction. Even where a distinction is made, as with Mann's differentiation between distributive and collective power, or where 'empowerment' rather than subordination is placed at the centre of power analysis, as with Foucault's 'positive' conception of power, there is an effective subversion of the distinction.

This dominant discourse can be recognised as involving more than a loss of analytic potential. In a very real sense, language is power (however, the unqualified converse is not true): the chronic articulation of certain dimensions of human experience to the virtual exclusion of others *can and does* make it difficult to think and act in ways which are dissonant with dominant forms. The general argument presented here suggests that the ubiquitous nature of power as strategic interaction should be regarded to be as mythical as globalisation. Nowhere is this 'mythologising' more evident than in the diffusion of postmodernist modes of thought and analysis. In so far, for example, as a Foucauldian emphasis upon the 'how' (as against the 'who' or the 'what') of power processes leads to recognition and investigation of those processes whereby diverse realities of inclusion and exclusion are implicated, indeed constituted, in discursive practices, there is certainly a potential advance in analytic potential. Otherwise 'naturalised' forms of mechanical essentialism and unproblematic and therefore dominating universalism may become accessible to critique and reassessment, as the discussion in Chapter 7 makes clear. However, to the very real extent that a such a development is implicated in a broader perspective which both proposes the redundancy of questions concerned with who and what and precludes their analysis, it becomes critically important to recognise the necessary political implications in the exclusion of definitive modern questions regarding justice and freedom.

The dominant discourse can be contested. A coherent and distinctive conceptualisation of social power can be explicated in the following terms: social power can be identified as an irreducibly relational and intersubjective phenomenon of concerted action. The analysis of power processes therefore concerns the genesis and maintenance of social processes expressive of such action. Consequently, in the explication of power relations, analytic priority must be given to processes as against outcomes, whereas in the explication of domination, priority is necessarily given to outcomes.

We can find the necessary alternative lexicon of power analysis in the work of Hannah Arendt and its subsequent Habermasian appropriation. However, both suffer from a critical limitation: the proposal that it is necessary – and, in Habermas' case, possible – to preserve authentic relations of power from contamination by other dimensions of social reality. Addressing this limitation requires that we recognise that, while accepting the ontological and analytical distinctiveness of power and domination, power relations are located in the context of broader and more obdurate relations of domination understood in terms of obstacles to corrigible realisations of justice in a world of plurality. In particular, the argument presented here suggests the possibility of relating power and domination through the identification of transformative struggles of control and recognition.

These considerations lead on to the second purpose of the book: the assessment of the possibilities for a transformative politics in late modern societies. While fully recognising the range of empirical changes subsumed under the heading 'postmodernisation', the argument rejects the proposition that such changes render redundant the political concerns definitive of a modernist agenda of political transformations in pursuance of autonomy and self-government. The book addresses these possibilities in two ways: first contextually, by means of a discussion of capitalism and states as major sites of social domination in modernity, addressing in particular their characteristics and tendential properties in late modernity. Tendentially, that is, in the absence of countervailing and regulatory constraints, capitalism has been and remains a system of domination and social destruction. As such, it is inherently expressive of structural antagonism(s), the realisations of which are complex, contingent and historically variable. In late modernity, the dynamics of capitalism are identified as those of post-Fordist restructuring and the virtual autonomy of finance capital. To the very real extent that for the foreseeable future capitalism will remain a dominant form of modernity, any transformative politics will of necessity continue to address issues of struggle and control within this context.

States and the state system have been equally central to modernity. In the context of the analysis of domination and power, this centrality has manifested itself internally in the form of dual tendential but conflictual possibilities: on the one hand, the interpenetration of state and economy produced what Habermas characterises as the statisation of the economy and the refeudalisation of the state. In the resultant circuit of power, democratic issues of participation and accountability are effectively marginalised and states can be viewed predominantly as sites of political domination. On the other hand, in so far as the welfare state social form has been identified with the potential for creating more inclusive political communities, states are viewed as arenas of critical struggle in terms of domination and empowerment. Assessing states in this context requires the identification of competing theorisations of the underlying rationale and periodisation of Welfare Statism. Analysis of Offe's evolving engagement with the issue identifies political struggle as the key factor determining the widespread stasis in the development and democratisation of welfare states. Wolin also locates Welfare Statism in the context of political struggles, but argues that its political rationale must be understood as that of domination and not empowerment.

States as central pillars of modernity therefore remain at the centre of power analysis. In late modernity, however, not only have their characteristics as the exclusive form of political order been increasingly subject to normative and comparative critique, but major changes in the determinate and determining contexts of politics have produced an ever growing body of analysis and advocacy exploring the transcendence of states in modernity.

With the end of the twentieth century, a number of factors provided the general context for the second perspective adopted here for assessing possibilities for transformative politics. The apparent stasis of Welfare Statism as the vehicle for social democratic transformation, widespread recognition of the destructive social consequences of the neo-liberal project in terms of social integration (both domestically and internationally), the apparent naturalising of capitalism as the 'only game in town' with the collapse of the Soviet Union – all in combination led to a disillusionment with and scepticism about the transformative possibilities of institutional politics. These developments served to accelerate an already well established shift in the nature of political projects, a shift, in Fraser's useful distinction, from the 'politics of distribution' to the 'politics of difference'.

In combination, this configuration has seen a growing concern with new possibilities for transformative politics. Part II analysed three such possibilities: the public sphere, citizenship and social movements. The transformative possibilities of each, which of course do not exhaust their analytic or political significance, were shown to lie in their character as sites of struggle and empowerment, expressed in the constitution through power of immanent political communities.

As we move into a new century, any brave new world order seems highly problematic. The risks are multiple and obvious: predatory globalised capitalism, militarism, both strategic and chaotic, a shared transnationalism of environmental disaster creating more inclusive communities of fate, exclusionary fundamentalisms of class, gender, race and religion. Equally, however, each of these threats is implicated in contestatory and transformative struggles seeking empowerment through concerted action.

References

Abercrombie, N., Hill, S., and Turner, B.S. (1980) *The Dominant Ideology Thesis*. London: Allen and Unwin.

Adler, P.S. (1992) *Technology and the Future of Work*. New York: Oxford University Press.

Agger, B. (1991) *A Critical Theory of Public Life: Knowledge, Discourse and Politics in an Age of Decline*. London: The Falmer Press.

Aglietta, M. (1979) *A Theory of Capitalist Regulation: the US Experience*. London: NLB.

Albrow, M. (1996) *The Global Age*. Cambridge: Polity Press.

Alexander, J. and Lara, M.P. (1996) Honneth's New Critical Theory of Recognition. *New Left Review*, 220, 126–36.

Anderson, B. (1991) *Imagined Communities: Reflections on the Origin and Spread of Nationalism*. London: Verso.

Anderson, P. (1974) *Lineages of the Absolutist State*. London: NLB.

Anderson, P. (1980) *Arguments within English Marxism*. London: Verso.

Andrews, G. (1991) *Citizenship*. London: Lawrence and Wishart.

Appelbaum, E. (1984) *Technology and the Redesign of Work in the Insurance Industry*. Stanford, CA: Stanford University Institute of Research on Educational Finance and Governance.

Archibugi, D., Held, D., and Kohler, M. (1998) *Re-imagining Political Community: Studies in Cosmopolitan Democracy*. Cambridge: Polity Press.

Arendt, H. (1963) *On Revolution*. Harmondsworth: Penguin.

Arendt, H. (1972) *Crises of the Republic*. London: Harcourt Brace Jovanovich.

Arendt, H. (1989) *The Human Condition*. London: University of Chicago Press.

Arendt, H. (1995) *Men in Dark Times*. London: Harcourt Brace.

Armstrong, P., Glyn, A., and Harrison, J. (1984) *Capitalism since World War II: the Making and Breakup of the Great Boom*. London: Fontana Paperbacks.

Arrighi, G. (1994) *The Long Twentieth Century: Money, Power and the Origins of our Times*. London: Verso.

Ashenden, S. and Owen, D. (1999) *Foucault contra Habermas*. London: Sage.

Askonas, P. and Stewart, A. (eds) (2000) *Social Inclusion: Possibilities and Tensions*. Basingstoke: Macmillan.

Bachrach, P. and Baratz, M.S. (1962) The Two Faces of Power. *American Political Science Review*, 56, 947–52.

Bader, V.M. (1995) Citizenship and Exclusion: Radical Democracy, Community, and Justice, or, What is Wrong with Communitarianism? *Political Theory*, 23, 211–46.

Bader, V.M. (1997) *Citizenship and Exclusion.* Basingstoke: Macmillan.

Bagguley, P. and Hearn, J. (eds) (1999) *Transforming Politics: Power and Resistance.* Basingstoke: Macmillan.

Ball, T. (ed.) (1987) *Idioms of Inquiry: Critique and Renewal in Political Science.* Albany, NY: SUNY Press.

Ball, T. (1988) *Transforming Political Discourse: Political Theory and Critical Conceptual History.* Oxford: Blackwell.

Barbalet, J.M. (1987) Power, Structural Resources and Agency. *Perspectives in Social Theory*, 8, 1–24.

Barbalet, J.M. (1988) *Citizenship: Rights, Struggle and Class Inequality.* Minneapolis: University of Minnesota Press.

Barber, B.R. (1996) *Jihad vs. McWorld: How Globalism and Tribalism are Reshaping the World.* New York: Ballantine Books.

Barber, B.R. (1998) *A Place for Us: How to Make Society Civil and Democracy Strong.* New York: Hill and Wang.

Barnet, R.J. and Cavanagh, J. (1994) *Global Dreams: Imperial Corporations and the New World Order.* New York: Simon and Schuster.

Barry, A., Osborne, T., and Rose, N. (1996) *Foucault and Political Reason.* London: UCL Press.

Baubock, R. (1994) *Transnational Citizenship.* Aldershot: Edward Elgar.

Bauman, Z. (1998) *Globalization: The Human Consequences.* Cambridge: Polity Press.

Beck, U. (1992) *Risk Society: Towards a New Modernity.* London: Sage.

Beck, U. (1994) The Reinvention of Politics: towards a Theory of Reflexive Modernization. In U. Beck, A. Giddens, and S. Lash (eds), *Reflexive Modernization: Politics, Tradition and Aesthetics in the Modern Social Order* (pp. 1–55). Cambridge: Polity Press.

Beck, U. (1997) *The Reinvention of Politics: Rethinking Modernity in the Global Social Order.* Cambridge: Polity Press.

Beck, U. (1999) *World Risk Society.* Cambridge: Polity Press.

Beiner, R. (1995) *Theorising Citizenship.* Albany, NY: SUNY Press.

Bendix, R. (1964) *Nation-Building and Citizenship.* London: John Wiley and Sons.

Benhabib, S. (1986) *Critique, Norm, and Utopia: A Study of the Foundations of Critical Theory.* New York: Columbia University Press.

Benhabib, S. (1992) *Situating the Self: Gender, Community and Post-Modernism in Contemporary Ethics.* London: Routledge.

Benhabib, S. (1996a) *Democracy and Difference: Contesting the Boundaries of the Political.* Princeton: Princeton University Press.

Benhabib, S. (1996b) *The Reluctant Modernism of Hannah Arendt.* London: Sage.

Benton, T. (1981) 'Objective' Interests and the Sociology of Power. *Sociology*, 15, 161–84.

Berg, M. (1991) On the Origins of Capitalist Hierarchy. In B. Gustafsson (ed.), *Power and Economic Institutions: Reinterpretations in Economic History.* Aldershot: Edward Elgar.

Berger, J. (1991) The Linguistification of the Sacred and the Delinguistification of the Economy. In A. Honneth and H. Joas (eds), *Communicative Action.* Cambridge: Polity Press.

Berman, M. (1998) Why Modernism Still Matters. In S. Lash and J. Friedman (eds), *Modernity and Identity*. Oxford: Blackwell.

Bernstein, R.J. (1991) *The New Constellation: the Ethical-Political Horizons of Modernity/Postmodernity*. Cambridge: Polity Press.

Blaug, R. (1999) *Democracy, Real and Ideal: Discourse Ethics and Radical Politics*. Albany, NY: State University of New York.

Bohman, J. and Rehg, W. (1997) *Deliberative Democracy: Essays on Reason and Politics*. Cambridge, MA: MIT Press.

Bottomore, T. (1992) Citizenship and Social Class, 40 Years On. In T.H. Marshall and T. Bottomore (eds), *Citizenship and Social Class*. London: Pluto Press.

Bourdieu, P. (1998) *Acts of Resistance: Against the New Myths of Our Time*. Cambridge: Polity Press.

Brand, A. (1990) *The Force of Reason: an Introduction to Habermas' Theory of Communicative Action*. London: Allen and Unwin.

Braudel, F. (1981–84) *Civilization and Capitalism*. London: Collins.

Braverman, H. (1974) *Labor and Monopoly Capital: the Degradation of Work in the Twentieth Century*. New York: Monthly Review Press.

Brubaker, W.R. (1989) *Immigration and the Politics of Citizenship in Europe and North America*. London: University Press of America.

Brubaker, W.R. (1992) *Citizenship and Nationhood in France and Germany*. Cambridge: Cambridge University Press.

Buechler, S.M. (2000) *Social Movements in Advanced Capitalism: The Political Economy and Cultural Construction of Social Activism*. Oxford: Oxford University Press.

Bull, H. (1977) *The Anarchical Society: A Study of Order in World Politics*. London: Macmillan.

Bulmer, M. and Rees, A.M. (1996) *Citizenship Today*. London: UCL Press.

Burawoy, M. (1978) Toward a Marxist Theory of the Labor Process: Braverman and Beyond. *Politics and Society*, 8, 247–312.

Burchell, G., Gordon, C., and Miller, P. (1991) *The Foucault Effect: Studies in Governmentality*. Chicago: University of Chicago Press.

Burnheim, J. (1985) *Is Democracy Possible?* Cambridge: Cambridge University Press.

Burnheim, J. (1986) Democracy, Nation-States, and the World System. In D. Held and C. Pollitt (eds), *New Forms of Democracy*. London: Sage.

Burnheim, J. (1995) Power-Trading and the Environment. *Environmental Politics*, 4, 49–65.

Calhoun, C. (1992) *Habermas and the Public Sphere*. London: MIT Press.

Canovan, M. (1992) *Hannah Arendt: a Reinterpretation of her Political Thought*. Cambridge: Cambridge University Press.

Carnoy, M. (1993) Multinationals in a Changing World Economy: Whither the Nation-State? In M. Carnoy, M. Castells, S.S. Cohen, and F.H. Cardoso (eds), *The Global Economy in the Information Age* (pp. 45–96). University Park, PA: Pennsylvania State University Press.

Castells, M. (1993) The Informational Economy and the New International Division of Labor. In M. Carnoy, M. Castells, S.S. Cohen, and F.H. Cardoso (eds), *The New Global Economy in the Information Age: Reflections on our Changing World*. University Park, PA: Pennsylvania State University Press.

Castells, M. (1996) *The Information Age: Economy, Society and Culture: Vol. I The Rise of the Network Society.* Oxford: Blackwell.
Castells, M. (1997) *The Information Age: Economy, Society and Culture: Vol. II The Power of Identity.* Oxford: Blackwell.
Chase-Dunn, C.K. (1989) *Global Formation: Structure of the World-Economy.* Oxford: Blackwell.
Clarke, P.B. (1978) *Liberals and Social Democrats.* Cambridge: Cambridge University Press.
Clarke, P.B. (1995) *Citizenship.* London: Pluto Press.
Clastres, P. (1987) *Society against the State.* New York: Zone Books.
Clegg, S. (1989) *Frameworks of Power.* London: Sage.
Cohen, J.L. (1979) Why More Political Theory? *Telos*, 40, 70–94.
Cohen, J.L. (1982) *Class and Civil Society: The Limits of Marxian Critical Theory.* Amherst, MA: University of Massachusetts Press.
Cohen, J. (1985) Strategy or Identity: New Theoretical Paradigms and Contemporary Social Movements. *Social Research*, 52, 663–716.
Cohen, J.L. and Arato, A. (1992) *Civil Society and Political Theory.* London: MIT Press.
Collini, S. (1979) *Liberalism and Sociology.* Cambridge: Cambridge University Press.
Connolly, W.E. (1984) Taylor, Foucault and Otherness. *Political Theory*, 65–76.
Connolly, W.E. (1991) *Identity/Difference: Democratic Negotiations of Political Paradox.* London: Cornell University Press.
Crick, B. (1992) *In Defence of Politics.* London: Penguin.
Crook, S. (1991) *Modernist Radicalism and its Aftermath: Foundationalism and Anti-Foundationalism in Radical Social Theory.* London: Routledge.
Crook, S., Pakulski, J., and Waters, M. (1992) *Postmodernisation: Change in Advanced Society.* London: Sage.
Crouch, C. and Pizzorno, A. (1978) *The Resurgence of Class Conflict in Western Europe since 1968.* London (Vol. I); New York (Vol. II): Macmillan (Vol. I); Holmes and Meier.
Curtis, B. (1995) Taking the State back out: Rose and Miller on Political Power. *British Journal of Sociology*, 46, 575–89.
Dahl, R.A. (1984) *Modern Political Analysis.* Englewood Cliffs, NJ: Prentice-Hall.
Dahl, R.A. (1989) *Democracy and its Critics.* London: Yale University Press.
Dahrendorf, R. (1988) *Modern Social Conflict.* London: Weidenfeld and Nicholson.
Dallmayr, F. (1985) *Praxis and Polis.* Boston, MA: MIT Press.
Dalton, R.J. and Kuechler, M. (1990) *Challenging the Political Order: New Social and Political Movements in Western Democracies.* Cambridge: Polity Press.
Davis, K., Leijenao, M., and Oldersma, J. (1991) *The Gender of Power.* London: Sage.
Davis, M. (1990) *City of Quartz: Excavating the Future in Los Angeles.* London: Verso.
Dean, M. (1999) *Governmentality: Power and Rule in Modern Society.* London: Sage.

della Porta, D. and Diani, M. (1999) *Social Movements: An Introduction*. Oxford: Blackwell.

della Porta, D., Kriesi, H., and Rucht, D. (1999) *Social Movements in a Globalizing World*. Basingstoke: Macmillan.

D'Entreves, M.P. (1994) *The Political Philosophy of Hannah Arendt*. London: Routledge.

Dews, P. (1984) Power and Subjectivity in Foucault. *New Left Review*, 144, 72–95.

Dews, P. (1999) *Habermas: a Critical Reader*. Oxford: Blackwell.

Dickenson, D. (1997) Counting Women in: Globalization, Democratization and the Women's Movement. In A. McGrew (ed.), *The Transformation of Democracy? Globalization and Territorial Democracy* (pp. 97–120). Cambridge: Polity Press.

Dietz, M. (1991) Hannah Arendt and Feminist Politics. In M.L. Shanley and C. Pateman (eds), *Feminist Interpretations and Political Theory*. Cambridge: Polity Press.

Disch, L.J. (1994) *Hannah Arendt and the Limits of Philosophy*. London: Cornell University Press.

Donati, P.R. (1992) Political Discourse Analysis. In M. Diani and R. Eyerman (eds), *Studying Collective Action* (pp. 136–67). London: Sage.

Donzelot, J. (1979) *The Policing of Families: Welfare versus the State*. London: Hutchinson.

Dreyfus, H. and Rabinow, P. (1982) *Michel Foucault: Beyond Structuralism and Hermeneutics*. Brighton: Harvester Press.

Dryzek, J.S. (1990) *Discursive Democracy: Politics, Policy and Science*. Cambridge: Cambridge University Press.

Dryzek, J.S. (1995) Political and Ecological Communication. *Environmental Politics*, 4, 13–30.

Eder, K. (1993) *The New Politics of Class: Social Movements and Cultural Dynamics in Advanced Societies*. London: Sage.

Edwall, T.B. (1992) *Chain Reaction: The Impact of Race, Rights, and Taxes on American Politics*. London: W.W. Norton.

Edwards, P.K. (1986) *Conflict at Work: a Materialist Analysis of Workplace Relations*. Oxford: Blackwell.

Edwards, R. (1979) *Contested Terrain: the Transformation of the Workplace in the Twentieth Century*. New York: Basic Books.

Elliott, L. and Atkinson, D. (1998) *The Age of Insecurity*. London: Verso.

Eyerman, R. and Jamison, A. (1991) *Social Movements: A Cognitive Approach*. Cambridge: Polity Press.

Falk, R. (1999) *Predatory Globalization: a Critique*. Cambridge: Polity Press.

Fay, B. (1996) *Contemporary Philosophy of Social Science*. Oxford: Blackwell.

Flyvbjerg, B. (1998) *Rationality and Power: Democracy in Practice*. Chicago: University of Chicago Press.

Forester, J. (1985) *Critical Theory and Public Life*. Cambridge, MA: MIT Press.

Foucault, M. (1977) *Discipline and Punish*. London: Allen Lane.

Foucault, M. (1979) Governmentality. *Ideology and Consciousness*, 6, 5–21.

Foucault, M. (1980) *Power/Knowledge*. Brighton: Harvester Press.

Foucault, M. (1982) The Subject and Power. In H. Dreyfus and P. Rabinow (eds), *Michel Foucault: Beyond Structuralism and Hermeneutics*. Brighton: Harvester.

Frankenberg, G. (1992) Disorder is Possible: An Essay on Systems, Laws, and Disobedience. In A. Honneth, T. McCarthy, C. Offe, and A. Wellmer (eds), *Cultural-Political Interventions in the Unfinished Project of Enlightenment*. Cambridge, MA: MIT Press.

Fraser, N. (1986) Towards a Discourse Ethic of Solidarity. *Praxis International*, 5, 425–9.

Fraser, N. (1989a) *Unruly Practices*. Cambridge: Polity Press.

Fraser, N. (1989b) What's Critical about Critical Theory: The Case of Habermas and Gender. In N. Fraser (ed.), *Unruly Practices*. Cambridge: Polity Press.

Fraser, N. (1992) Rethinking the Public Sphere: a Contribution to the Critique of Actually Existing Democracy. In C. Calhoun (ed.), *Habermas and the Public Sphere*. London: MIT Press.

Fraser, N. (1997) *Justice Interruptus: Critical Reflections on the 'Postsocialist' Condition*. London: Routledge.

Fraser, N. and Gordon, L. (1994) Civil Citizenship against Social Citizenship. In B. van Steenbergen (ed.), *The Condition of Citizenship* (pp. 90–107). London: Sage.

Fraser, N. and Nicholson, L.J. (1989) Social Criticism without Philosophy: An Encounter between Feminism and Postmodernism. In L.J. Nicholson (ed.), *Feminism/Postmodernism* (pp. 19–38). London: Routledge.

Geller, J. (1979–80) Forms of Capitalist Control over the Labour Process. *Monthly Review*, 31 (7), 39–46.

Gerth, H.H. and Mills, C.W. (1946) *From Max Weber: Essays in Sociology*. New York: Oxford University Press.

Gianni, M. (1998) Taking Multiculturalism Seriously: Political Claims for a Differentiated Citizenship. In K. Slawner and M. Denham (eds), *Citizenship after Liberalism* (pp. 33–55). New York: Peter Lang.

Giddens, A. (1976) *New Rules of Sociological Method*. London: Hutchinson.

Giddens, A. (1977) *Studies in Social and Political Theory*. London: Hutchinson.

Giddens, A. (1979) *Central Problems in Social Theory*. London: Macmillan.

Giddens, A. (1982a) Class Division, Class Conflict and Citizenship Rights. In A. Giddens (ed.), *Profiles and Critiques in Social Theory*. London: Macmillan.

Giddens, A. (1982b) Power, the Dialectic of Control and Class Structuration. In *Social Class and the Division of Labour*. Cambridge: Cambridge University Press.

Giddens, A. (1984) *The Constitution of Society*. Cambridge: Polity Press.

Giddens, A. (1985a) Reason without Revolution? Habermas' Theorie des kommunikativen Handelns. In R.J. Bernstein (ed.), *Habermas and Modernity* (pp. 95–121). Cambridge: Polity Press.

Giddens, A. (1985b) *The Nation-State and Violence*. Cambridge: Polity Press.

Giddens, A. (1991a) *Modernity and Self-Identity: Self and Society in the Late Modern Age*. Cambridge: Polity Press.

Giddens, A. (1991b) *The Consequences of Modernity*. Cambridge: Polity Press.
Giddens, A. and Mackenzie, G. (1982) *Social Class and the Division of Labour: Essays in Honour of Ilya Neustadt*. Cambridge: Cambridge University Press.
Giugni, M.G., McAdam, D., and Tilly, C. (1998) *From Contention to Democracy*. Oxford: Rowman and Littlefield.
Giugni, M., McAdam, D., and Tilly, C. (1999) *How Social Movements Matter*. Minneapolis: University of Minnesota Press.
Goldthorpe, J.H. (1984) *Order and Conflict in Contemporary Capitalism: Studies in the Political Economy of Western European Nations*. Oxford: Clarendon Press.
Gordon, D., Edwards, R., and Reich, M. (1982) *Segmented Work, Divided Workers: the Historical Transformation of Labor in the United States*. Cambridge: Cambridge University Press.
Gorz, A. (1982) *Farewell to the Working Class*. London: Pluto.
Greider, W. (1998) *One World Ready or Not: the Manic Logic of Global Capitalism*. London: Penguin.
Habermas, J. (1971) *Toward a Rational Society: Student Protest, Science and Politics*. London: Heinemann.
Habermas, J. (1973) *Theory and Practice*. Boston: Beacon Press.
Habermas, J. (1976) *Legitimation Crisis*. London: Heinemann Educational Books.
Habermas, J. (1977) Hannah Arendt's Communications Concept of Power. *Social Research*, 44, 3–23.
Habermas, J. (1978) *Knowledge and Human Interests*. London: Heinemann.
Habermas, J. (1983) Hannah Arendt: On the Concept of Political Power. *Philosophical-Political Profiles*. Cambridge, MA: MIT Press.
Habermas, J. (1984) *The Theory of Communicative Action* (Vol. 1). Boston: Beacon Press.
Habermas, J. (1989a) *The Structural Transformation of the Public Sphere: An Inquiry into a Category of Bourgeois Society*. Cambridge: Polity Press.
Habermas, J. (1989b) *The Theory of Communicative Action* (Vol. 2). Cambridge: Polity Press.
Habermas, J. (1990a) Some Questions regarding the Theory of Power: Foucault Again. In *The Philosophical Discourse of Modernity*. Cambridge: Polity Press.
Habermas, J. (1990b) *The Philosophical Discourse of Modernity*. Cambridge: Polity Press.
Habermas, J. (1994) Citizenship and National Identity. In B. van Steenbergen (ed.), *The Condition of Citizenship*. London: Sage.
Habermas, J. (1996) *Between Facts and Norms: Contributions to a Discourse Theory of Law and Democracy*. Cambridge: Polity Press.
Habermas, J. and Luhmann, N. (1971) *Theorie der Gesellschaft oder Sozialtechnologie*. Frankfurt/Main: Suhrkamp.
Hall, J.A. and Ikenberry, G.J. (1989) *The State*. Milton Keynes: Open University.
Hall, S. and Held, D. (1989) Citizens and Citizenship. In S. Hall and M. Jacques (eds), *New Times: The Changing Face of Politics in the 1990s*. London: Lawrence and Wishart.

Hall, S. and Jacques, M. (1989) *New Times: The Changing Face of Politics in the 1990s*. London: Lawrence and Wishart.

Halsey, A.H. (1986) *Change in British Society*. Oxford: Oxford University Press.

Hammar, T. (1990) *Democracy and the Nation-State: Aliens, Denizens and Citizens*. Aldershot: Gower.

Harvey, D. (1989) *The Condition of Postmodernity*. Oxford: Blackwell.

Hay, C. (1996) *Re-Stating Social and Political Change*. Buckingham: Open University Press.

Haynes, J. (1997) *Democracy and Civil Society in the Third World*. Cambridge: Polity Press.

Heater, D. (1990) *Citizenship: The Civic Ideal in World History, Politics and Education*. Cambridge: Cambridge University Press.

Held, D. (1991) *Political Theory Today*. Cambridge: Polity Press.

Held, D. (1995) *Democracy and the Global Order: from the Modern State to Cosmopolitan Governance*. Cambridge: Polity Press.

Held, D. (1996) *Models of Democracy*. Cambridge: Polity Press.

Hernes, H. (1987) *Welfare State and Woman Power*. Oslo: Norwegian University Press.

Hilton, R. (1978) *The Transition from Feudalism to Capitalism*. London: New Left Books.

Hinchman, L.P. and Hinchman, S.K. (1994) *Hannah Arendt: Critical Essays*. Albany, NY: SUNY Press.

Hindess, B. (1982) Power, Interests and the Outcomes of Struggles. *Sociology*, 16, 498–511.

Hindess, B. (1993) Citizenship in the Modern West. In B. Turner (ed.), *Citizenship and Social Theory*. London: Sage.

Hirschman, A.O. (1991) *The Rhetoric of Reaction*. Cambridge, MA: Harvard University Press.

Hirst, P. (1997) *From Statism to Pluralism: Democracy, Civil Society and Global Politics*. London: UCL Press.

Hirst, P. and Thompson, G. (1996) *Globalization in Question*. Cambridge: Polity Press.

Hoffman, J. (1995) *Beyond the State*. Cambridge: Polity Press.

Hollingsworth, J.R. and Boyer, R. (1997a) *Contemporary Capitalism: the Embeddedness of Institutions*. Cambridge: Cambridge University Press.

Hollingsworth, J.R. and Boyer, R. (1997b) Coordination of Economic Actors and Social Systems of Production. In J.R. Hollingsworth and R. Boyer (eds), *Contemporary Capitalism: The Embeddedness of Institutions*. Cambridge: Cambridge University Press.

Hollingsworth, J.R., Schmitter, P.C., and Streeck, W. (1994) *Governing Capitalist Economies*. New York: Oxford University Press.

Holton, R.J. (1985) *The Transition from Feudalism to Capitalism*. London: Macmillan Educational.

Holton, R.J. (1998) *Globalization and the Nation-State*. Basingstoke: Macmillan.

Holub, R.C. (1991) *Jürgen Habermas, Critic in the Public Sphere*. London: Routledge.

Honig, B. (1993) *Political Theory and the Displacement of Politics*. Ithaca, NY: Cornell University Press.

Honneth, A. (1993) *The Critique of Power*. Cambridge, MA: MIT Press.

Honneth, A. (1995) *The Fragmented World of the Social: Essays in Social and Political Philosophy*. Albany, NY: SUNY Press.

Honneth, A. (1996) *The Struggle for Recognition: The Moral Grammar of Social Conflicts*. Cambridge: Polity Press.

Horsman, M. and Marshall, A. (1994) *After the Nation-State: Citizens, Tribalism and the New World Disorder*. London: HarperCollins.

Howard, R. (1986) *Brave New Workplace*. Harmondsworth: Penguin Books.

Ingram, D. (1987) *Habermas and the Dialectic of Reason*. London: Yale University Press.

Isaac, J.C. (1998) *Democracy in Dark Times*. Ithaca, NY: Cornell University Press.

James, S. (1992) The Good-enough Citizen: Citizenship and Independence. In G. Bock and S. James (eds), *Beyond Equality and Difference*. London: Routledge.

Jameson, F. (1995) *Postmodernism, or, The Cultural Logic of Late Capitalism*. Durham, NC: Duke University Press.

Janowski, T. (1998) *Citizenship and Civil Society: A Framework of Rights and Obligations in Liberal, Traditional, and Social Democratic Regimes*. Cambridge: Cambridge University Press.

Jenkins, J.C. and Klandermans, B. (1995) *The Politics of Social Protest: Comparative Perspectives on States and Social Movements*. London: UCL.

Jessop, B. (1978) Corporatism and Liberal Democracy. In G. Littlejohn, B. Smart, J. Wakeford, and N. Yuval-Davis (eds), *Power and the State* (pp. 10–51). London: Croom Helm.

Jessop, B. (1990) *State Theory: Putting Capitalist States in their Place*. Cambridge: Polity Press.

Jessop, B. (1999) Narrating the Future of the National Economy and the National State: Remarks on Remapping Regulation and Reinventing Governance. In G. Steinmetz (ed.), *State/Culture: State-Formation after the Cultural Turn*. London: Cornell University Press.

Johansson, A. (1991) Taylorism and the Rise of Organised Labour: United States and Sweden. In B. Gustafsson (ed.), *Power and Economic Institutions: Reinterpretations in Economic History* (pp. 302–36). Aldershot: Edward Elgar.

Kapstein, E.B. (1996) *Governing the Global Economy: International Finance and the State*. Cambridge, MA: Harvard University Press.

Keane, J. (1988) *Civil Society and the State: New European Perspectives*. London: University of Westminster Press.

King, D.S. and Waldron, J. (1988) Citizenship, Social Citizenship and the Defense of Welfare Provision. *British Journal of Political Science*, 18, 415–43.

Kitschelt, H. (1993) New Social Movements, Political Parties, and Democratic Theory. *Annals of the AAPSS*, 528, 13–29.

Korten, D.C. (1995) *When Corporations Rule the World*. London: Earthscan Publications.

Koselleck, R. (1987) *Critique and Crisis: the Parthenogenesis of Modern Society*. Leamington Spa: Berg.

Kriesi, H., Koopmans, R., Dyvendak, J.W., and Giugni, M.G. (1995) *New Social Movements in Western Europe: a Comparative Analysis*. London: UCL Press.

Kuttner, R. (1997) *Everything for Sale: The Virtues and Limits of Markets*. New York: Alfred A. Knopf.

Kymlicka, W. (1989) *Liberalism, Community and Culture*. Oxford: Oxford University Press.

Kymlicka, W. (1991) Liberalism and the Politicization of Ethnicity. *Canadian Journal of Law and Jurisprudence*, 4, 239–56.

Kymlicka, W. (1995) *Multicultural Citizenship: A Liberal Theory of Minority Rights*. Oxford: Clarendon Press.

Kymlicka, W. (1998) *Finding Our Way: Rethinking Ethnocultural Relations in Canada*. Toronto: Oxford University Press.

Kymlicka, W. and Norman, W. (1994) Return of the Citizen: A Survey of Recent Work on Citizenship Theory. *Ethics*, 104, 352–81.

Landes, J.R. (1988) *Women and the Public Sphere in the Age of the French Revolution*. London: Cornell University Press.

Landes, J.B. (1998) *Feminism, the Public and the Private*. Oxford: Oxford University Press.

Lash, S. and Urry, J. (1987) *The End of Organised Capitalism*. Oxford: Polity Press.

Latour, B. (1987) *Science in Action*. Milton Keynes: Open University Press.

Layder, D. (1985) Power, Structure and Agency. *Journal for the Theory of Social Behaviour*, 15, 131–49.

Layder, D. (1997) *Modern Social Theory*. London: UCL Press.

Leadbetter, C. (1999) *Living on Thin Air: The New Economy*. London: Viking.

Leca, J. (1992) Questions on Citizenship. In C. Mouffe (ed.), *Dimensions of Radical Democracy*. London: Verso.

Lembruch, G. (1977) Liberal Corporatism and Party Government. *Comparative Political Studies*, 10, 91–126.

Lembruch, G. and Schmitter, P.L. (1982) *Patterns of Corporatist Policy-Making*. London: Sage.

Linklater, A. (1998) *The Transformation of Political Community*. Cambridge: Polity Press.

Lipietz, A. (1986) New Tendencies in the International Division of Labour: Regimes of Accumulation and Modes of Regulation. In A. Scott and M. Storper (eds), *Production, Work, Territory: the Geographical Anatomy of Industrial Capitalism*. London: Allen and Unwin.

Lister, R. (1997) *Citizenship: Feminist Perspectives*. Basingstoke: Macmillan.

Lockwood, D. (1981) The Weakest Link in the Chain? Some Comments on the Marxist Theory of Action. *Research in the Sociology of Work*, 1, 435–81.

Lockwood, D. (1992) *Solidarity and Schism*. Oxford: Clarendon Press.

Luhmann, N. (1982) *The Differentiation of Society*. New York: Columbia University Press.

Luke, T. (1990) *Social Theory and Modernity*. London: Sage.

Lukes, S. (1974) *Power: A Radical View*. London: Macmillan.

Lukes, S. (1977) *Essays in Social Theory*. New York: Macmillan.

Lyon, D. (1994) *The Electronic Eye: The Rise of Surveillance Society*. Cambridge: Polity Press.

Lyotard, J.-F. (1984) *The Postmodern Condition: a Report on Knowledge*. Manchester: Manchester University Press.

MacIntyre, A. (1985) *After Virtue*. London: Duckworth.

Mair, L.P. (1962) *Primitive Government*. Harmondsworth: Penguin.

Mander, J. and Goldsmith, E. (eds) (1996) *The Case against the Global Economy and for a Turn toward the Local*. San Francisco: Sierra Club Books.

Mann, M. (1984) The Autonomous Power of the State: Its Origins, Mechanisms and Results. *Archives européennes de sociologie*, 25, 185–213.

Mann, M. (1986) *The Sources of Social Power* (Vol. 1). Cambridge: Cambridge University Press.

Mann, M. (1987) Ruling Class Strategies and Citizenship. *Sociology*, 21, 339–54.

Mann, M. (1993) *The Sources of Social Power* (Vol. 2). Cambridge: Cambridge University Press.

Mann, M. (1997) Has Globalisation Ended the Rise and Rise of the Nation-state? *Review of International Political Economy*, 4, 472–96.

Mansbridge, J.J. (1980) *Beyond Adversary Democracy*. New York: Basic Books.

Marglin, S. (1974) What do Bosses Do? The Origins and Functions of Hierarchy in Capitalist Production. *Review of Radical Political Economics*, 6 (Part I), 60–112.

Marglin, S.A. (1991) Understanding Capitalism: Control versus Efficiency. In B. Gustafsson (ed.), *Power and Economic Institutions: Reinterpretations in Economic History* (pp. 225–52). Aldershot: Edward Elgar.

Marglin, S.A. and Schor, J.B. (1989) *The Golden Age of Capitalism: Reinterpreting the Postwar Experience*. Oxford: Clarendon Press.

Markoff, J. (1996) *Waves of Democracy: Social Movements and Political Change*. London: Sage.

Marquior, J.G. (1991) *Foucault*. London: Fontana.

Marshall, T.H. (1963) Citizenship and Social Rights. In T.H. Marshall (ed.), *Sociology at the Crossroads and Other Essays* (pp. 67–127). London: Heinemann.

Marshall, T.H. (1981) *The Right to Welfare and Other Essays*. London: Heinemann.

Martin, B. (1996) *Politics in the Impasse: Explorations in Postsecular Social Theory*. Albany, NY: SUNY Press.

Marx, K. (1970) *Capital* (Vol. 1). London: Lawrence and Wishart.

Matthews, J. (1989) *Age of Democracy: The Politics of Post-Fordism*. Oxford: Oxford University Press.

McAdam, D. (1982) *Political Processes and the Development of Black Insurgency*. Chicago: University of Chicago Press.

McAdam, D. and Rucht, D. (1993) The Cross-National Diffusion of Movement Ideas. *The Annals of the AAPSS*, 528, 56–74.

McAdam, D., McCarthy, J., and Zald, M. (1996) Introduction: Opportunities, Mobilizing Structures and Framing Processes – Toward a Synthetic, Comparative Perspective on Social Movements. In D. McAdam, J. McCarthy, and M. Zald (eds), *Comparative Perspectives on Social Movements: Political Opportunities, Mobilizing Structures, and Cultural Framings*. New York: Cambridge University Press.

McCarthy, J.D. (1987) Pro-Life and Pro-Choice Mobilization: Infra-Structure Deficits and New Technologies. In M.N. Zald, and J.D. McCarthy (eds), *Social Movements in an Organizational Society*. New Brunswick, NJ: Transaction Books.

McCarthy, T. (1984) *The Critical Theory of Jürgen Habermas*. Cambridge: Polity Press.

McCarthy, T. (1985) Complexity and Democracy: the Seducements of Systems Theory. *New German Critique*, 35 (spring/summer), 27–53.

McCarthy, T. (1990) The Critique of Impure Reason. *Political Theory*, 18 (3), 437–69.

McCarthy, T. (1992) Complexity and Democracy: The Seducements of Systems Theory. In A. Honneth, T. McCarthy, C. Offe, and A. Wellmer (eds), *Cultural-Political Interventions in the Unfinished Project of Enlightenment*. Cambridge, MA: MIT Press.

McGrew, A. (1997) *The Transformation of Democracy? Globalization and Territorial Democracy*. Cambridge: Polity Press.

McNay, L. (1997) *Foucault and Feminism*. Cambridge: Polity Press.

McNeish, W. (1999) Resisting Colonisation: the Politics of Anti-Roads Protesting. In P. Bagguley and J. Hearn (eds), *Transforming Politics: Power and Resistance*. Basingstoke: Macmillan.

Meehan, E. (1993) *Citizenship and the European Community*. London: Sage.

Meehan, J. (1995) *Feminists Read Habermas: Gendering the Subject of Discourse*. London: Routledge.

Melucci, A. (1989) *Nomads of the Present*. London: Radius.

Melucci, A. (1996a) *Challenging Codes: Collective Action in the Information Age*. Cambridge: Cambridge University Press.

Melucci, A. (1996b) *The Playing Self: Person and Meaning in the Planetary Society*. Cambridge: Cambridge University Press.

Meyer, W.J. (1998) The Politics of Differentiated Citizenship. In K. Slawner and M.E. Denham (eds), *Citizenship after Liberalism* (pp. 57–79). New York: Peter Lang.

Meyer, D.S. and Tarrow, S. (1998) The Social Movement Society: Contentious Politics for a New Century. In J.C. Green (ed.), *People, Passions, and Power*. Oxford: Rowman and Littlefield.

Michels, R. (1959) *Political Parties: a Sociological Study of the Oligarchical Tendencies of Modern Democracy*. New York: Dover.

Miller, P. and Rose, N. (1990) Governing Economic Life. *Economy and Society*, 19, 1–31.

Miller, P. and Rose, N. (1995) Political Thought and the Limits of Orthodoxy: a Response to Curtis. *British Journal of Sociology*, 46, 590–7.

Mills, C.W. (1956) *The Power Elite*. New York: Oxford University Press.

Misgeld, D. (1985) Critical Hermeneutics Versus Neoparsonianism? *New German Critique*, 35 (spring/summer), 55–87.

Mohanty, C.T. (1991) Introduction: Cartographies of Struggle: Third World Women and the Politics of Feminism. In C.T. Mohanty, A. Russo, and L. Torres (eds), *Third World Women and the Politics of Feminism*. Bloomington: Indiana University Press.

Moore, J.B. (1978) *Injustice: The Social Bases of Obedience and Revolt*. London: Macmillan.

Mosca, G. (1939) *The Ruling Class*. New York: McGraw-Hill.

Moscovici, S. and Doise, W. (1994) *Conflict and Consensus: A General Theory of Collective Decisions*. London: Sage.

Mouffe, C. (1993) *The Return of the Political*. London: Verso.

Mouzelis, N. (1990) *Post-Marxist Alternatives: The Construction of Social Orders*. Basingstoke: Macmillan.

Mouzelis, N. (1991) *Back to Sociological Theory*. London: Macmillan.

Mouzelis, N. (1992) Social and System Integration: Habermas' View. *British Journal of Sociology*, 43 (2), 267–88.

Nairn, T. (2000) *After Britain*. London: Granta.

Nettl, J. (1967–8) The State as a Conceptual Variable. *World Politics*, 20, 559–92.

Nicholson, L.J. (1986) *Gender and History: The Limits of Social Theory in the Age of the Family*. New York: Columbia University Press.

Nicholson, L. and Seidman, S. (1995) *Social Postmodernism: Beyond Identity Politics*. Cambridge: Cambridge University Press.

Nicholson, P. (1984) Politics and Force. In A. Leftwich (ed.), *What Is Politics: the Activity and its Study*. Oxford: Blackwell.

Offe, C. (1984) *Contradictions of the Welfare State*. London: Hutchinson.

Offe, C. (1985) *Disorganised Capitalism*. Cambridge: Polity Press.

Offe, C. (1996) *Modernity and the State*. Cambridge: Polity Press.

Offe, C. and Ronge, V. (1975) Theses on the Theory of the State. *New German Critique*, 6, 139–47.

Offe, C. and Wiesenthal, H. (1980) Two Logics of Collective Action: Theoretical Notes on Social Class and Organisational Form. In M. Zeitlin (ed.), *Political Power and Social Theory*. Greenwich, CT: JAI Press.

Ohmae, K. (1990) *The Borderless World: Power and Strategy in the International Economy*. London: Fontana.

Ohmae, K. (1996) *The End of the Nation State*. London: HarperCollins.

Okin, S.M. (1989) *Justice, Gender and the Family*. New York: Basic Books.

Oldfield, A. (1990a) Citizenship: an Unnatural Practice. *Political Quarterly*, 61 (2), 177–87.

Oldfield, A. (1990b) *Citizenship and Community: Civic Republicanism and the Modern World*. London: Routledge.

Parekh, B. (1981) *Hannah Arendt and the Search for a New Political Philosophy*. Atlantic Highlands: Humanities Press.

Parsons, T. (1967a) On the Concept of Political Power. *Sociological Theory and Modern Society*. London: Free Press.

Parsons, T. (1967b) Voting and the Equilibrium of the American Political System. *Sociological Theory and Modern Society*. London: Free Press.

Parsons, C. (1987) *Flexible Production Technology and Industrial Restructuring: Case Studies of the Metalworking, Semiconductor, and Apparel Industries.* Berkeley: University of California Press.

Pateman, C. (1988) *The Sexual Contract.* Cambridge: Polity Press.

Pateman, C. (1992) Equality, Difference and Subordination: The Politics of Motherhood and Women's Citizenship. In G. Bock and S. James (eds), *Beyond Equality and Difference: Citizenship, Feminist Politics, and Female Subjectivity.* London: Routledge.

Perraton, J., Goldblatt, D., Held, D., and McGrew, A. (1997) The Globalization of Economic Activity. *New Political Economy*, 2, 257–77.

Phillips, A. (1991) *Engendering Democracy.* Cambridge: Polity Press.

Phillips, A. (1992) Democracy and Difference: Some Problems for Feminist Theory. *Political Quarterly*, 63, 79–90.

Phillips, A. (1993) *Democracy and Difference.* Cambridge: Polity Press.

Phillips, A. (1995) *The Politics of Presence.* Oxford: Oxford University Press.

Phillips, A. (1999) *Which Equalities Matter?* Cambridge: Polity Press.

Piore, M. and Sabel, C. (1984) *The Second Industrial Divide.* New York: Basic Books.

Piven, F.F. and Cloward, R. (1977) *Poor People's Movements: Why They Succeed, How They Fail.* New York: Vintage Books.

Pizzorno, A. (1970) An Introduction to the Theory of Political Participation. *Social Science Information*, 9, 29–61.

Plant, R. (1988) *Citizenship, Rights and Socialism.* London: Fabian Society.

Plant, R. (1990) Citizenship and Rights. In R. Plant and N. Barry (eds), *Citizenship and Rights in Thatcher's Britain: Two Views.* London: IEA Health and Welfare Unit.

Plant, R. (1992) Citizenship, Rights and Welfare. In A. Coote (ed.), *The Welfare of Citizens.* London: Institute of Public Policy Research/Rivers Oram Press.

Poggi, G. (1978) *The Development of the Modern State.* London: Hutchinson.

Polanyi, K. (1957) *The Great Transformation.* Boston: Beacon Books.

Pollin, R. (1996) Contemporary Economic Stagnation in World Historical Perspective. *New Left Review*, 109–18.

Polsby, N. (1980) *Community Power and Political Theory: a Further Look at Problems of Evidence and Influence.* New Haven: Yale University Press.

Procacci, G. (1989) Sociology and its Poor. *Politics and Society*, 17, 163–87.

Ransom, J.S. (1997) *Foucault's Discipline: The Politics of Subjectivity.* London: Duke University Press.

Rasmussen, D. (1990) *Reading Habermas.* Oxford: Basil Blackwell.

Ray, L.J. (1993) *Rethinking Critical Theory: Emancipation in the Age of Global Social Movements.* London: Sage.

Rees, A.M. (1996) T.H. Marshall and the Progress of Citizenship. In M. Bulmer and A.M. Rees (eds), *Citizenship Today.* London: UCL Press.

Reich, R. (1992) *The Work of Nations: Preparing Ourselves for 21st-Century Capitalism.* New York: Vintage.

Revkin, A. (1990) *The Burning Season: the Murder of Chico Mendes and the Fight for the Amazon Forest.* London: Collins.

Roberts, S. (1979) *Order and Dispute: an Introduction to Legal Anthropology.* Oxford: Martin Robertson.

Robertson, R. (1992) *Globalisation: Social Theory and Global Culture.* London: Sage.

Roche, M. (1992) *Rethinking Citizenship.* Cambridge: Polity Press.

Roche, M. and van Berkel, R. (1997) *European Citizenship and Social Exclusion.* Aldershot: Ashgate.

Rohrschneider, R. (1993) Impact of Social Movements on the European Party System. *Annals of the AAPSS,* 528, 157–70.

Rose, N. (1993) Government, Authority and Expertise in Advanced Liberalism. *Economy and Society,* 22, 283–99.

Rose, N. (1996) The Death of the Social? Refiguring the Territory of Government. *Economy and Society,* 25, 327–56.

Rose, N. (1999) *Powers of Freedom: Reforming Political Thought.* Cambridge: Cambridge University Press.

Rose, N. and Miller, P. (1992) Political Power beyond the State: Problematics of Government. *British Journal of Sociology,* 43, 172–205.

Rosenberg, J. (1994) *The Empire of Civil Society: a Critique of the Realist Theory of International Relations.* London: Verso.

Roseneil, S. (1995) *Disarming Patriarchy: Feminism and Political Action at Greenham.* Buckingham: Open University Press.

Rowlinson, M. and Hassard, J. (1994) Economics, Politics and Labour Theory. *Capital and Class,* 53 (summer), 65–94.

Rucht, D. (1996) The Impact of National Contexts on Social Movement Structures: A Cross-Movement and Cross-National Comparison. In D. McAdam, D. McCarthy, and M. Zald (eds), *Comparative Perspectives on Social Movements: Political Opportunities, Mobilizing Structures and Cultural Framings* (pp. 185–204). Cambridge: Cambridge University Press.

Ruggie, J. (1993) Territoriality and Beyond: Problematising Modernity in International Relations. *International Organisation,* 47, 139–74.

Ryan, M.P. (1997) Gender and Public Access: Women's Politics in Nineteenth Century America. In C. Calhoun (ed.), *Habermas and the Public Sphere* (pp. 259–88). London: MIT Press.

Sandel, M.J. (1996) *Democracy's Discontent: America in Search of a Public Philosophy.* Cambridge, MA: Harvard University Press.

Saunders, P. (1993) Citizenship in a Liberal Society. In B. Turner (ed.), *Citizenship and Social Theory.* London: Sage.

Sayer, A. and Walker, R. (1992) *The New Social Economy: Reworking the Division of Labor.* Oxford: Blackwell.

Schapera, I. (1956) *Government and Politics in Tribal Societies.* London: Watts.

Schmitter, P.C. (1974) Still the Century of Corporatism? *Review of Politics,* 36, 85–131.

Schmitter, P.L. and Lembruch, G. (1979) *Trends towards Corporatist Intermediation.* London: Sage.

Scott, A. (1997) *The Limits of Globalization: Cases and Arguments.* London: Routledge.

Seidman, S. (1989) *Jürgen Habermas on Society and Politics: a Reader.* Boston: Beacon Press.

Seidman, S. (1994) *The Postmodern Turn: New Perspectives on Social Theory*. Cambridge: Cambridge University Press.

Shaiken, H. (1986) *Work Transformed: Automation and Labor in the Computer Age*. Lexington, MA: Lexington Books.

Shaiken, H. (1993) Beyond Lean Production. *Stanford Law and Policy Review*, 5 (1), 41–52.

Shearing, C. (1995) Reinventing Policing: Police as Governance. In O. Marenin (ed.), *Policing Change: Changing Police* (pp. 285–307). New York: Garland Press.

Sklair, L. (1991) *Sociology of the Global System*. New York: Harvester.

Smith, J. (1994) *The Globalization of Social Movements: The Transnational Social Movement Sector 1983–93, ASA* Conference.

Smith, J. (1997a) Transnational Political Processes and the Human Rights Movement. In S.M. Buechler and F.K.J. Cylke (eds), *Social Movements*. Mountain View, CA: Mayfield.

Smith, J. (1997b) Characteristics of the Modern Transnational Social Movement Sector. In J. Smith, C. Chatfield, and R. Pagnucco (eds), *Transnational Social Movements and Global Politics: Solidarity beyond the State*. Syracuse, NY: Syracuse University Press.

Smith, J., Pagnucco, R., and Romeril, W. (1994) Transnational Social Movement Organizations in the Global Political Arena. *Voluntas*, 5, 2.

Smith, N. (1984) *Uneven Development*. Oxford: Blackwell.

Smith, T. (1994) Flexible Production and the Capital Wage/Labour Relation in Manufacturing. *Capital and Class*, 53 (summer), 39–64.

Spinosa, C., Flores, F., and Dreyfus, H.L. (1997) *Disclosing New Worlds: Entrepreneurship, Democratic Action, and the Cultivation of Solidarity*. London: MIT Press.

Stewart, A. (1995) Two Conceptions of Citizenship. *British Journal of Sociology*, 46 (1), 63–78.

Stewart, A. (2000) Never Ending Story: Inclusion and Exclusion in Late Modernity. In P. Askonas and A. Stewart (eds), *Social Inclusion: Possibilities and Tensions* (pp. 55–72). Basingstoke: Macmillan.

Stone, D.A. (1984) *The Disabled State*. Philadelphia: Temple University Press.

Swyngedouw, E. (1986) The Socio-spatial Implications of Innovations in Industrial Organisation. *Johns Hopkins European Center for Regional Planning and Research*, working paper no. 20.

Tarrow, S. (1996) *Power in Movement: Social Movements, Collective Action and Politics*. Cambridge: Cambridge University Press.

Tassin, E. (1992) Europe: A Political Community? In C. Mouffe (ed.), *Dimensions of Radical Democracy: Pluralism, Citizenship, Community*. London: Verso.

Taylor, C. (1986) Foucault on Freedom and Truth. In D.C. Hoy (ed.), *Foucault: A Critical Reader* (pp. 69–102). Oxford: Blackwell.

Taylor, C. (1991) Shared and Divergent Values. In R.L. Watts and D.G. Brown (eds), *Options for a New Canada*. Toronto: University of Toronto Press.

Taylor, C. (1992) The Politics of Recognition. In A. Gutmann (ed.), *Multiculturalism and 'The Politics of Recognition'*. Princeton: Princeton University Press.

Thompson, E.P. (1963) *The Making of the English Working Class.* London: Gollancz.

Thompson, E.P. (1978) Eighteenth-century English Society: Class Struggle without Class. *Social History,* 3, 133–64.

Thompson, J. and Held, D. (1982) *Habermas: Critical Debates.* London: Macmillan.

Tilly, C. (1975) *The Formation of National States in Western Europe.* Princeton: Princeton University Press.

Tilly, C. (1978) *From Mobilization to Revolution.* New York: McGraw-Hill.

Tilly, C. (1979) Repertoires of Contention in America and Britain, 1750–1830. In M. Zald and J.D. McCarthy (eds), *The Dynamics of Social Movements.* Cambridge, MA: Winthrop.

Tilly, C. (1984) Social Movements and National Politics. In C. Bright and S. Harding (eds), *Statemaking and Social Movements.* Ann Arbor: University of Michigan Press.

Tilly, C. (1995) *Popular Contention in Great Britain, 1758–1834.* Cambridge, MA: Harvard University Press.

Tolliday, S. and Zeitlin, J. (1991) *The Power to Manage: Employers and Industrial Relations in Comparative Historical Perspective.* London: Routledge.

Touraine, A. (1977) *The Self-Production of Society.* London: University of Chicago Press.

Touraine, A. (1981) *The Voice and the Eye: An Analysis of Social Movements.* Cambridge: Cambridge University Press.

Touraine, A. (1992) Two Interpretations of Contemporary Social Change. In H. Haferkamp and N.J. Smelser (eds), *Social Change and Modernity* (pp. 55–77). Berkeley: University of California Press.

Trey, G. (1998) *Solidarity and Difference: the Politics of Enlightenment in the Aftermath of Modernity.* Albany, NY: State University of New York Press.

Turner, B. (1986) *Citizenship and Capitalism: The Debate over Reformism.* London: Allen and Unwin.

Turner, B. (1988) *Status.* Milton Keynes: Open University Press.

Turner, B. (1990) Outline of a Theory of Citizenship. *Sociology,* 24, 189–217.

Urry, J. (1995) Rethinking Class. In L. Maheu (ed.), *Social Movements and Social Classes: The Future of Collective Action* (pp. 169–81). London: Sage.

van Dyke, V. (1985) *Human Rights, Ethnicity and Discrimination.* Westport, CT: Greenwood.

van Gunsteren, H.R. (1978) Notes on Theory of Citizenship. In P. Birnbaum, J. Lively and G. Parry (eds), *Democracy, Concensus and Social Contract.* London: Sage.

van Gunsteren, H.R. (1998) *A Theory of Citizenship: Organizing Plurality in Contemporary Democracies.* Oxford: Westview Press.

van Steenbergen, B. (1994) *The Condition of Citizenship.* London: Sage.

Vogel, U. and Moran, M. (1991) *The Frontiers of Citizenship.* Basingstoke: Macmillan.

Walby, S. (1993) Post-Post-Modernism? Theorising Social Complexity. In M. Barrett and A. Phillips (eds), *Destabilizing Theory: Contemporary Feminist Debates.* Cambridge: Polity Press.

Wallerstein, I. (1974) *The Modern World System.* New York: Academic Press.

Walzer, M. (1983) *Spheres of Justice.* New York: Basic Books.

Walzer, M. (1986) The Politics of Michel Foucault. In D.C. Hoy (ed.), *Foucault: A Critical Reader.* London: Blackwell.

Walzer, M. (1992) The Civil Society Argument. In C. Mouffe (ed.), *Dimensions of Radical Democracy.* London: Verso.

Watanabe, S. (1986) Labour-saving versus Work-amplifying Effects of Microelectronics. *International Labour Review,* 125 (3), 243–59.

Waters, M. (1995) *Globalization.* London: Routledge.

Weiss, L. (1998) *The Myth of the Powerless State: Governing the Economy in a Global Era.* Cambridge: Polity Press.

Weiss, L. and Hobson, J.M. (1995) *State and Development: a Comparative Historical Analysis.* Cambridge: Polity Press.

White, S.K. (1990) *The Recent Work of Jürgen Habermas.* Cambridge: Cambridge University Press.

White, S.K. (1991) *Political Theory and Postmodernism.* Cambridge: Cambridge University Press.

Whitebook, J. (1996) *Perversion and Utopia: a Study in Psychoanalysis and Critical Theory.* London: MIT Press.

Wilensky, H. (1975) *The Welfare State and Equality: Structural and Ideological Roots of Public Expenditures.* Berkeley: University of California Press.

Witte, J.F. (1980) *Democracy, Authority, and Alienation in Work.* London: University of Chicago Press.

Wolin, S. (1987) Theorising the Welfare State. *Political Theory,* 15, 467–500.

Wolin, S. (1989) *The Presence of the Past.* London: Johns Hopkins University Press.

Wolin, S. (1992) What Revolutionary Action Means Today. In C. Mouffe (ed.), *Dimensions of Radical Democracy.* London: Verso.

Wolin, S. (1996) Fugitive Democracy. In S. Benhabib (ed.), *Democracy and Difference: Contesting the Boundaries of the Political* (pp. 31–45). Princeton: Princeton University Press.

Womack, J., Jones, D., and Roos, D. (1990) *The Machine that Changed the World.* New York: Rawson Associates.

Wood, S. (1982) *The Degradation of Work? Skill, Deskilling and the Labour Process.* London: Hutchinson.

Wright, E.O. (1995) *Associations and Democracy: The Real Utopias Project.* London: Verso.

Yeatman, A. (1994) *Post-modern Revisionings of the Political.* London: Routledge.

Young, I.M. (1989) Polity and Group Difference: A Critique of the Ideal of Universal Citizenship. *Ethics,* 99, 250–74.

Young, I.M. (1990) *Justice and the Politics of Difference.* Princeton: Princeton University Press.

Young, I.M. (1996) Communication and the Other: Beyond Deliberative Democracy. In S. Benhabib (ed.), *Democracy and Difference: Contesting the Boundaries of the Political* (pp. 120–35). Princeton: Princeton University Press.

Zald, M.N. and McCarthy, J.D. (1979) *The Dynamics of Social Movements.* Cambridge: Winthrop.

Zald, M.N. and McCarthy, J.D. (eds) (1987) *Social Movements in an Organizational Society.* New Brunswick, NJ: Transaction Books.

Zuboff, S. (1988) *In the Age of the Smart Machine.* London: Heinemann.

Index